LANCASHIRE LIBRARY
BURNLEY
ASEMEI

D0586438

RS

WITHDRAWN FROM
LANCASHIRE LIBRARIES

LL 60

02. 09. 94

AUTHOR	CLASS
PERMUTT, C.	771
TITLE Collecting photographic antiques	No 01407968 ✓

Lancashire
County
Council

This book should be returned on
or before the latest date shown above
to the library from which it was borrowed
LIBRARY HEADQUARTERS
143, CORPORATION ST. PRESTON PR1 2TB

a30118 014079689b

Collecting
Photographic
Antiques

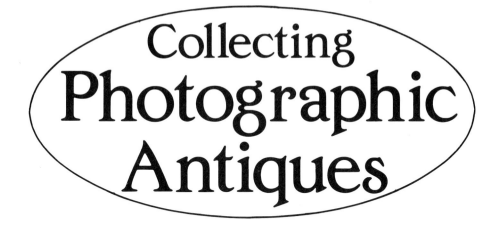

Collecting Photographic Antiques

CYRIL PERMUTT

Patrick Stephens, Wellingborough

LANCASHIRE LIBRARY

01407968

UB

© Cyril Permutt 1986

All rights reserved. No part of this publication may be
reproduced, stored in a retrieval system or transmitted,
in any form or by any means, electronic, mechanical,
photocopying, recording or otherwise, without prior
permission in writing from Patrick Stephens Limited.

First published in 1986

British Library Cataloguing in Publication Data

Permutt, Cyril
Collecting photographic antiques.
1. Photography—Apparatus and supplies—
Collectors and collecting
I. Title
771'.075   TR196

ISBN 0-85059-689-0

*Patrick Stephens Limited is part of the
Thorsons Publishing Group*

Photoset in 10 on 11 pt Palacio by MJL Typesetting
Services Limited, Hitchin, Herts. Printed in Great
Britain on Consort Bulky 110 gsm, and bound, by
Butler and Tanner, Limited, Frome, Somerset, for the
publishers, Patrick Stephens Limited, Denington
Estate, Wellingborough, Northants, NN8 2QD,
England.

Contents

To my dear wife Sadie
and our children
Philip, Elaine, Richard, Pamela and Jeffrey
and particularly to Elaine
my pretty secretary and darling daughter
with my thanks for their help
with both the collection and this book
and especially to our granddaughters
Rachel, Melanie and Bettina to whom
the future belongs.

Introduction

A photographic antique may be any one of the unusual items that preceded and led to the invention of photography or were made for a photographic purpose or produced by a photographic process. They range from the pre-photographic camera lucidas, camera obscuras and solar microscopes used by the early experimenters and all the other items that preceded the photographic camera right up to those 'modern' cameras which were landmarks on the road to the future like the first Kodaks, the first 35 mm cameras, the first Polaroid Land Instant Print cameras and the Hasselblad cameras used by American astronauts on the surface of the moon. Examples of all the different processes and photographs produced as well as the accessories and bric-a-brac of the first 150 years of photography are equally collectable.

Although it sounds as if all this is an inexhaustible source of collectable material, because of natural wastage and the frailty of many of the items, their disposable nature and the built-in obsolescence caused by constant innovations and inventions, the vast majority of the millions of cameras, the thousands of millions of photographs and the multitude of accessories that have been produced have now disappeared and this is especially true of the early and more desirable and collectable items. So much so that in many cases there are only one or two examples of rare items left in existence and some we only know of from an illustration or mention in an early photographic book, catalogue or journal.

It is this very rarity of these early and unusual photographic antiques that adds spice to our search for them and to our joy when one is discovered and although such items have become very valuable today they can still be occasionally picked up inexpensively in a flea market or general auction sale by the lucky collector who is knowledgeable enough to recognise them.

Collecting rare old cameras, photographs and photographic antiques has been the hobby of a few of us for over thirty years and the best examples have not only kept in line with inflation but since the quantum jump in collecting that occurred in the early 1970s, with the entry of Christie's, Sotheby's and other large salesrooms into the field, many of them have achieved spectacular advances particularly in the last few years. At the same time however something that all serious collectors hate has occurred, people who are not interested in photographic antiques but only in investing money or making quick profits have jumped into the market and as a result collectors are more than ever in need of the expert knowledge and sensible advice that they can only obtain from books like this written by a collector for collectors.

The question of value is of great interest to collectors and although it should not be the reason for collecting photographic antiques it is nice to know that the *Practical Investor* for July 1981 headlined one page with the line 'Saleroom: small is beautiful' and went on to say 'Small portable items of value are the best hedges against inflation in the view of 120 specialists employed by Phillips, the international fine art auctioneers.' Phillips of course have their own old camera and photograph department, and like the other large auction rooms hold regular sales of photographic antiques. One of the reasons for the strong price performance of photographic antiques is the international demand that they enjoy now that collecting them has become a world-wide hobby with well-known collectors and large collections in every civilized part of the world.

I trust that all collectors of photographic antiques from the newest tyro to the most experienced expert will find this book exciting and interesting and an invaluable work of reference. I hope that reading it will give you all as much enjoyment as writing it has given to me.

To help spark your imagination here is an A-Z of just some potential subject areas for a photographic collection:

A   Albums, ambrotypes and actinometers.
B   Box cameras and books about photography.
C   Cartes de visite, calotypes and camera obscuras.
D   Daguerreotype and dark room apparatus.
E   Eastman cameras and Edison inventions.
F   Fox Talbot photographs and flashlight apparatus.
G   Gelatine dry plates and graphoscopes.
H   Holmes stereoscopic viewers and Hill and Adamson photographs.
I   Instruction books for old cameras.
J   Jewellery with inset photographs and photographic journals.
K   Kodak cameras and Ives Kromscopes.
L   Leather photographs and Lorraine glasses.
M   Magic lanterns and medals.
N   Niepce's cameras and photographs and early negatives.
O   Opal prints.
P   Portraits of Presidents and Royalty and photogenic drawings.
Q   Queues, rationing and other war time photographs.
R   Rejlander, O.G. and Robinson, H.P.'s combination photographs.
S   Stereoscopes and stereoscopic photographs.
T   Transparencies and tintypes.

U Union cases and other photographic cases.
V Voigtlander cameras and Victorian photographs.
W Waistcoat cameras and wet-collodion negatives.
X X-ray photographs and equipment.
Y Yosemite Park photographs.
Z Zeiss Ikon cameras and Zeiss lenses.

Any of these would make a wonderful specialized collection but you will find it even more interesting and enjoyable if you can discover a field of your own and so help to fill in yet another of the blank spaces in the history of photography.

Cyril Permutt
October 1986

Acknowledgements

It gives me great pleasure to thank Brian Coe, for many years Curator of the Kodak Museum and now with the Royal Photographic Society at Bath, and fellow collector B.E.C. Howarth-Loomes for the friendship, information and assistance that they have given to me so freely over the years.

I would also like to express my gratitude to Bill Rodgers, Thurman F. (Jack) Naylor, Fred Spira, Philippe Garner and Hilary Kay of Sotheby's Bond Street, and David Allison and Edward Holmes of Christie's South Kensington for the information and photographs that they have made available to me and for their kind permission to use them in this book, and I am grateful to all the other collectors, curators and keepers of collections, camera and film manufacturers and dealers who have helped.

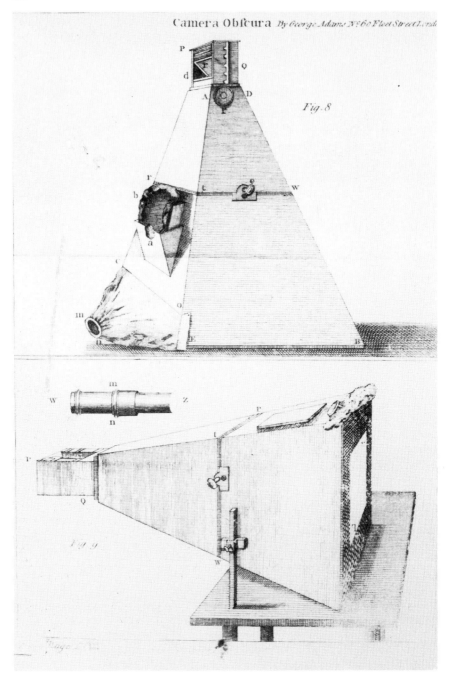

Camera Obſcura *By George Adams Nº 60 Fleet Street Lond.*

Fig. 8

Fig. 9

Chapter 1

The first great period of photographic antiques

Collecting photographic antiques encompasses so many different facets of photography that the collector soon has to decide which area of the history of photography is the most appealing and then try to specialize in that particular area. In this book I have tried to signpost some of the less obvious paths that a collector of photographic antiques can follow.

The beginnings of photography go far back in time. The handbook of the Compass camera made by Le Coultre et Cie of Switzerland in 1937 said that a museum in Oxford has fragments of a ten thousand year old clay pot which has the image of the wickerwork that was woven around it to hold it in shape whilst it was drying burnt into its surface by the action of the sun and this must surely be the earliest known sun picture. Most collectable photographic antiques are not as old as that, and although many examples of photographic history are now in museums and private collections all over the world valuable early items are still being unearthed by knowledgeable collectors.

The first collectable items associated with the history of photography began to appear with the development of the camera obscura in the sixteenth and seventeenth centuries and by the end of the eighteenth century portable camera obscuras, solar microscopes and the Lorraine glass, a convex mirror of black glass that gave a reduced size reflection, were being used to capture the images of the world about them. Optical viewers like the Zograscope were being used to enhance the perspective of the pictures that they produced. The camera lucida, a small optical drawing device introduced by William Hyde Wollaston in 1807 which used a prism to superimpose a view of the scene to be traced upon the drawing paper and was not a camera at all, and the many optical amusements and toys that were popular at that time are all now sought after by collectors of photographic antiques.

The camera obscura, originally a dark room with a small hole in a wall or the shutter of a window had been known to astronomers from the fourth

Left *A camera obscura by George Adams of 60 Fleet Street, London from* Micrographica Illustra *1771.* (Courtesy of Christie's South Kensington.)

LANCASHIRE LIBRARY

century BC and was mentioned by the Arabian scholar Alhazan in the tenth century AD, by Levi Ben Gershon a Jewish philosopher and mathematician in the fourteenth century AD and by Leonardo da Vinci (1452-1519) who wrote: 'When the images of illuminated objects pass through a small round hole into a very dark room . . . you will see on the paper all those objects in their natural shapes and colours. They will be reduced in size, and upside down, owing to the intersection of the rays at the aperture.'

Girolamo Cardano of Milan in Book IV of his scientific encyclopedia *De Subtilitate,* 1550, was the first to point out the advantage of placing a convex lens in the hole and in his book *Delicia physico-mathematicae,* 1651, Daniel Schwenter improved on this by describing the scioptric ball, a wooden ball with a hole bored through it and a lens fitted at each end. When the ball is fitted in to a hole in a window shutter and rotated it greatly extends the field of view. The camera obscuras became very fashionable and were built in to many private homes and public buildings and a few still are in existence today.

During the seventeenth and eighteenth centuries portable camera obscuras were made in many shapes and sizes ranging from collapsible wooden huts and room sized constructions to sedan chairs, tents, tables and small wooden boxes that could be held in the hand, all of which are highly desirable collectors items today. Wooden scioptric balls and the later brass Victorian versions occasionally come to light and lucky collectors are still finding the brass tops of tent camera obscuras complete with their lenses and prisms, although in most cases the material of the tent itself has long since perished.

The hand held camera obscura, a small wooden box with a lens in the front focussing the external view on to a ground glass screen, was improved during the eighteenth century becoming two wooden boxes sliding into each other for easier focussing of the image which was usually reflected by a mirror on to a ground glass screen in the top of the rear box and in this form it was the immediate precursor of the photographic camera. These small sliding box camera obscuras were very popular with artists and although they are now very rare and much sought after by collectors they are still sometimes to be found.

From the notes left by the pioneers of photography we can clearly see how these early optical devices and images signposted the path that led to the invention of photography.

The industrial revolution had brought a prosperous and growing middle class into being and created a mass demand for personal portraits. Mechanical methods were evolved to satisfy this demand and silhouettes became very popular by the early part of the eighteenth century. In his *Miscellanies,* 1745, Swift described a method of tracing the shadow of a profile and although they were often sketched or painted the cheapest versions were cut out with a pair of scissors and mounted on to thin card. They were called silhouettes after the French finance minister of the time Etiene de Silhouette

Pocket camera obscura, 7 in long, English 1800. Sold at Sotheby's Belgravia on 20 March 1981 for £1,400.

whose pennypinching practices had made his name synonymous with cheapness. The success of the silhouette was not rivalled until 1786 when Gilles Louis Chrétien invented the physionotrace. With this device the outline of a person's shadow was thrown on to a glass plate and by the use of a pointer connected to an engraving tool traced on to a copper plate which with added details of face and clothing could be inked and used to provide a series of prints. Although not strictly photographic these and similar items should be all included at the beginning of a collection as they help to fill in the background of the birth of photography.

The first of the pioneers of photography was Thomas Wedgwood youngest son of Josiah Wedgwood the famous potter. Born into a scientific background, he was well educated and in 1792 when he was 21 years old he submitted a paper *Experiments and Observations on the Production of Light from Different Bodies by Heat and Attrition* to the Royal Society. Wedgwood knew of J.H. Schulze's and C.H. Scheele's observations on the blackening action of light on the salts of silver and was well acquainted with his father's use of a camera obscura whilst working on the scenes of the English countryside and stately homes which were used to decorate his famous dinner and tea services.

During the 1790s he began experimenting with the light sensitive salts of silver and by the end of the eighteenth century he was making light images on sensitized paper and leather. Whilst engaged on these experiments he became friendly with Humphry Davy, the famous chemist, and partly as a result of this friendship the first report of Wedgwood's photographic experiments 'An account of a method of copying paintings-upon-glass and of making profiles by the agency of light upon nitrate of silver. Invented by T. Wedgwood Esq., with observations by H. Davy.' was published in *The Journals of the Royal Institution* of which Davy was then the editor on June 22nd 1802.

The report said '. . . white paper, or white leather, moistened with a solution of nitrate of silver, undergoes no change when kept in a dark place; but, on being exposed to the day light, it speedily changes colour, and, after passing through different shades of grey and brown, becomes at length nearly black . . . outlines and shades of paintings on glass may be copies or profiles of figures procured, by the agency of light . . . The copy of a painting, or the profile, immediately after being taken, must be kept in an obscure place. It may indeed be examined in the shade but, in this case, the exposure should be only for a few minutes; by the light of candles or lamps, as commonly employed, it is not sensibly affected . . . the images formed by means of a camera obscura, have been found to be too faint to produce, in any moderate time, an effect upon the nitrate of silver. To copy these images, was the first object of Mr Wedgwood, in his researches on the subject . . . Nothing but a method of preventing the unshaded parts of the delineation from being coloured by exposure to the day is wanting, to render the process as useful as it is elegant'.

Wedgwood's efforts to fix the images seen in the camera obscura were not successful although had he given an exposure of six or eight hours as was given later by Joseph Nicéphore Niepce instead of what he called 'any moderate time', he may well have achieved his aim and become the world's first photographer. Wedgwood had been a sick man all his life and finally died in 1805 before perfecting his process and although he did not succeed in permanently fixing any of the pictures that he produced they were without a doubt the original forerunners of photography.

There are no surviving examples of Wedgwood's 'heliotypes' in either the Wedgwood Museum or amongst the Wedgwood manuscripts deposited at the Keele University Library but in her book *A Group of Englishmen* published in 1871 Eliza Meteyard refers to the two heliotypes still then existing and researchers are even now looking through old files and manuscripts in several different locations in the hope of locating further examples of what would be a most wonderful find for a collector.

The first really permanent photographs were finally made by the Frenchman Joseph Nicéphore Niepce in the course of his experiments to improve the lithographic processes then in use. After what seem to have been abortive attempts in 1814 and 1815 to copy engravings by oiling them to make them transparent, putting them onto pewter plates coated with concoctions that he hoped would be light sensitive and then exposing them to sunlight, in April 1816 he obtained a successful view from the window of the attic workroom in his family home at Gras using paper sensitized with chloride of silver exposed in a camera obscura.

At this time Niepce was using three home made camera obscuras in his photographic experiments, one made from a jewel box fitted with a microscope lens giving an image a little less than 3 cm square, another slightly larger than that and a third one about 15 cm square. Although he used nitric acid to fix the images he obtained they were not permanent and the action of

An exposure of more than eight hours was necessary when Niepce took this, the world's earliest surviving photograph made in a camera, from the window of his study in Gras.

the fixing acid itself eventually bleached them entirely.

Continuing his experiments using plates of pewter, glass, copper and zinc he discovered that a coating of bitumen of Judea dissolved in lavender oil hardened under the influence of light. When it was exposed to the sun under an engraving oiled to make it transparent, the bitumen under the clear parts of the engraving became hard whilst under the dark lines it remained soluble and could be washed away by the oil of lavender. He made his first permanent copy of an engraving, one of Pope Pius VII, on a glass plate coated in this way in July 1822.

Niepce called these images heliographs and in his notes and correspondence differentiated between copies of engravings which he called 'copies de gravure' and photographic images made in the camera obscura which he called 'point de vue', and these are amongst the earliest real photographic images that the collector can hope to find. Niepce produced several copies of engravings during the next few years, the best known of these is a copy of an engraving of Cardinal d'Amboise one of Louis XII's ministers. At least three copies of this engraving were made by Niepce on his pewter plates and several proofs made from these plates have been discovered. In the course of time more will probably be found and one of them would be an ideal item for a collection of photographic antiques.

The world's earliest surviving photograph was taken by Niepce in 1826. Made on a pewter plate 8 in by 6½ in and taken from his attic workroom at his home in Gras, in the village of Saint-Loup-de-Varennes which is four miles south of Chalon-sur-Saône in France it shows from left to right, an upper loft that was called their pigeon-house, a tree with the sky showing through a hole in its foliage, the sloping roof of a barn and on the right another wing of the house. Missing since it had been loaned to an exhibition in 1898, this photograph was brought to light in 1952 thanks to the research and endeavours of Helmut Gernsheim and together with other of Niepce's

Carte de visite portrait of Louis Jacques Mandé Daguerre. Photograph by Mayer and Pierson, copied from the original daguerreotype of 1848-9 attributed to the Meade Brothers of New York. (Courtesy of Sotheby's Belgravia.)

relics that had been found with it were presented by the owner to the Gernsheim Collection, now housed at the University of Texas, which as any collector will agree was a fitting reward for the work involved. Three more of these pewter plate photographs made at about the same time are in the Museum of the Royal Photographic Society, Octagon, Bath, which also houses many other photographic treasures and is well worth a visit.

Niepce had worked with home made cameras until January 1926 when he purchased his first professionally made camera obscura from Charles & Vincent Chevalier the leading Paris opticians of the day, whose apparatus is still highly valued by collectors. Niepce took his first successful photographs from nature with their camera. The day long exposure needed by Niepce's process rendered it impractical however and although he produced a few more examples and tried using several different cameras and formulae he made no real further progress before his death in 1833 and the first really practical method of photography was to be invented by Louis Jacques Mandé Daguerre a decade later.

Daguerre, a highly successful scenic artist and showman, was well known in both Paris and London as the originator of the Diorama, an entertainment in which the audience was surrounded by vast translucent painted panoramas which were given dramatic effects by varying the colour, direction and density of the specially controlled lighting so that daylight scenes were changed into night, the fires in burning buildings quenched, empty courtyards filled with people and enormous edifices changed into ruins before the audience's very eyes.

Daguerre had been using the camera obscura as an aid in preparing the realistic images he painted for the Diorama and had also made unsuccessful efforts to record the images seen in the camera obscura on silver chloride paper. Like Niepce, Daguerre was buying his equipment from the Chevaliers who learning of his experiments told him of Nicéphore Niepce's efforts and in June 1926 Daguerre commenced corresponding with Niepce. Niepce was very discrete in his replies, but whilst visiting his brother Claude who was lying sick at Kew, he approached members and wrote a memoire to the Royal Society with which he enclosed several of his heliographs in an effort to publicise his invention. This memoire was not published by the society because Niepce did not include the full details of his discoveries and it is this correspondence that was re-discovered by Gernsheim. Niepce returned to France and after further correspondence and meetings with Daguerre they formed a ten year partnership in which they agreed to pool their knowledge and work together to develop a practical process of photography.

The Musée Denon at Chalon-sur-Saône has several of Niepce's cameras on display including one made of zinc 65 cm by 36 cm by 36 cm which is labelled 'Chambre noire envoyée par Daguerre aJ .N. Niepce', and there must be many more cameras and items of equipment used by these two famous Frenchmen still waiting to be discovered by collectors.

All collectors search for extremely rare and valuable items such as these but it takes a combination of knowledge and good luck to track one down. The work put in to such a search is well worth while because even if the original quest is unsuccessful other exciting and desirable photographic antiques are often found along the way and dedication in following a trail should not cause you to neglect any lesser finds that you may make during the journey.

When Niepce died in 1833 his son Isadore continued the partnership although nothing was achieved until Daguerre accidentally happened upon the secret of developing a latent image in 1835. Daguerre had been experimenting with silvered copper plates made sensitive to light by iodine vapour but the iodide of silver created was not sensitive enough to produce a visible image. Storing one of these unsuccessful plates in his chemical cupboard so that he could repolish it and use it again he was amazed to find when he took it out a few days later that a picture had appeared on it. Repeating this with other plates and removing his stock of chemicals one by one he determined that it was the vapour given off by mercury spilt from a broken thermometer that had developed the latent image on the plate but it was not until 1837 that he discovered the secret of permanently fixing the image on his silver plates with a solution of salt in hot water.

Daguerre called these photographs daguerreotypes. The earliest known example is a still life taken in 1837 which is now in the Société Francais de Photographie in Paris. Daguerre had stumbled across the world's first practical process of photography and its public announcement by Francois Arago on 7 January 1839 led to the production of what is now a flood of photographic antiques for the modern collector. In return for pensions for himself and Isadore Niepce, Daguerre published full details of his invention

Above *The earliest known daguerreotype, a still life taken in his studio and signed and dated 1837 by L.J.M. Daguerre. The original is preserved at the Société Francais de Photographie, Paris.*

Below *Daguerreotype camera and outfit c 1846.* (Courtesy of Christie's South Kensington.)

on 19 August 1839 after which it was to be used freely throughout the world—except for England where he had patented five days earlier.

Like Niepce's pewter plate photographs the daguerreotype gave a direct positive image. To produce this image the silvered sheet of copper was first polished and then buffed to a fine mirror like surface. It was then placed face down over a dish of iodine crystals in a wooden box until the iodine vapour had reacted with the polished silver to make the light sensitive silver iodide and then exposed in a camera. Light coming through the camera lens produced an invisible latent image and to develop this image the copper plate was placed silver side down in a box over a bowl containing mercury which was heated by a spirit lamp. The rising mercury vapour reacted with the silver iodide where it had been exposed to light forming a positive image which was visible because of the contrast between the brightness where the mercury adhered to those parts of the image that had been exposed to light and the darkness of the remaining silver iodide that had not been affected and the image was finally fixed by soaking the plate in a strong solution of common salt.

The items of equipment used in the daguerreotype process are as eagerly sought after today as the cameras and images themselves and are perhaps even harder to find. The plate boxes, iodine sensitizing boxes, mercury fuming chambers, spirit lamps and polishing buffs, all the paraphenalia of the process have now become wonderful photographic antiques and fetch high prices in salesrooms and auctions.

The daguerreotype became immensely popular and improved cameras and improvement to the process came thick and fast. The first daguerreotype camera available commercially was made by Daguerre's relative Alphonse Giroux in June 1839. Using 6½ in by 8½ in plates they had Daguerre's signature and Giroux's seal on the side as a guarantee of their authenticity and although they were sold as fast as they could be produced they are very rare and valuable today. These sliding box cameras were to be the most popular type for the next twenty or thirty years and later examples come up fairly frequently at antique camera sales. When smaller cameras were later made this 6½ in by 8½ in size became known as whole plate and the smaller sizes became half plate and quarter plate etc.

Later that same year Baron Pierre Armand Seguir an amateur daguerreotypist made the first folding daguerreotype camera which was fitted with two sets of bellows which opened each way from a central frame so that when folded the camera and all the daguerreotype processing equipment could be stored in a wooden box for the travelling photographer. Then early in 1840 Chevalier marketed a wooden folding camera 'The Photographe' in which the hinged sides folded flat when the lens board and ground glass screen were removed. These were amongst the leaders in a flood of novel camera designs that are still being discovered by collectors today.

The magic of the mirror with a memory captured all who saw the early daguerreotypes although these were almost all outdoor scenes or still life representations as portraits taken in Europe needed exposures of up to twenty or thirty minutes even in full sunshine. The world's first professional photographic portrait studio was opened early in March 1840 in New York City by Alexander Wolcott and John Johnson using an unusual camera that Wolcott had invented which used a concave mirror instead of a lens. The camera was an open fronted box measuring 8½ in by 8 in by 15 in. Light coming in from the front was reflected by the mirror at the back on to a small sensitized plate held in a moving frame and facing backwards towards the mirror. The 7 in mirror reflected several more times the light than any lens then in use and with it portraiture became a practical proposition.

The only known surviving example of a Wolcott mirror camera is in the York Institute, Saco, Maine, USA. I have not seen one of these cameras offered for sale nor do I know of one in any private collection although a number of them must have been made and sold because when Richard Beard opened the first English photographic studio at the Royal Polytechnic Institution in London on 23 March 1841 he too used a Wolcott camera, and daguerreotype portraits in the distinctive Beard case are still to be found fairly easily.

In 1840 mathematician Joseph Petzval designed a new camera lens with an f 3.6 aperture which passed through almost sixteen times as much light as the f 17 lens used on the Daguerre camera. This Petzval lens was first fitted to an all metal Voigtlander camera introduced on 1 August 1841 and was later used on wooden ones. Some seventy Voigtlander cameras fitted with the Petzval lens were sold by the end of 1841. In the late 1950s Voigtlander made a number of replicas of this first all brass Voigtlander camera and although these are now also highly desirable collectors items they should not be mistaken for originals. All these replicas are based on the immaculate example in the Deutches Museum, Munich, West Germany and are engraved with the serial number 84.

All cameras from these early days of photography are highly valued by collectors but even amongst these rare items the first Daguerre, Walcott and Voigtlander cameras reign supreme and are the most eagerly sought after.

The daguerreotype was the most popular photographic process in the early days of photography and it remained in use until the mid 1850s and even later than that in the United States, but the real father of photography was the Englishman William Henry Fox Talbot. After spending the autumn of 1833 with his wife touring Europe and unsuccessfully trying to sketch the countryside using a camera lucida he determined 'that on his return to England he would try to cause these natural images to imprint themselves durably and remain fixed upon the paper.'

After his return to his home at Lacock Abbey in Wiltshire in January 1834 he began experimenting with paper sensitized with silver chloride and made negative images of pieces of lace and leaves which he fixed in a strong solution of salt. By the early part of 1935 he was using these negatives to make positive contact prints and used the moist sensitized paper in a

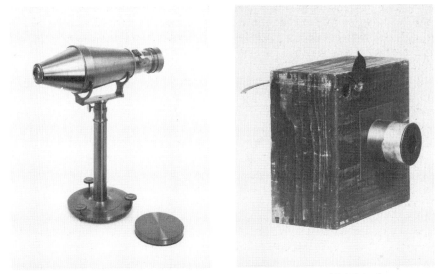

Above left *Replica of the 1840 Voigtlander daguerreotype camera with 3¼ in daguerreotype holder. Sold at Phillips on 12 March 1980 for £750.* **Above right** *One of Fox Talbot's earliest cameras.* (Courtesy of the Royal Scottish Museum.)

Below *Trafalgar Square during the construction of Nelson's Column. A talbotype, 7¼ in by 8¾ in, by William Henry Fox Talbot, late 1843. Sold at Sotheby's Belgravia on 29 October 1982 for £7,480.*

camera obscura that he had made out of a large box in an attempt to take a view of Lacock Abbey. The picture was still insufficiently exposed after a couple of hours and in an effort to speed up the process he had some tiny 2¼ in by 2¼ in miniature camera obscuras made by Joseph Foden, the Lacock carpenter, and fitted them with microscope lenses. He set several of these tiny cameras up around Lacock Abbey and taking them indoors after an exposure of ten minutes found a miniature image in each. One of these miniature negatives was a photograph of the latticed window of the library at Lacock Abbey taken in August 1835. It is now the world's earliest surviving negative and is preserved in the Science Museum, London, together with about 6,000 calotypes including many of Fox Talbot's earliest attempts, most of his waxed negatives and several of his cameras.

Many of Fox Talbot's accessories and scientific instruments are held by the Royal Scottish Museum at Edinburgh and the Royal Photographic Society at Bath houses many of his prints and various early cameras. Much of the apparatus on display at the Fox Talbot Museum at Lacock Abbey is on loan from my personal collection but the museum which stands at the gates of Lacock Abbey also houses some 10,000 letters and about 1,000 calotypes by Fox Talbot and his contemporaries the Reverends Bridges and Calvert Jones. These letters and calotypes are all that remain in the family estate as Fox Talbot's granddaughter Miss Matilda Talbot, who had inherited the estate and wanted to honour her grandfather's name, allowed the keepers of the Science Museum, the Royal Photographic Society and the Royal Scottish Museum to come down to Lacock and take whatever they liked of Fox Talbot's material in 1936.

Valuable discoveries of photographic antiques are still being made and there still remain many more awaiting discovery by some lucky collector. Only a little while ago a young man clearing out the attic of a recently inherited large suburban house on the outskirts of London found an early sliding body daguerreotype camera in an old trunk. A farmer drove up to Sotheby's with a Land Rover full of wet plate cameras, equipment and lenses discovered in an old derelict farm hut, while a dealer clearing out an old house due for demolition found a brand new folding whole plate wet plate camera made by Horne and Thornthwaite in about 1858 together with a chest full of photographs, equipment and other associated photographic antiques in a small boarded up room, so keep looking it may be your turn next!

Chapter 2

Collectable antiques from the wet plate era

In 1851 an English photographer, Frederick Scott Archer, described a revolutionary new photographic process which was to be instrumental in creating a flood of wonderful photographic antiques for collectors. The daguerreotype process had proved to be a dead end and the fibrous structure of paper negatives made them far from ideal but glass plates coated with a film of collodion, gun cotton dissolved in ether, and made sensitive to light by immersion in a solution of silver nitrate were not only capable of fine resolution but were also far more sensitive than either the daguerreotype or calotype process which meant that successful photographs could be taken giving exposures of only a few seconds or even less.

The very nature of this new process, because the plates had to be exposed in the camera and then developed and fixed whilst still wet or they became very insensitive, meant that the photographer had to carry a portable dark room with all its accompanying impedimenta with him finally leaving what are now wonderfully collectable photographic antiques scattered almost everywhere that he went.

Niepce had used glass for his first heliographs and using glass for the sensitized material had been suggested by Sir John Herschel and others. A photograph made by Herschel in September 1839 on glass made sensitive to light by precipitated silver chloride is preserved in the Science Museum, London, but this took several days to prepare and was not practical and the first really useable glass plate process was that introduced in 1847 by Abel Niepce de Saint-Victor, a cousin of Nicéphore Niepce, in which a glass plate was coated with a thin film of albumen (white of egg) mixed with a few drops of potassium iodide, allowed to dry and then sensitized when required for use by a rinse with acid silver nitrate solution.

After being exposed in a camera the plate was developed in gallic acid, and although these albumen plates were even slower than the other processes then in use they could register great detail and were ideal for architecture, landscapes, lantern slides, and later, transparencies for stereoscopes. Examples of these can still be found fairly easily by collectors today.

In another innovation in 1852 Scott Archer described a method of treating a collodion wet plate negative with a solution of mercuric bichloride which whitened the image so that if the plate was backed with black varnish or black paper or velvet the lightened negative image appeared as a positive. This collodion positive was called an ambrotype and was very popular for portraiture becoming 'the poor man's daguerreotype' and often being sold in similar cases and presentation but at much cheaper prices. One interesting and fairly rare version was the 'Relievo' ambrotype introduced in 1854. In this only the sitter and studio furniture were varnished black or brown, the rest of the photograph was scraped off and the picture was mounted on a fairly thick piece of plain glass backed by white or light coloured card or paper which caused the image to stand out and gave it a three dimensional effect in line with the then current interest in stereoscopic photography. A few even more rare ambrotypes were made on blue Bristol glass.

Collodion positive photographs on black paper, called melanographs, and on black or brown enamelled tinplate, called ferrotypes or tintypes, were introduced in 1853 and collodion positive photographs on leather in 1854. The paper proved to be too perishable and the leather was inclined to crack so these melanographs and leather photographs are great rarities today. The ferrotypes or tintypes which were the cheapest and easiest to produce of all of the photographic processes then in use, had by the 1860s become the one used by itinerate beach and fairground photographers and were still being used in England until just a few years ago. These collodion positives like daguerreotypes were each a unique image that was sold in a protective case or at least a cardboard holder.

Glass collodion negatives were occasionally printed on salted calotype paper although examples of these are relatively rare but albumen printing paper described by Louis-Désiré Blanquart-Évrard in 1850, which was made by coating paper with albumen containing a small amount of ammonium chloride and then sensitizing it with silver nitrate, gave results that proved ideal for the glass collodion wet plate negatives and was used by almost all photographers until well into the 1890s. The paper was placed in direct contact with a glass negative in a printing frame and printed in strong sunlight until the colour was deep enough and then fixed in hypo and toned in a solution of chloride of gold which gave it that rich sepia colouring that we find so charming in Victorian photographs.

In 1854, André Adolphe Disderi of Paris patented a method of photographing several portraits on a single negative plate which greatly reduced cost. He popularized this small mounted print size, 4 in by 2½ in which became known as the carte de visite. These became immensely popular in the 1860s when almost everyone collected carte de visite photographs not only of their family and friends but also of celebrities and famous people of all kinds. It has been estimated that whilst a few million photographs were probably produced in the first ten years after the invention of photography in 1839, in the next twenty years they were numbered in hundreds of

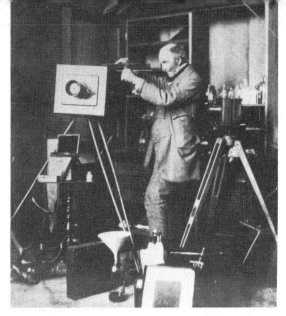

Captain Horatio Ross in his home photographic studio preparing a collodion plate, 1860. (Courtesy of Christie's South Kensington.)

millions and the vast majority of these were cartes de visite. This will give collectors some idea of the relative rarity and value of these early photographs, a large proportion of which were made by one of the many variants of Scott Archer's process.

Because of the vast quantities produced, cartes de visite, visiting cards with a portrait instead of a name, are more easily found by collectors than any other form of early photograph and some collectors have amassed large quantities of them. William Culp Darrah a famous American collector well known for his enormous collection of stereographs has a vast collection of carefully conserved cartes de visite filed, indexed and cross indexed under photographer, subject matter, price, and a host of other headings. Whilst such large and comprehensive collections are perhaps a little beyond many collectors we should all try to emulate this careful listing and indexing of all items of collectabilia. Too many collectors end up with boxes full of unidentified and unsorted items from forgotten sources instead of the carefully laid out collection that can be made with surprisingly little extra effort.

The collecting craze for cartes de visite that reached a peak between 1860 and 1866 left behind many specialized collections in albums that are much sought after by collectors today such as family albums of famous people like the carte de visite album of members of the Wedgwood family found for me by a very good friend, or the album of carte de visite spirit photographs belonging to Georgina Houghton progeny of George Houghton who became a partner in Antoine Claudet's glass business in 1836 and imported the very first daguerreotypes and daguerrotype cameras into England. The connection with the early history and pre-history of photography makes these albums of great interest and value to collectors.

Collectors can specialize in cartes by one photographer, cartes from one area, of one famous or infamous person, of one subject matter, of one period of time, or one of almost any number of different types of cartes that were produced, the operative word in every case being 'one'. Collectors have even specialized in the backs of the cartes. These carry a great number of designs, the same stock design often being used by several different photographers with just the name of the photographer, often varied over the years, getting more elaborate as the years went by.

The albums in which collections of cartes de visite were kept are themselves now valuable collectors pieces. As with all collectabilia only the most unusual albums in the best of condition should be kept in a collection. We all of course pick up tatty items from time to time, we buy dirty dogeared old albums because of the beautiful old photographs that they contain and we accumulate piles of well worn or uninteresting cartes because we want one or two of them for our collections but such debris should be disposed of as soon as possible as it will otherwise almost inevitably overwhelm a fine collection and end up discouraging rather than encouraging the aspiring collector.

With the increase in the popularity of photography in the 1850s and 1860s many shopkeepers and itinerant traders introduced photography as a profitable sideline and barbers, coffee shops, shoe shines and tobacconists vied with each other and with the professional photographers for the public's custom. Collectors of photographic antiques will delight in the cartoons that abounded in periodicals such as Punch which had a field day with photographers almost as much as they will enjoy collecting the photographic artifacts that were left behind as photographic establishments opened up and then closed down again in large numbers.

The dying away of the craze for collecting cartes in 1866 prompted F.R. Window a partner in Window and Bridge, London portrait photographers, to suggest the cabinet portrait, a photograph 5½ in by 4 in mounted on a 6½ in by 4½ in card and by 1868 this new size had been adopted by almost all the photographers still in business. Cameras, lenses and albums for these new size photographs proliferated. Albums and frames to take both cartes and the new cabinet photographs were created in a profusion of bindings colours and designs, and during the 1870s larger photographs were

London Stereoscopic Company 5 in by 4 in mahogany wet plate sliding box camera, 1860. Sold at Christie's South Kensington on 12 October 1974 for £682.

Right *A ferrotype 'mug' camera with an f3.5–60mm Laack Rathenow Schnellarbeter lens, 29 cm high, German 1895. Sold at Sotheby's Belgravia on 7 July 1978 for £550.*

Below *A whole plate ambrotype group portrait of three Unionist soldiers, identified with contemporary label as Norman H. Chamberlain, Joseph Shaw and Henry S. Williams. Contemporary manuscript information gives details of their deaths. The photograph is contained in a plush lined leather case and dates from the early 1860s. Sold at Sotheby's Belgravia on 26 June 1975 for £160.*

produced framed for standing on mantlepieces, pianos or sideboards or to hang on walls. These larger photographs however, ranging up to the imperial mounted on a 8¾ in by 5 in card and the panel on a 13 in by 8 in mount were expensive, a giant 24 in by 20 in photograph framed for wall hanging costing as much as £8 8s 0d, a vast amount in those days when a labourer's pay was about 10s 6d a week.

Cartes and cabinet photographs were the most popular and it is these that the collector will find today. They remained popular right up to the First World War and, together with the almost universal tintype photograph that covered a similar span of time, can be found fairly readily on stalls in flea markets, in junk shops and anywhere where the debris of our Victorian ancestors abound. The most interesting and those sought after by discerning collectors are of course those with unusual subject matter or unusual backs or those made by famous photographers. Outdoor scenes, country-people and tradesmen with the tools of their craft or trade, royalty, and of course photographs of photographers and their studios and cameras are all highly desirable and fetch premium prices in sales rooms or when purchased from dealers. The collector's answer to this is to painstakingly sort through the piles of old photographs yourself in street markets, antique fairs and garage or car boot sales, as always, discarding the ordinary and dirty and seeking for the finer and unusual examples and all the while keeping an alert eye open for early cameras and other items of equipment and the finer photograph albums with ornate covers of carved wood, Japanese lacquer, finely worked leather, mother of pearl and plush.

Left *Carte de visite photograph of Miss Georgina Houghton with a ghost which she believed to be St Paul. Taken by 'spirit' photographer Frederick A. Hudson on 21 November 1872.*

Above right *A small lavender coloured velvet album, decorated with gold, pearls and blue enamel* (courtesy of Christopher Pearce) *and a red leather album decorated with gold and silver flowers and butterflies* (courtesy of B.E.C. Howarth-Loomes).

Centre right *A rare 11½ cm Unghams disc musical photographic album. The periphery driven movement is contained in the back of a leather bound album and a compartment at the back holds seven spare discs. German, 1910. Sold at Sotheby's Belgravia on 18 July 1980 for £260.*

Right *'Photographing the first-born' a* Punch *cartoon by Gerald du Maurir, 1876.*

Chapter 3

Kodak collectables

The nicest Kodak collectable in my collection is the blue plush covered copy of the 1947 catalogue of the Kodak Museum given to me when I first visited the Kodak Museum at Harrow in the early 1960s. It was a red letter day for me and also a day of some importance for the museum because in those years before collecting photographic antiques became the popular hobby that it is today and before old cameras and photographs became 'object-de-vertu' and as such were transformed into investors items as well as collectors items individual visits to the museum by private collectors were the exception rather than the rule.

In those early days there were only a handful of enthusiastic private collectors of photographica and as we all happily seemed to specialize in different fields of photography we co-operated with and assisted each other rather than competed with each other as most collectors seem to do today.

In November 1969 Brian Coe was appointed Curator of the Kodak Museum and at the kind invitation of Messrs Kodak Ltd, we often gathered together at Harrow for enjoyable evenings of lectures, entertainments and refreshments, at one of which, a collector laughingly mentioned that he had just returned from a visit to a remote outpost in the Shetland Islands where seeing an antique shop he had asked if they had any old cameras or photographs only to be told that 'a man called Cyril Permutt has just been in and bought the lot!' It was not quite true of course but it demonstrates the conditions that existed for collectors of photographic antiques in those days when collectors were few and far between and interesting collectable items abounded.

These 'Friends of the Kodak Museum' evenings often ended with everyone being given lists of old photographic books and collectabilia that were available for exchange or which had been offered to the museum but were surplus to the museum's requirements and I am indebted to Brian Coe and Kodak Ltd for several interesting items which came to me in this way.

The Victorian Image Photography, an exhibition drawn from the collections of the Kodak Museum, Bernard Howarth-Loomes and myself held at the Church Farm House Museum, Hendon, from 16 October to 21 November 1971 was perhaps instrumental in awakening a new public interest in

Right *George Eastman.* (Courtesy of the Kodak Museum, Harrow.)

Below *Eastman's Gelatine Dry Plates. George Eastman was one of the first makers of dry plates in America.* (Courtesy of the Kodak Museum, Harrow.)

photographic antiques and the much larger exhibition at the Victoria and Albert Museum in the next year and the commencement of large sales of photographica by the prestigious auction houses such as Christie's, Sotheby's and Phillip's put the cachet of respectability on a hobby that had until then been perhaps looked at a little askance.

The all embracing and mouth-watering displays to be seen at the Kodak Museum are well worth a visit. They range from the pre-history of photography through daguerreotype, calotype and wet plate items right up to modern cameras used in space. Of course, large and comprehensive selections of Kodak cameras and examples of other Kodak contributions to the progress of photography from the Eastman dry plates, Eastman paper roll films and the first Kodak camera are displayed.

For collectors the Kodak saga starts when George Eastman began the commercial production of dry plates in Rochester, New York in 1880. A bank clerk who was also an enthusiastic photographer, he had begun making photographic emulsions for his own use in 1878 using a formula from an English magazine, and by 1879 had invented an emulsion coating machine for the mass production of dry plates which he patented and used to establish his new enterprise.

Unused packets of these early dry plates are now very scarce and collectors find them almost impossible to obtain, but George Eastman's next innovation the Eastman-Walker roll holder, invented by Eastman and William H. Walker an associate in 1885, which made it possible to use rolls of negative paper in the ordinary plate cameras of the day can still sometimes be found. The introduction of readily available commercial dry plates and roll film brought a revolutionary change to photography and produced a flood of potential photographic antiques for collectors.

Although the wet collodion plate process remained popular with photographers for nearly thirty years and has left lovely photographic relics for us to collect today, its great drawback was the need to prepare each plate immediately before exposure and develop it immediately afterwards, which meant that photographers were either chained to their studio and dark room or if they ventured abroad had perforce to carry with them in addition to their cumbersome camera and tripod, a portable dark room complete with all the complex and varied panopalia involved in the chemistry of the wet collodion process, from bottles of water and chemicals to a supply of the heavy glass plates themselves.

In his brief biography of George Eastman in *Image*, Volume II No 8, November 1953 the late O.N. Solbert, a former Director of the George Eastman House of Photography, described the making of a wet plate photograph. 'A group of curious tourists draped themselves on the bridge to pose for the picture and watch George Eastman set up and focus his camera, crawl into his tent on his hands and knees to sensitize his plates, crawl out again with them ready to take the picture. It was a hot day but the fascinated group remained for the long and intricate operation and waited breathlessly

A No 1 Kodak Roll Film Camera, 1888. Sold at Sotheby's Belgravia on 29 October 1976 for £1,300.

for him to emerge from his steaming dark tent after developing his plate.' It was the liberation from all this brought about by the new processes and materials that led to the great growth of photography at that time.

The Kodak camera first marketed by Eastman in June 1888 was a photographic milestone and is of course the Kodak collector's item par excellence. Examples in good condition which cost five guineas when new now fetch prices in the region of £1,000 at photographic auctions. The Kodak camera was sold ready loaded with a stripping paper film that gave a hundred 2½ in diameter circular photographs. After the hundred photographs were taken the entire camera had to be posted back to the factory, where for two guineas the film was removed the camera reloaded and immediately returned to the owner. The film was developed and printed and the mounted prints were returned in about ten days.

George Eastman had sought for a distinctive name for his new cameras. He liked the letter K and its association with the hard C of camera and after considering large number of words that began and ended with a K he refined his lists to a few short words that could be spelled and pronounced easily in almost any language. He finally chose the name Kodak which was registered as a trademark in 1888 and eventually became so popular that almost every box camera made for a generation became a Kodak in the eyes of the public.

The first Kodak camera which had a capacity up to a hundred and fifty exposures, was fitted with a cylindrical barrel type shutter. An improved version with a sector type shutter, the No 2 Kodak Camera taking up to a hundred 3½ in diameter photographs and the first commercial transparent film were introduced in 1889. The No 3 Kodak Camera for up to a hundred 4¼ in by 3¼ in photographs, the No 3 Kodak Junior Camera taking sixty 4¼ in by 3¼ in photographs, the No 4 Kodak camera taking up to a hundred 5 in by 4 in photographs and the No 4 Kodak Junior Camera taking 48 exposures the same size were introduced in January 1890.

Silver Medal at Minneapolis Convention
P. A. of A. for most important invention
of the year.

⁕⁓THE⁓⁕

KODAK

CAMERA.

PHOTOGRAPHY REDUCED TO THREE MOTIONS.

And so on for 100 Pictures.

1. Pull the Cord.   *2. Turn the Key.*   *3. Press the Button.*

✦ ANYBODY CAN USE IT. ✦

Size of Camera, 3¼ x 3¼ x 6½ inches.

Weight, 1 lb. 10 oz.

Size of Picture, 2⅝ in. diameter.

➤➤ PRICE, $25.00. ◄◄

Price includes hand-sewed sole leather Carrying Case,
with shoulder strap and film for 100 exposures.

Uncapping for Time Exposures

➤➤ PRICE ◄◄

For Developing, Printing and Mounting 100 Pictures,
   Including spool 100 films for reloading Camera..... $10 00

Spool for reloading only..................................... 2 00

THE EASTMAN DRY PLATE AND FILM CO.,

Rochester, N. Y.

15 Oxford Street, London.

The first folding Kodak, the No 4 Folding Kodak camera holding 48 4 in by 5 in exposures was also introduced in 1890 and was rapidly followed by the No 4 Folding Kodak Improved Camera in 1893, also for 48 4 in by 5 in exposures, the No 5 Folding Kodak Camera for 54 5 in by 7 in pictures and in 1893 the No 5 Folding Kodak Improved Camera for 54 5 in by 7 in pictures and the No 6 Folding Kodak Improved Camera for 48 6½ in by 8½ in pictures.

This wonderful band wagon was soon jumped on by other manufacturers. The Luzo camera using Eastman roll films was patented in England by H.J. Redding in 1888. The Blair Camera Company of Boston, USA, acquired the rights to the roll film camera patented in England in 1889 by H.B. Good and marketed a camera called the Blair Kamaret based on this patent in 1892. The Cristallos Folding Camera, the Prisⁱ Camera and several other copy Kodaks were introduced in Europe in 1890 and 1891, and in 1892 the Boston Camera Company introduced the Bull's-Eye Camera, the first camera to use the numbered roll film and a red window at the back for the accurate location of each negative, invented by S.N. Turner.

George Eastman fought back with fresh innovations and marketed the first daylight loading cameras and packaged roll film in 1891. These Daylight Kodak Cameras came in three sizes the 'A' Daylight taking 24 2¾ in by 3¼ in exposures, the 'B' taking 24 2½ in by 4 in exposures and the 'C' taking 24 4 in by 5 in exposures and although they were called Daylight Kodaks photographers were told to change the films by subdued light in an ordinary room or by lamplight.

Three Ordinary Kodak Cameras similar in capacity and size to the Daylight Kodaks but lower in price and not daylight loading were manufactured from December 1891. They were not as successful as the other early Kodaks and are relatively rare today. Because of this and because they were the only Kodak box camera made of polished wood they are much sought after by collectors and tend to be expensive when found, the same camera often being chased by Kodak collectors, collectors of wooden cameras and collectors of box cameras for their own collections.

The first films for the daylight loading Kodaks had black paper leaders and trailers attached to the celluloid film but films with black cloth trailers were soon brought into production. The films were sold in light tight cardboard cartons with a velvet slot through which the black leader protruded and were wound through the camera into another similar carton. This meant that amateur photographers were now able to load and unload the cameras themselves and was another step forward in the simplification of photography and created yet another choice item for collectors to look for today.

George Eastman's Daylight Kodak Cameras and the Boston Camera Company's Bull's-Eye Camera were not as successful as had been expected,

Left *The operation of a Kodak camera, from an early advertisment, 1888.* (Courtesy of the Kodak Museum, Harrow.)

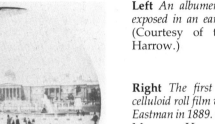

Left *An albumen print from a negative exposed in an early Kodak camera, 1890. (Courtesy of the Kodak Museum, Harrow.)*

Right *The first commercial transparent celluloid roll film was introduced by George Eastman in 1889. (Courtesy of the Kodak Museum, Harrow.)*

Bottom right *A Luzo roll film camera of 1896, sold at Christie's South Kensington on 22 January 1975 for £294.*

but realising that owners of cameras with the red windows would also have to buy the patented numbered film, Eastman commenced manufacture of his Bullet Camera using Turners invention at the end of 1894. In May 1895 he introduced the Pocket Kodak Camera which was the first camera to be manufactured by mass production methods. It was a tiny camera by the standards of the day, measuring only 2¼ in by 2⅞ in by 3⅞ in and taking a twelve exposure roll film giving 1½ in by 2 in negatives. Although only in production for five years the little Pocket Kodak proved to be the most popular camera of the nineteenth century, outselling any other camera that had been made until that time. This should not however lead collectors to believe that they are plentiful or easily found today as any example in nice condition that does turn up at a sale is eagerly bid for by enthusiastic collectors of early Kodak cameras.

These new cameras and the new cartridge roll film for them sold so successfully that in August 1895, instead of continuing to pay royalties, George Eastman bought the entire Boston Camera Company together with Turner's patent. Production of the various versions of the No 2 Bullet Camera which took eighteen 3½ in by 3½ in photographs was carried on until 1903, and the No 2 Bull's-Eye Improved Camera which followed the model previously made by the Boston Camera Company was produced from 1897 to 1913.

Between 1894 and 1897 Eastman made a series of Kodet Cameras which could take plates or roll holders, most of them in two sizes, the No 4 taking 4 in by 5 in pictures and the No 5 taking 5 in by 7 in pictures. By the end of the century several different sizes and versions of the Bull's-Eye Camera including the No 2 Folding Bull's-Eye Camera, one of the rarer examples of the breed, and the No 2 Falcon Kodak Camera, all using roll film, and the No 2 and No 4 Eureka Cameras which used the roll holder and the No 2 Eureka Junior Camera using plates were all also sold.

Cartridge Kodaks introduced in 1897 were of a much better quality than

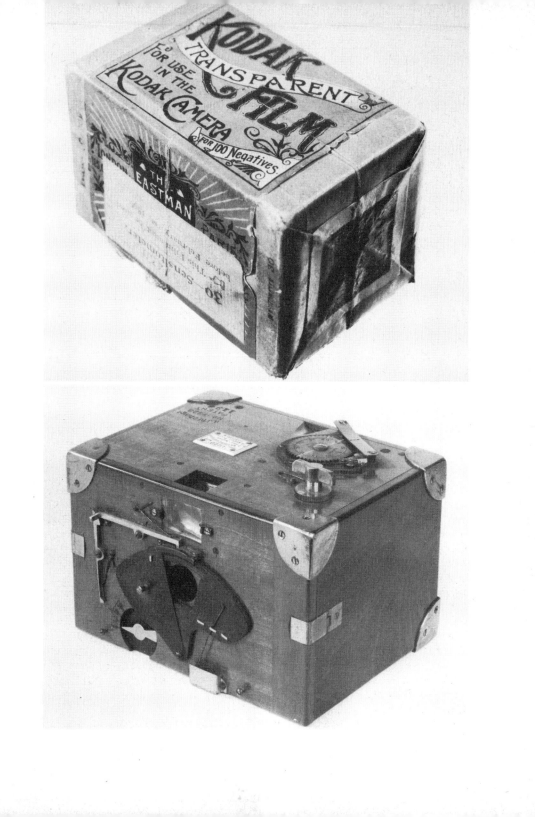

The Daylight Kodak Camera of 1891 with a carton of the film which could be loaded into the camera in subdued light. (Courtesy of the Kodak Museum, Harrow.)

the earlier Kodak cameras. They were more elaborate and could use either roll film or plates, and their quality has meant that they have lasted longer and are now found more frequently, but it was the No 1 Folding Pocket Kodak of 1898 that became the real Kodak best seller. The first of the range of folding Kodak cameras created by George Eastman's camera designer Frank Brownell it was the first camera to take 2¼ in by 3¼ in negatives on what was later numbered 120 roll film which proved to be the most popular amateur size for the next fifty years and measuring just over 1½ in thick when closed it took the world by storm and contributed to the estimated more than a million cameras that were in amateur's hands at the turn of the century.

The Brownie Box Cameras were another of Frank Brownell's designs that proved a winner for Kodak. Sold as a children's camera for one dollar in the United States and for five shillings in Great Britain, it took six 2¼ in by 2¼ in photographs on a cartridge roll film which cost ten cents for paper film or fifteen cents for celluloid film and only another forty cents for developing, printing and mounting. Named for the fairy like creatures so popular with American children at that time it was an instant success, an estimated 50,000 being sold in America and an equal number in Great Britain within the first year of production.

The back of the first production models of this camera just pushed on like the lid of a box but this proved to be unsafe in use and after the first month the camera was made with a hinged back secured by a sliding catch. Early Brownie cameras with the loose back are the hardest to find and much sought after by collectors today. They demonstrate how examples of even simple cameras that were produced in large numbers can still have a rarity value. It is however usually the more unusual types of Kodak cameras such as the Panoram and Stereo Kodaks that catch the collector's eye today.

Panoram Kodaks were made in several sizes from the No 4 taking 3½ in by 12 in photographs introduced in 1899 and made in various versions until

EASTMAN KODAK CO.'S BROWNIE CAMERAS $1.00

Make pictures 2¼ x 2¼ inches. Load in Daylight with our six exposure film cartridges and are so simple they can be easily

Operated by any School Boy or Girl.

Fitted with fine Meniscus lenses and our improved rotary shutters for snap shots or time exposures. Strongly made, covered with imitation leather, have nickeled fittings and produce the best results.

Forty four page booklet giving full directions for operating the camera, together with chapters on "Snap Shots," "Time Exposures," "Flash Lights," "Developing" and "Printing," free with every instrument.

Brownie Camera for 2¼ x 2¼ pictures,	$1.00
Transparent-Film Cartridge, 6 exposures, 2¼ x 2¼,	.15
Paper-Film Cartridge, 6 exposures, 2¼ x 2¼,	.10
Brownie Developing and Printing Outfit.	.75

Advertisement for Eastman Kodak Co's Brownie Cameras, 1900.

June 1924, to the No 1 taking 2¼ in by 7 in photographs made from April 1900 until the No 1 Model D patented 18 June 1914 was discontinued in 1926 and the No 3A made from May 1926 until 1928. The No 1 Panoram Kodak is the one that is most popular with collectors as it uses the still readily available 120 roll film and so, unlike most early collectable cameras, it can still be used easily today, most collectors feeling as I do that these lovely old cameras should whenever possible be kept in use and not just left on the shelf.

Panoramic cameras were not a novel idea, in fact the all time collectors award would probably go to the Thomas Sutton Panoramic Wet Plate

Camera made by Thomas Ross of London in 1861, fitted with a Suttons patent spherical water lens also made by Ross and using special curved plates, fine examples of this camera are now fetching prices well in excess of £10,000 at collectors' sales, however collectors are more likely to be able to find examples of the contemporary competitors of the Panoram Kodaks like the Al-Vista and the Hinton panoramic cameras.

Like the Panoram Kodaks, the Al-Vista made by the Multiscope and Film Company, Burlington, Wisconsin, USA in 1898, taking a 4 in by 12 in negative, took advantage of the flexibility of roll film to take the panoramic photograph by holding the film in a curved position behind a rotating lens. It was first marketed in Great Britain by Hinton and Company in 1899 but by 1903 Hinton and Company were making their own panoramic camera which took the same size negative as the Al-Vista but had the added advantage of a rising front and a central lens fixing with which the camera could be used to take photographs measuring 4 in by 6 in.

Stereoscopic cameras are another interesting field for collectors of photographic antiques. The No 2 Stereo Kodak made in 1901 was a box camera using 101 film, but all the other Kodak stereoscopic cameras made until the 1920s, the Stereo Weno No 1 made in 1902, the Stereo Weno No 2 also known as the Stereo Hawkeye No 1 made in 1904, the No 2 Stereo Brownie made in 1905, the Stereo Hawkeye No 5 also known as the No 3 1907, the Stereo Hawkeye No 6 also known as the No 4 1907, and the Stereo Kodak Model 1 made in 1917 were all folding cameras and make beautiful exhibits in a collection of Kodak or stereoscopic photographic antiques. The alternative numbers and identifications for some of these cameras came about because those sold in Great Britain and other countries overseas were sometimes given different names or numbers to those originally used in the United States.

Other Kodak collectables from the beginning of the twentieth century include the No 2 Flexo Kodak of 1900, which was a simplified version of the Bullet and Bull's-Eye cameras, the No 3B Quick Focus Kodak of 1906 a box camera in which the front springs out to a pre-set focusing distance at a touch of a button, the No 4 Screen Focus Kodak of 1906 which could be focussed on the ground glass screen by just swinging out the roll film holder or by detaching the roll film holder used with a plate holder, and the No 1A and 4A Speed Kodaks which were fitted with focal plane shutters giving speeds of up to one thousandth of a second.

Top left *The original Brownie Camera of February 1900. After the first four or five weeks the back was altered to a hinged type secured by a sliding latch. The optional clip-on viewfinder was available after July 1900. (Courtesy of the Kodak Museum, Harrow.)*

Centre left *Panoramic study of a bridge by Adolphe Braun. Albumen print 8 in by 11 in, 1860, sold at Sotheby's Belgravia on 28 June 1978 for £40.*

Left *Thomas Sutton panoramic wet plate camera made by Ross of London 1861 and fitted with Sutton's patent spherical water lens. This camera was sold at Christie's South Kensington on 25 April 1974 for £11,550.*

The No 1 Folding Pocket Kodak of 1897 was followed by a series of Folding Pocket Kodak cameras of varying sizes and specifications many of which staying in production right up until 1915. The nicest and most collectable one of these is the No 3 Folding Pocket Kodak Deluxe camera made from 1901 to 1903 which had Persian Morocco covered silk bellows and was the first Kodak camera to be fitted with a Bausch and Lomb automatic shutter. *The Kodak Collector,* a booklet by Allen R. Feinberg of Illinois, USA, first published in 1972, gives detailed lists of these and most other Kodak cameras and although several other books and booklets on Kodak collectabilia have been published since then I still find Feinberg's detailed listings most helpful.

These folding cameras were very successful but Kodak's next big hit was the Vest Pocket Kodak first produced in their Rochester NY factory in April 1912. Taking eight 1⅝ in by 2½ in exposures on 127 roll film, the original model fitted with a Meniscus Achromatic lens in a Kodak Ball Bearing shutter was made until 1914 but Vest Pocket Kodaks proliferated in such large numbers that they became another in the long line of Kodak best sellers.

As with all the successful Kodak cameras they became available fitted with a variety of lenses and shutters. They included such delightful collectable cameras as the Vanity Kodak Camera 1928 to 1933, the Vest Pocket Kodak Series III in a choice of five colours, blue, brown, gray, green or red, the Vanity Kodak Ensemble 1928-1931, Vanity Kodak Model B with a lipstick, compact, mirror and change pocket, the Kodak Petite Camera 1929-1934, a Vest Pocket Kodak made in colour, the Boy Scout Kodak 1930-1934, the Girl Scout Kodak 1929-1934, the Camp Fire Girls' Kodak 1931-34, the Kodak Ensemble 1929-1933, a Kodak Petite Camera in a suede case with a lipstick compact and mirror, the Kodak Coquette 1930 to 1931, a Kodak Petite Camera with a matching lipstick holder and compact, and last but not least the Jiffy Kodak VP Camera that was marketed from April 1935 until 1942.

In 1914 H.J. Gaisman patented a new type of roll film with a layer of carbon paper between the film and its backing paper. Pressing on the backing paper with a metal stylus made the carbon paper transparent so that if one wrote a message or date with the stylus light would penetrate the backing paper and imprint the message on the film. George Eastman was always on the lookout for new photographic ideas and ways of keeping his cameras ahead of and different from the evergrowing flood of look alike imitation Kodak cameras that followed hard on the heels of each new Kodak innovation. In 1914 the Eastman Kodak Company paid Gaisman the then almost unheard of sum of $300,000 for the rights to his patent and produced four Autographic Kodak Cameras the No 1 Junior, No 1A, No 3 and No 3A all using the new film and fitted with a little spring operated trap-door in the camera back which opened at a touch revealing the backing paper which was written on with the small metal stylus provided with each camera, and exposed for two or three seconds before re closing the trap-door. This proved to be yet another success for the Eastman Kodak Company and the first four Autographic Kodaks were followed by Autographic Vest Pocket Kodaks in 1915 and the No 2C Junior Autographic Camera in 1916.

The No 3A Autographic Kodak Special also introduced in 1916 and the No 1A Autographic Kodak Special of 1917 are of outstanding interest to collectors as they were the first cameras ever made with built in coupled rangefinders, but the Autographic back was soon available on almost the entire range of Kodak folding cameras and owners of the older Folding Pocket Kodak Cameras could buy a replacement Autographic back for use on their cameras. This updating of old cameras was a Kodak feature at the time and they would replace the lenses and shutters on old cameras with new and better versions for a reasonable charge, often taking the old ones in part exchange. Because of this collectors must be careful when using the patent dates or types of lens and shutters to date Kodak cameras.

There were of course many later Kodak cameras that are of great interest to collectors from simple box cameras like the brown leatherette covered gilt trimmed Anniversary Hawkeye Camera of 1930 made by George Eastman to mark the fiftieth anniversary of his company and given away free to any child whose twelfth birthday fell in 1930. Other examples of particular interest are the art deco No 2 and No 2A Beau Brownie Cameras of 1930 and the moulded plastic Baby Brownie of 1934, the Kodak Bantam Special of 1936 which used the new 828 roll film and the Super Kodak Six-20 introduced in 1938 which was the first camera with a fully automated exposure control system. Most of these delightful cameras were designed for George Eastman by the artist Walter Dorwin Teague and would make attractive additions to a collection or exhibition of Kodak cameras.

Kodak collectors should also look out for the copies of Kodak cameras made by other manufacturers. Each new Kodak innovation brought a horde of imitation and look alike box cameras and folding cameras in its wake mostly using the same film sizes that had been introduced by Kodak and these films and the film cartons themselves are also very collectable items today. A special size roll film was made for each of the early Kodak cameras and was referred to by that camera's name. The film for the No 1 Folding Pocket Kodak introduced in 1898 being called Eastmans Transparent Film, light proof Kodak Cartridge, six exposures 2¼ in × 3¼ in, No 1 Folding Pocket Kodak (also for three exposures, No 1 Panoram Kodak).

The rolls of film were all called cartridges until 1930, but these listings became unwieldy and in 1913 the films were given numbers. The Kodak lists for 1914 were the first to give these numbers together with the cameras names and from 1919 onwards only the numbers themselves were used. The various sized Kodak cartridges were assigned arbitrary numbers commencing with No 101 in the order in which they were first put on the market. No 101 giving 3½ in by 3½ in negatives was for the No 2 Bullet Camera introduced in 1895, No 102 giving 1½ in by 2 in negatives for the

Left *The Vanity Kodak Camera of 1928. The Vanity Kodaks were a new range of Vest Pocket Cameras Series III made in blue, green, red and grey and sold with a matching silk-lined case.* (Courtesy of the Kodak Museum, Harrow.)

Below *The No 1 Autographic Kodak Junior of 1914. The pressure of the stylus caused the backing paper to become transparent so that notes could be written and light penetrating the backing paper would expose them on the film.* (Courtesy of the Kodak Museum, Harrow.)

The Kodak Bantam Special of 1936 was a precision built miniature camera, taking the then newly introduced 828 roll film. (Courtesy of the Kodak Museum, Harrow.)

Pocket Kodak of 1895, No 115 giving 7 in by 5 in negatives for the No 5 Cartridge Kodak of 1898, No 120 giving the still popular 2¼ in by 3¼ in negatives for the No 2 Brownie of 1901 and No 122 giving 3¼ in by 5½ in post card size negatives for the No 3A Folding Pocket Kodak of 1903 and so on. As far as I know no private collector has as yet gathered together an entire set of the Kodak roll films but it would be an interesting exercise and I am including a list of them here for the benefit of any collector who would like to make the effort.

Film number	Negative size	Introduced	Discontinued
101	3½ in by 3½ in	1895	July 1956
102	1½ in by 2½ in	1895	September 1933
103	3¾ in by 4¾ in	1896	March 1949
104	4¾ in by 3¾ in	1897	March 1949
105	2¼ in by 3¼ in	1898	March 1949
106	3½ in by 3½ in	1898	1924
107	3¼ in by 4¼ in	1898	1924
108	4¼ in by 3¼ in	1898	October 1929
109	4 in by 5 in	1898	1924
110	5 in by 4 in	1898	October 1929
111	6½ in by 4¾ in	1898	
112	7 in by 5 in	1898	1924

113	9 cm by 12 cm	1898	
114	12 cm by 9 cm	1898	
115	6¾ in by 4¾ in	1898	March 1949
116	2½ in by 4¼ in	1899	
117	2¼ in by 2¼ in	1900	March 1949
118	3¼ in by 4¼ in	1900	August 1961
119	4¼ in by 3¼ in	1900	July 1940
120	2¼ in by 3¼ in	1901	
121	1⅝ in by 2½ in	1902	November 1941
122	3¼ in by 5½ in	1903	
123	4 in by 5 in	1904	March 1949
124	3¼ in by 4¼ in	1905	August 1961
125	3¼ in by 2½ in	1905	March 1949
126	4¼ in by 6½ in	1906	March 1949
127	1⅝ in by 2½ in	1912	
128	1½ in by 2¼ in	1912	November 1941
129	1⅞ in by 3 in	1912	January 1951
130	2⅞ in by 4⅞ in	1916	August 1961
616	2½ in by 4¼ in	1932	
620	2¼ in by 3¼ in	1932	
135	24 mm by 36 mm	1934	
828	28 mm by 40 mm	1935	
126	28 mm by 28 mm	1963	

Numbers 106 to 114 inclusive in this list are cartridge roll holders. The No 120 roll film can be substituted for No 105 and the No 122 for 124.

An interesting sub-section of an exhibition of Kodak collectables could show all the different types of Kodak films made in one particular film size. For instance the Eastman Kodak Company of Rochester, New York, has kindly let me have the following listing of all the different films that were made for their 3¼ in by 5½ in postcard cameras.

1903	Eastman's Transparent Film
1903 to 1943	Eastman's non-curling (NC) film (Kodak NC Film from 1930)
1910 to 1916	Eastman Speed Film
1914 to 1941	Eastman Autographic Film (Kodak Autographic from 1930) (Available only on special order after 1934)
1912 to 1924	Hawk-Eye Film
1931 to 1955	Kodak Verichrome Film
1933 to 1939	Kodak Super Sensitive Panchromatic Film
1935 to 1939	Kodak Panatomic Film
1938 to 1955	Kodak Super XX Panchromatic Film
1939 to 1943	Kodak Panatomic X Panchromatic Film
1941 to 1956	Kodak Plus X Panchromatic Film

1941 to 1945   Kodacolor
1955 to 1970   Kodak Verichrome Pan Film

Another sub-section of Kodak collectabilia perhaps shown in association with these films could consist of all the Kodak and Brownie cameras using No 122 roll film, and again the list shown here is by courtesy of the Eastman Kodak Company.

No 3A	Folding Pocket Kodak Camera	May 1903-1915
No 3A	Folding Brownie Camera	April 1909-1915
No 3A	Special Kodak Camera	April 1910-1914
No 3A	Six-Three Kodak Camera	April 1913-1915
No 3A	Autographic Kodak Camera	July 1914-1934
No 3A	Autographic Kodak Special Camera	July 1914-1915
No 3A	Autographic Kodak Special Camera with Coupled Rangefinder	February 1916-1934
No 3A	Folding Autographic Brownie Camera	July 1916-1926
No 3A	Autographic Kodak Junior Camera	April 1918-1927
No 3A	Panoram Kodak Camera	May 1926-1928
No 3A	Pocket Kodak Camera	February 1927-1933
No 3A	Kodak Series II Camera	April 1936-1941
No 3A	Kodak Series III Camera	July 1941-1945

The Kodak cameras provide a wonderful field for the collector and when associated with the other collectable Kodak antiques such as early Kodak advertisements and ephemera, Kodak Magazines, cartoons showing Kodaks, the George Eastman Medal awarded to Kodak employees, Kodak daylight developing machines and tanks, examples of early Eastman dry plates and films and Kodak films, and all the other Eastman Kodak innovations and inventions they would provide a lifetime of happy hunting for a specialist collector. If you are extra lucky you may even discover cameras like the two Kodaks used by Orville and Wilbur Wright when they were inventing the aeroplane, which were found by Dr Robert Bingham a California surgeon some years ago and which Dr Bingham has since donated to the University of California, Riverside, together with the other more than 3,000 items in his collection. So get out and get collecting now.

Chapter 4

Collecting detective and miniature cameras

The period of transition from the wet plate era to the dry plate and roll film eras of photography which gave birth to the Kodak cameras and their host of imitators also brought into being a burgeoning flood of detective and spy cameras that are much sought after by collectors today.

Using the new dry plates the photographer was no longer encumbered with the dark tent, tripod and other appurtenances of the wet plate period, the exposed plates could be developed at home or given out to one of the new processing firms that were springing up, and the photographer was no longer the unmistakable object of the public's curiosity. Taking advantage of this and of the speed of the new gelatine dry plates which meant that hand held exposures of 1/25 second could be given outdoors, photographs taken whilst the subject was unaware became popular and this lead to the introduction of detective cameras disguised to look like almost anything else except a conventional camera. The name detective camera was first used by Thomas Bolas for two cameras which he designed for the police to use to take surreptitious photographs of suspects in January 1881, one of which he disguised as a wooden box the other as a book.

By 1881 most photographers were changing over to the new dry plates at first using them in their old cameras but gradually changing over to the new types of cameras that were rapidly evolving. In the 1880s one could not just go up to a stranger in the street and ask him or her to pose for a photograph as one might do today, so elaborating on Bolas' original ideas, cameras were disguised in many different ways. Cameras were fitted into shoe boxes and workmen's lunch boxes or wrapped in brown paper and tied with string to look like a parcel with only the lens visible through a hole in the end and cameras were even disguised as Gladstone bags, handbags and picnic baskets.

The concealed detective cameras were usually quarter plate or 4 in by 5 in magazine cameras but camera makers soon introduced specially made small sized detective cameras that successfully masqueraded as books, cravats, field glasses, guns, hats, opera glasses, pocket watches, pistols, purses and walking sticks, or were in some cases worn under the waistcoat with the lens poking through a buttonhole in lieu of the button. Few of them

ADAMS & CO.'S
"HAT" DETECTIVE CAMERA.

ADAMS & Cº

ADAMS & Cº

THIS folds inside the same as an ordinary opera hat, and the lens can be removed in a moment, it simply fitting in with a bayonet joint. It takes pictures 4¼ × 3¼, and is fitted with a best quality Rectilinear Lens, working at *f* 11. The shutter works in the diaphgram slot and time as well as instantaneous exposures may be given. A focussing screen is also supplied. This is really a good instrument, and is not to be classed with the small postage stamp so-called cameras, like the scarf, purse, and button-hole. By taking 4¼ × 3¼ it becomes a useful instrument. They are sent out all ready for fitting, or we fit them free of expense if hat is sent.

Price £3 3s. net, with two Slides. Extra Slides, 4/- each.

Above *Adam and Co's Hat Detective Camera, 1891.*

Below *Scovill and Adams Co's Book Detective Camera, disguised as a set of three leather bound books. 4 in by 5 in, American 1892. Sold at Sotheby's Belgravia on 19 May 1983 for £4,180.*

Watson's Stereoscopic Binocular Detective Camera, 1902. The left hand barrel took its pictures at right angles to the direction in which one appeared to be looking and the right hand barrel was the magazine for twelve 5 in by 2 in plates. Sold at Sotheby's Belgravia on 16 November 1978 for £1,250.

made pictures of any great quality but all of them make wonderful exhibits in a collection of photographic antiques today. Very small cameras that could be used almost by sleight of hand such as Marion and Company's Academy Cameras and the later Kombi and Expo Police Cameras were also called detective cameras and many collectors have put together excellent collections of these tiny cameras.

Fox Talbot was the first photographer to use very small cameras. In the summer of 1835 he had a number of tiny cameras made by the local carpenter and fitted them with microscope lenses. They were so small that his wife called them his mousetraps. These miniature cameras took a 1 in square negative and shortened the exposure time required by his sensitized paper sufficiently for him to be able to take his first successful photographs. The earliest negative known, a photograph of a lattice window in the library at Lacock Abbey, which is preserved in the Science Museum, London was taken with one of these miniature cameras. By 1840 John B. Dancer was making enlarged copies of daguerreotypes with a view to using very minute plates with a very minute camera and then magnifying them subsequently to any required size.

Thomas Skaife's metal Pistolgraph Camera first mentioned in June 1856 using 1½ in circular wet plates, M Millot-Brulé's French Pistol Camera which followed soon after and Ottewill's Miniature Camera of 1860 all used miniature formats. C. Piazzi Smyth the Astronomer Royal for Scotland used a miniature camera of his own design when he photographed the interior of the Great Pyramid in Egypt in 1865. Made of tin it measured 3½ in by 3½ in and was 2 in long with an added 6 in extension that acted as a lens hood. It took 1 in square negatives on the end of a 1 in by 3 in microscope slide which was sensitized in an ebonite nitrate of silver bath that was built into the camera. Many other ingenious inventors also produced extra small cameras.

These early miniature cameras are all of great interest to collectors and of great value today because few were made at the time and even fewer have survived the passing years. Also of great interest because of their rarity and ingenuity of design, but perhaps more readily obtainable by collectors today, are the multitude of miniature detective and spy cameras that were introduced in the early days of the dry plate and roll film eras of photography.

It would be well to note however that the very rarity and hence the value of these beautiful little cameras has set the wolves amongst the sheep and some cameras of great interest to collectors such as the Ben Akiba Walking Stick Camera have recently been withdrawn from sales because a thorough investigation has shown them to be the work of unscrupulous forgers and not the original antiques that they professed to be. This is of course no reflection upon the integrity of reputable camera manufacturers such as Voigtlander whose replicas of their original daguerreotype camera of 1840 or Leitz whose replicas of their original prototype UR Leica camera of 1912 are highly valued by collectors but it is a warning to all collectors and would be collectors of photographic antiques to be cautious and 'not judge the jam by the label on the jar.'

Whilst some miniature cameras like those of Marion and Company made in the early 1880s bring very high prices when offered for sale today others such as the Ticka Pocket Watch Camera of 1906 can still be bought fairly reasonably and one of these in fine condition would make a nice starting point for a collection of this kind. The Ticka was made in several versions and collectors should look for the Focal Plane Ticka and the Watch Face Ticka which had a glass covered watch dial on the back, both introduced in 1908, and the Expo Watch Cameras which were American made versions of the Ticka cameras.

At a time when most men carried a pocket watch, a pocket watch camera must have been an almost perfect design for a detective camera. It could be taken out casually and held in the hand as if consulting it for the correct time and a photograph could be taken without attracting anyone's attention. Pocket watch detective cameras had been made before the Ticka, the rarest one of all probably being Lancaster's Patent Watch Camera of 1886. Originally fitted with a rotary shutter the improved model introduced in 1890 had a spring activated drop shutter. By then two versions were being made, a ladies' model for 1 in by 1½ in dry plates and a slightly larger gentleman's model for 2 in by 1½ in dry plates. These collapsible cameras are opened by turning the 'winding' knob at the top of the camera and are kept rigid by internal springs.

The Photoret Pocket Watch Camera introduced in 1890 was followed by the Kombi in 1893, the Phototake in 1896, the Presto Pocket Camera in 1899, the Expo Police Camera in 1911, and a host of other miniature cameras many of which seem to have been little more than toys and most of which seem to have been made more for today's collector than for the contemporary photographer. The exception to this are the few precision miniature cameras that were made between the two world wars and the outstanding examples of these were the Compass Camera made in Switzerland in 1937 to the design of Noel Pemberton-Billing who incorporated almost every available development in its construction, and the Minox Subminiature first

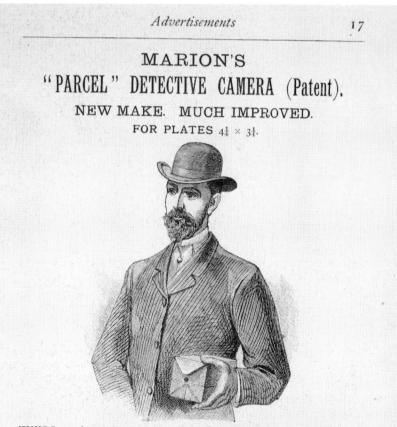

Advertisements　　　　　17

MARION'S
"PARCEL" DETECTIVE CAMERA (Patent).
NEW MAKE.　MUCH IMPROVED.
FOR PLATES 4¼ × 3¼.

THIS Camera is made box-shape, is neatly covered with brown linen-lined paper, and tied with string like an ordinary parcel, of which it has the exact appearance. The object is to disguise its real use, and to permit a Photograph to be taken without raising the slightest suspicion. After slipping the plates in from the holder, which may be done in daylight, it is only necessary to adjust the focus and to touch a spring to obtain a sharp Negative; the Plate is then returned to its holder. These Plate-holders are made of india-rubber, impervious to light and atmosphere, and being flexible, thin, and light, will pack in a very small compass. The Camera is fitted with a good double combination quick-acting Lens. It can easily be opened, when desirable, to clean from dust, etc.

Many of the beautiful pictures taken by Mr. T. C. Hepworth were done with this Camera. We can highly recommend it.

		£ s. d.
PARCEL CAMERA complete, with one Plate-Holder	.	4 0 0
Extra India-Rubber Plate-Holders	per doz.	1 0 0
Above Camera covered in Leather instead of Paper, with Leather Straps and Handle	.	4 14 0
Marion's Instantaneous Plates, suitable for this Camera	per doz.	0 1 6

MARION & CO., 22 & 23 Soho Square, London, W.

Right *The Ticka Pocket Watch Camera, 1907, made by Houghtons Ltd of London. When every man wore a pocket watch it was obviously a good design for a novelty camera. (Courtesy of the Kodak Museum, Harrow.)*

Left *Marion's Parcel Detective Camera, 1892.*

Below *A postcard advertising the Ticka Pocket Watch Camera.*

Taken with a "TICKA."

These Pictures were all taken on a single spool, by an Amateur, almost the first time he used the Camera.

made in Latvia in 1935 which was the camera used by many police agencies and intelligence networks in their daily work.

In the 1920s and 1930s almost any camera taking 2¼ in by 2¼ in negatives or smaller was called a miniature camera. Although many highly successful miniature plate cameras, including the outstanding Ermanox of 1924 which used 1¾ in by 2¼ in plates and with its enormous f 2 lens was the first of the candid cameras, and its many imitators plus the 2¼ in by 2¼ in roll film cameras such as the Rolleiflex and Rolleicord series, introduced by Franke and Heidecke in 1928, were produced it was the miniature 35 mm camera using cine film that swept the board and is still the most significant film size.

Pedants may quibble about the inclusion of such recent items in a book devoted to collecting photographic antiques, but the early 35 mm cameras are most important milestones in the development of modern photography and many collectors have made wonderfully complete collections of them, some covering the entire field and others specializing in one particular make, Leica or Contax perhaps, whilst others still have specialized in one period or even in the 35 mm cameras made in one country only.

The earliest known still camera to use 35 mm cine film was the camera invented by Dr Lucien G. Bull whilst working at the Institute Marey in Paris in 1903. It was not only the first 35 mm still camera but was also the world's first 35 mm stereoscopic camera. Designed for the high speed photography of objects illuminated by an electric spark, it could take up to 2,000 photographs per second on perforated or unperforated 35 mm cine film. As early as 1904 Dr Marey achieved spectacular results showing a dragonfly in flight and a bursting soap bubble taken at well over 1,000 frames per second.

The octagonal mahogany case of the Bull Camera is 5¼ in wide and 14¾ in high. Inside two 36 in strips of 35 mm cine film are wrapped around a metal

The very rare Lancaster's Patent Watch Camera, men's model. 1½ in by 2 in with an f8-60 mm lens, drop shutter and nickel plated watch form case with hinged covers front and rear opening to a telescopic body. English, 1890s. (Courtesy of Sotheby's Belgravia.)

Above left *The Photoret Magazine Snap-shot Watch Camera of 1893 by the Magic Introduction Co, New York, took six exposures on a 1¾ in diameter celluloid film disc. Sold at Christie's South Kensington on 26 January 1984 for £240.*

Above right *Brass and nickel Presto Miniature Camera for either roll film or glass plates. 3½ in long, American, 1908. Sold at Sotheby's Belgravia on 29 June 1981 for £260.*

Below *The Kombi subminiature combined camera and graphoscope of 1893 took 25 1½ in diameter circular negatives on a roll of film. This camera was sold at Sotheby's Belgravia on 21 March 1975 for £75. Similar Kombi cameras were sold at Christie's South Kensington on 30 November 1978 for £150 and on 17 May 1979 for £120.*

Compass camera with Kern lens, range finder, exposure meter, ground glass focussing screen, spirit level, stereoscopic head and filter control in metal case. Sold at Sotheby's Belgravia on 22 February 1980 for £380.

drum which is driven by an electric motor at speeds of up to forty revolutions per second with 54 electric sparks being produced at each turn of the drum. Only two of Dr Bull's cameras have been found; one is in the Science Museum at London, the other in the outstanding collection of Thurman F. Naylor in Massachusetts, USA, but more than two must have been made and this gives collectors yet another masterpiece of photographica to look for.

The first patent application for a 35 mm still camera was recently rediscovered by Brian Coe. Dated 9 March 1908, the patent number 5336 was issued to Dr Alberto Lleo, Pablo Audouard and Claudio Baradat all of Barcelona in Spain on 25 June 1908 and although no production of this camera has been recorded there is doubtless a prototype or two lying around somewhere waiting to be discovered.

The first 35 mm film camera using the 24 mm by 36 mm double cine frame format was handmade by George P. Smith in America in 1912 but the Homeos Stereoscopic Camera made by Richard Frères in Paris in 1913 was the first commercially produced 35 mm film still camera. A hundred and fifty Homeos Cameras were made before the end of 1913. The Homeos was rapidly followed by the Tourist Multiple in late 1913 and the Simplex Multi-Exposure patented by Walter H. Moses Jr in 1914, both made in the United States, the Centus Film Camera a 35 mm box camera made by James H. Sinclair of London and the Levy Roth Minigraph made in Berlin, but the First World War stopped the production of all of these cameras and no more were made until after the war.

The production of several imaginative 35 mm cameras like Talbot's Invisible Belt Camera, designed by Walter Talbot of Berlin in 1915 to take fifteen 24 mm by 24 mm pictures whilst being worn under the jacket with the lens protruding through a button hole, was also stopped by the war but Le Cent Vues, a 35 mm camera taking a hundred half frame 18 mm by 18 mm negatives on perforated film patented in Great Britain in 1914 was manufactured by its inventor Etiene N. Mollier in France in May 1924.

Production of the Homeos Stereoscopic 35 mm Camera was also

recommenced after the war and by the time that production ceased in the early 1920s an estimated 1,500 had been made but sales were slow and the stocks were not finally cleared until the early 1930s.

One of the smallest of the early 35 mm cameras was designed by M. Maroniez in 1913. Again stopped by the war it was finally produced by E. Guerin in Paris in 1923 and sold as Le Furet, 'The Ferret'. It seems to have been made with today's collectors in mind and was available with bodies of plain black metal, of polished brass, covered in black leather and in a beautiful Luxus model that was covered in red snakeskin. To add further interest for collectors all these different versions could be obtained in a standard 24 mm by 36 mm format or in a factory adapted single frame 18 mm by 24 mm format. As far as I know no collector has yet assembled a complete set of all the models of the Le Furet Camera but they would make a wonderful display in any collection.

The Phototank made by Henri Bayle in France in 1922 is another camera that is unusual enough to stand out in any collection. It was designed in metal on the lines of a World War 1 army tank and although it looks strong enough to survive several World Wars very few are seen today.

Right *French World War 2 espionage camera, similar to the Kodak Matchbox Camera of the same period.* (Courtesy of H. Keith Melton.)

Below *Two views of the Bull 35 mm high speed stereo camera of 1903. This was probably the first camera to use 35 mm film for still photos.* (Courtesy of Thurman F. Naylor.)

Left *Le Furet 35 mm camera designed by M. Maroniez in 1913 but not introduced until it was manufactured by E. Guerin in Paris in 1923. It was one of the smallest 35 mm cameras then made.* (Courtesy of Thurman F. Naylor.)

Below *The No 00 Cartridge Premo, the first 35 mm Kodak camera. It was introduced in February 1916 and took six 32 mm by 44 mm exposures on a roll of No 35 Kodak film.* (Courtesy of Thurman F. Naylor.)

The Sica, a wonderfully collectable camera manufactured by Simons and Company of Bern Switzerland in 1923, took 25 30 mm by 40 mm exposures on unperforated paper backed 35 mm film and the Eka made by M.E. Krauss in France early in 1924 also used unperforated 35 mm film taking supposedly 35 mm by 45 mm negatives on 25 or a hundred exposure films although the actual frame size seems to have been nearer 30 mm by 44 mm. The Eka was a precision made camera but because of its cost and non-standard film format it is very rare today and few collectors can boast of having one in their collections.

The Sept Camera manufactured by André Debrie of Paris and distributed by the Société Francais Sept in 1922 is a clear landmark in the use of 35 mm motion picture film for still pictures. Sold as a three in one camera that could be used for taking motion pictures, snapshots or time exposures it was designed to take 250 18 mm by 24 mm exposures on standard perforated 35 mm cine film either one at a time or in rapid succession it is a direct ancestor of the modern half frame 35 mm camera and is in the line of descent to today's 35 mm cameras with a built in motor drive.

The Sept was a redesigned version of an Italian camera the Autocinephot, first patented in 1918 and made in small numbers in Italy from early 1919 but the Autocinephot sank without trace whilst the Sept made in France under licence from the inventor Guiseppe Tartara became popular with professional newspaper photographers and is still occasionally used for short animation sequences in one or two film studios so that whilst examples of the Sept camera are offered for sale comparatively frequently the Autocinephot has become one of the rarer collectable 35 mm cameras.

Across the Atlantic Kodak introduced their own first 35 mm camera the Kodak 00 Cartridge Premo in February 1916. A small box camera which took six 32 mm by 42 mm negatives on a No 35 Kodak film, it sold reasonably well but although Kodak made an estimated 315,000 of these early 35 mm box cameras few are to be found today.

The Ansco Memo first announced in December 1926 was a more successful American camera that was made in a number of highly collectable versions. It was a small black leather covered wooden camera measuring only 2 in by 2½ in by 4 in. Weighing only 12 oz when loaded with film, it took half frame 18 mm by 24 mm negatives on standard perforated 35 mm cine film in specially loaded cassettes. The first Memos were fitted with wooden cassettes but these were soon superseded by metal ones and the camera eventually became available in fixed focus and several different focusing models. Production was carried on after the 1928 merger of Ansco and Agfa but was stopped in the early 1930s and the remaining stock was cleared at very low prices.

A few early examples finished in polished wood like tropical cameras have been found and as was the case with many cameras at the time, the Memo was made in green Boy Scout, Girl Scout and Campfire Girl versions. Examples of these and the many Memo accessories that included a developing machine, film printer, filters, printing frames, copier, copying camera and an enlarger can still be put together to form a small but complete Ansco Memo collection.

The prototype Leica 35 mm film camera built by Oskar Barnack in 1913 was another of the casualties of the First World War but although its development was stopped and another ten years were to pass before the Leica, named for the first syllables of the words Leitz camera, was finally produced the Leica has become a landmark in the history of photography.

Collecting Leica cameras is now an established speciality and one that still holds spectacular opportunities for collectors. It is known that at least two and probably three of the first prototype Leicas were built in 1913 and that one was used by Oskar Barnack and another by Ernest Leitz II but the only known survivor is kept in the Leica Museum in Wetzlar and every collector hopes that if one of the others still exists he or she will be the lucky one to find it. In the recent past Leitz have produced several hundred replicas of the original prototype Leica camera for collectors and museums. These are engraved Nachbildung der Ur-Leica, the Ancestor Leica, and have the Leitz trademark on the back of the camera.

In 1923, after the hiatus of the First World War and post-war years, a run of 31 pre-production models was made of the finished camera. These Model 'O', in German the 'nullserie', Leica cameras were made to test the methods of production and are numbered from 100 to 130 inclusive. Less than half of these have been traced to date but there must still be several more in existence somewhere waiting for persevering collectors to find them.

Manufacture of the first regular production model the Leica I commenced in 1924 and it was first introduced to the public at the Leipzig Spring Fair of 1925. Although known to the public as the Leica I it was called the Model A in the factory and in some of the countries to which it was exported. Similarly the second model fitted with a compur shutter was called the Model B. The official Leica production lists give the numbers of 600 Leicas that were made fitted with a dial set compur shutter from 1926 to 1929 and of another 882 made in 1929 and 1930 that were fitted with a rim set compur shutter, but collectors have found several compur Leicas with numbers different to those listed and it would be safe to assume that at least two unrecorded batches were made.

The ideal collector's Leica is probably the Luxus Leica of 1930. These were Leica Is with the metal parts gold plated and the camera body covered with lizard skin instead of the usual black vulcanite. The official lists record the making of only fifteen of these Luxus Leicas with numbers from 34,803 to

Left *Self-portrait of Oskar Barnack, inventor of the Leica, taken in 1914.* (Courtesy of Ernst Leitz GmbH, Wetzlar.)

Right *UR Leica, a replica of Oskar Barnack's first prototype 35 mm camera.* (Courtesy of Thurman F. Naylor.)

34,817 but again Luxus with numbers other than these are known to collectors. The Luxus Leica in the Leitz Museum at Wetzlar is No 9,781 and is possibly the original Luxus prototype.

Although most of the early Leicas had nickel plated knobs and lens mounts and had the normal black imitation leather covering a few were covered with calf skin and No 35,000 which was otherwise normal had a lizard skin covering.

Leitz also produced several specialized Leica cameras that are highly valued by collectors today. They include the Leica Reporter of 1937 which was a Leica IIIa with the film chambers enlarged to take 10 m of film allowing 250 or more exposures to be made without reloading, a medical Leica made just before World War 2, code named RYOOK, for taking 24 mm by 24 mm negatives of X-ray screens, several different military models made during the war and not included in the factory records for security reasons, the Mifilmca Leica Microscope Film Camera, the Leica MD 'Post' Camera taking a 24 mm by 27 mm negative that was used by the postal authorities to record the telephone meter readings and several other special Leicas that were made by the Leitz subsidiary companies in Canada and the USA.

The collection at the Leitz Factory at Wetzlar houses many unusual prototype cameras that would make mouth-watering additions to any collection. They include the 'doppel' Leica, a stereoscopic camera made personally by Oskar Barnack in 1935, an amazing 35 mm Leica panoramic camera, the Leica 75 which was a little larger than the normal Leica and a little smaller than the Leica 250 Reporter, and the prototype Leica IV of 1935 which was the predecessor of the Leica M3, but in addition to these and the many other delightful items in the Leitz Museum there have been persistent rumours of

prototype Leicas that were 'liberated' during and just after the war and may yet one day become part of some lucky collector's Leica exhibit.

Leitz have also produced an enormous variety of accessories for the Leica camera. Until 1960 these were given code words ranging from ABCOO film cutting knife for cutting films in the camera, 1936, to ZWTOO intermediate thread for using the Elmar 50 mm lens on the universal copying device, 1936, and many collectors have made specialized collections of these too.

The very success of the Leica cameras triggered off a spate of copy Leicas, imitation Leicas and downright Leica forgeries. The earliest of these were probably the three Soviet Leica copies made in a juvenile rehabilitation centre, the F.E. Dzerzhinsky Labour Commune at Kharkov in the Ukraine in October 1932. These straightforward copies of the Leica I were called FEDs after the initials of Felix Edmundovich Dzerzhinsky, the founder of the Soviet secret police for whom the labour commune had been named.

The production of these first Soviet copy Leicas seems to have been only a pilot run and by the end of 1933 only thirty complete cameras had been made. In 1934 a new model FED was introduced. This was a straight copy of the Leica II except for the omission of the accessory shoe. Ten cameras numbers 31 to 40 were completed in January 1934. The early FED IIs had a smooth black celluloid like covering and plated metal parts but FED IIIs were soon being made with black painted metal parts. A few were made with a burnished finish on the plated brass and on some the black covering had a more leather-like finish. The name FED/Trudkommuna/im./F.E. Dzerzhinskogo/Khar'kov (FED, F.E. Dzerzhinsky Labour Commune, Kharkov) was engraved on the top of the rangefinder of these early FED cameras, the lens was engraved FED 1;3.5 F=50m/m, and some 4,000 cameras were produced in 1934.

The lenses for the first few of these FEDs were made by the VOOMP Opytnyi Zavod (VOOMP Experimental Factory). VOOMP also made a few copy Leica I cameras in 1933 and a copy Leica II which they called the Pioner (Pioneer) in 1934. About 300 Pioneer cameras were made in 1934 and early

It is estimated that only about 24 of these gilt finished, snakeskin covered Luxus Leicas were made. (Courtesy of Hans Edwards.)

The Dopple Leica of 1935. Oscar Barnack's 193 mm long prototype 35 mm stereo camera. (Courtesy of Ernst Leitz GmbH, Wetzlar.)

1935 but production seems to have ceased after that and the FAG the third Soviet copy of the Leica seems to have suffered a similar fate. The FAG was another Leica II copy made this time in the Geodeziya Zavod (Geodesy Factory). Some 50 FAG cameras were produced in early 1934 and early in 1935 the introduction of a new model with a detachable back was reported but only a few hundred FAG cameras seem to have been made.

In July 1934 the administration of the Dzerzhinsky Commune was changed. Production of the FED was increased and the quality of the camera improved with a better satin chrome finish and a rectangular viewfinder frame which was made flush with the top of the rangefinder housing towards the end of 1935. By this time production of both the Pioneer and FAG cameras had ceased and all production of the Soviet copy Leicas was concentrated in the FED factory.

A few of the FED copy Leicas that have reached the West have 'Ernst Leitz Wetzlar' and the Leica symbol engraved on them and some are even fitted with counterfeit Leitz Summar and Elmar lenses, but these seem to have been engraved privately rather than to have been deliberate factory counterfeits and nobody who has handled a real Leica would be taken in by one. Novices should beware because although the FED was much inferior in workmanship it bears a marked resemblance to a genuine Leica, but for collectors of course a FED with Leica markings must be a more rare find than a genuine Leica itself.

Only about forty of a new model FED-B of 1937 which was a copy of the Leica IIIa were produced but the 1938 FED-S (known as such because the third letter of the Russian alphabet is pronounced like the English 'S') which was the standard FED with a faster f 2 lens and an additional top speed of a thousandth was more successful and in all about 175,000 FED cameras were produced before the Germans invaded the Soviet Union and occupied Kharkov.

The Hansa Canon (originally called Kannon) of 1936 and the Leotax of 1941 were the best of the early Japanese copies of the Leica cameras. Other collectable copies like the Honor and the Nicca made in Japan and the Zorki from the Soviet Union were joined by the Foca from France, the Kardon from the United States, the Kristall from Italy, the Meopta from Czechoslovakia, the Wica from Austria and the best copy Leica of them all, the Reid from Great Britain could make a dream theme for collectors.

The first real competition to the Leica came from the Contax camera introduced by Zeiss Ikon of Dresden, Germany, in March 1932. A de luxe miniature camera the Contax I as it became known was a little larger and heavier than the Leica II of that same year. It was a solid and well made camera and sold well although it never outsold the Leica. A second version of the original Contax introduced in 1934 which had the additional slower shutter speeds of 1/10, 1/5 and ½ second was originally known as the Contax II but this designation was subsequently given to the new chromium plated Contax introduced in 1936. The Contax III introduced at the same time was the new Contax II with an additional built-in, but not coupled, photo-electric exposure meter. The Contax cameras also suffered from a rash of copies and imitations such as the 1954 Soviet Kiev III which was an exact copy of the Contax II.

In 1935 Zeiss introduced another camera that has become a land mark for collectors. This was the Zeiss Ikon Contaflex the world's first 35 mm twin lens reflex and the first camera to have a built-in photo-electric exposure meter. Its Contax metal focal plane shutter with coupled film wind and the six interchangeable taking lenses that were produced made it an outstanding camera and one that is now much sought after by collectors.

Collectors have often asked me for some date beyond which old cameras and the other photographic collectabilia are no longer considered collectable photographic antiques and the answer of course is that there is no such date. Many collectors are only interested in items from the nineteenth century or even earlier, and these are all highly desirable, but other equally dedicated collectors only collect dry plate cameras, equipment, negatives and contemporary prints made with them, whilst others concentrate on roll film, 35 mm, sub-miniature items, or other specialities which bring collecting right up to date.

How about, for instance, a collection of 'instant' cameras, equipment and images ranging from the early tintype (which were first called melainotype or ferrotype) examples from the 1850s right through to the several variations of the first Polaroid Land Model 95 instant camera of 1948 with its unique ball and mast sight which became the improved 95A in 1954 and the 95B in 1958, the model 700 Polaroid produced from 1955 to 1957 which was basically a 95A with an uncoupled rangefinder next to the flip up optical viewfinder, the model 150 produced from 1957 to 1960, a 95B with a coupled rangefinder, the 1954 model 110, the 110A of 1957, the 110B of 1960 and so on up to and including examples of all the current models and of course including the range of Kodak Instant Print cameras that are now competing for the instant print market.

The Telephot Button Camera made by the British Ferrotype Co, Blackpool in 1900. Sold at Sotheby's Belgravia on 7 July 1978 for £580.

Even the new Kodak Disc cameras and the derivatives made by other camera manufacturers, new though they may be now, will one day be valued collectors, items so why not look for a few examples of the first Disc cameras made by each of the modern manufacturers and then perhaps work your way backwards to the original cameras that used discs of glass or film.

Disc cameras have been made in almost every size and shape imaginable from strange revolver like pieces of apparatus to wrist watches and almost everything else in between. One of the first cameras to use a disc was Thompson's revolver camera. Designed by an Englishman it was made by A. Brois of Paris, France, and first demonstrated at a meeting of the Société Francais de Photographie on 4 July 1862 as the Revolver Photographie. Four separate exposures were made on a circular plate housed in a cylinder in the mid-section of the camera and the rear of the cylinder was revolved one quarter turn after each exposure until all four had been taken.

In 1867 Alfred A. Pollock, an English amateur photographer, suggested using a rotating circular plate to take a series of instantaneous photographs of a man walking and then printing them onto another circular plate so that they could be viewed as a phenakistiscope or stroboscope disc. Pierre Jules César Janssen, a French astronomer, used his photographic revolver, an automatic camera taking a series of 48 photographs at seventy second intervals around the edge of a circular daguerreotype plate which was rotated by clockwork, to take photographs of the transit of the planet Venus across the Sun on 8 December 1874. In his efforts to record the movement of birds in flight Dr Etienne Jules Marey incorporated Janssen's idea in his photographic gun of 1882. Used like a rifle, Marey's photographic gun took a series of photographs around the edge of a revolving circular plate at the rate of twelve a second.

A few years later an American inventor Robert D. Gray showed his disc detective camera to the world at a meeting of the New York Society of Amateur Photographers on 22 December 1885. This camera patented on 27

July 1886 was manufactured by the Western Electric Co, New York. Covered by a false waistcoat front, it took six 1⅝ in diameter exposures on a 5½ in diameter dry plate. A second model in May 1886 no longer had a false waistcoat front attached to it but was worn under an ordinary waistcoat or jacket so that only the lens protruding through a button hole could be seen.

C.P. Stirn of Stirn and Lyon of New York purchased the rights to the camera from Gray in 1886 and on 28 July 1886 patented it in Germany. Stirn's brother Rudolph Stirn began producing a new improved model in Berlin in October of that year, this new model which was hinged at the bottom and closed by a knob at the top was called 'C.P. Stirn's Patent Concealed Vest Camera'. Made in two sizes, the No 1 took six 1⅝ in diameter exposures on a 5½ in plate and the larger, No 2, which was 7 in in diameter took four 2½ in diameter exposures on each plate. They sold extremely well and were marketed under several different names all over the world. They were sold in England as Perken Son and Rayment's 'Waistcoat Detective Camera' and also as the London Stereoscopic & Photographic Company's 'Secret Camera', in France as A. Schaeffner's 'Le Cuirasse' and in Germany as the 'Geheim Camera' (Secret Camera).

The Stirn Concealed Vest Camera most often seen by collectors is the smaller No 1 model which was the more popular of the two. It was produced until 1892 although production of the larger model had ceased in 1890.

The next collectable disc camera was the Magic Photoret manufactured by the Magic Introduction Co of New York who marketed it in 1894. The first American made pocket watch type miniature camera, made three years after the introduction of the Lancaster Pocket Watch Camera in England in 1891, the Photoret was designed by W.K.L. Dickson who had developed the Mutoscope whilst working for Thomas A. Edison and patented by Herman Casler in 1893. It took six exposures, ½ in square with the corners cut off, on a 1¾ in diameter sheet of celluloid film. A simple camera, it had the advantage over the Lancaster Pocket Watch Camera of being always ready for use and was capable of producing good quality enlargement if used carefully.

The British Journal of Photography for 8 September 1911 described a 'Circular Pocket Camera' patented in London on 3 August 1910 by John Arnold which took six photographs on a flat circular film after the fashion of the Stirn's Vest Camera but as far as I can make out Arnold's camera was never put into production.

A similar fate was to be in store for the disc cameras designed by American inventor James J. Dilks in the 1930s and 1940s. An engineer from New Jersey, Dilks made several different disc cameras ranging from a 5 in square, ¾ in thick metal camera taking twenty ½ in by ⅝ in exposures on a 4½ in diameter disc of film, to a circular camera taking twelve exposures on a disc of film and even a stereoscopic version that could take single exposures or stereo pairs on the film disc, but although Dilks offered to sell the patents of his 'Rotadisc' cameras to the Eastman Kodak Co in the 1940s and 1950s his

Stirn's Waistcoat Detective Camera. When worn suspended around the neck by the cord the lens protruded through a button hole in place of the button. Sold at Sotheby's Belgravia on 26 June 1981 for £320.

offers were not taken up and his cameras were never produced commercially.

Japan produced the tiny octagonal Petal disc camera in 1948. Made by Sakura, it took six circular approximately 7/32 in exposures on a circular film disc the size of a 5p piece and with the round version of the same camera made by Konica in 1950 it makes a nice pair of disc cameras for the collector to look for.

The Steinbeck ABC wristwatch camera made in Germany in 1950 had a similar film format to the Petals taking eight 5.5 mm diameter exposures on a 24 mm film disc but was by all accounts a better camera. The shutter setting, film wind and counter were all interlocked. The film was supplied in special daylight loading cassettes and the manufacturers made a special enlarger for the film discs so that with care enlargements of up to 8 in by 10 in could be made.

Several other cameras using discs of film were also made before Kodak introduced their modern versions of the disc camera but it was Kodak's introduction of space age technology and new high resolution films that has led to today's outburst of disc cameras and established a whole new spectrum of collectable cameras for us to find and preserve for the edification of future photographic historians.

Chapter 5

Collecting old photographs

Collecting old photographs is a fascinating introduction to collecting photographic antiques and your own old family photographs can become the nucleus of a wonderful photographic collection. The grim-visaged images of our Victorian ancestors, grim-visaged because of the concentration necessitated by the head clamps and long exposure times used in the early days of photography are stern reminders of our forefathers Victorian morals and customs. They illustrate the value of preserving old photographs and if by happy chance were taken by a famous photographer they will become a prized part of your collection of old photographs.

The first time that the painter Paul Delaroche saw a daguerreotype he is reported to have exclaimed, 'From today painting is dead!' Whilst this was poetic exaggeration, photography did indeed develop into a new art form. Not one which replaces painting as Delaroche had anticipated but rather one which supplements it and develops our perception of space and time in newer and perhaps more vivid directions, and as photography developed it has left behind a multitude of collectable images many of which connoisseurs are only now beginning to appreciate. Early photography became an extension of the existing art forms and many artists and miniature painters put out of work by the new invention became photographers themselves.

The earliest daguerreotype still in existence, a still life taken by Daguerre in 1837 and now preserved at the Société Francais de Photographie, Paris, shows the influence of art even at this early stage, whilst the scenes of the towns and countryside which the early photographers recorded are often reminiscent of the landscape paintings that were fashionable then and which early photographers strove to emulate. Collectors will know that early 'art' photographs of this kind are extremely rare and hard to find today and when they do appear in salesrooms they fetch extremely high prices.

William Henry Fox Talbot announced his first paper process which he called 'Photogenic Drawing' in January 1839, six months before the daguerreotype process was made public. His paper process provided both negative and positive prints but like the daguerreotype was at first too slow to be used for successful portraiture. Fox Talbot exposed his sensitized material in the camera until the image became visible as Daguerre had, but his discovery of the latent image in the autumn of 1840 led to his patenting a major modification of his process on 8 February 1841. He called these new improved photographs calotypes after a Greek word meaning beautiful, but soon changed their name to talbotypes.

The shorter exposure time made possible by the talbotype process at last made portraiture practical and further improvements to the daguerreotype and the introduction of new improved cameras led to the opening of the first professional photographic portrait studio in Britain by Richard Beard on 23 March 1841 and to photography becoming finally accepted as a popular art form.

Most of the earliest photographs that come to light are daguerreotype portraits and as well as those made by Beard and other pioneers, collectors should look for portraits of well known people, photographs of everyone from artisans to scientists and the photographers themselves with their instruments or the tools of their trade, and daguerreotypes of outdoor scenes and landscapes, all of which are highly desirable photographic antiques. When unusual daguerreotypes of this kind are offered for sale in the better auction rooms, particularly if they are in good condition and accompanied by contemporary documentation they command very high prices, often up to £1,000 or more, but the diligent collector can still make a lucky find if he or she is observant and knowledgeable and one of the purposes of this book and my previous book *Collecting Old Cameras* is to provide the collector with just the knowledge needed to sort the wheat from the chaff.

Although painting has influenced photography since its inception photographers gradually evolved individual styles which were purely photographic. Daguerrian artists like Antoine Jean Francois Claudet, William

Half plate daguerreotype portrait in a gilt and plush lined brown leather case, 1850s. Sold at Sotheby's Belgravia on 27 March 1981 for £110.

Beard quarter plate daguerreotype portrait, tinted, with a gilt and plush lined red leather case gilt embossed with photographer's credit 'Beard's Photographic Institutions 35 King William Street, 34 Parliament Street and the Royal Polytechnic Institution, London and 34 Church Street, Liverpool', 1850. Sold at Sotheby's Belgravia on 21 March 1980 for £190.

Edward Kilburn, John Jabez Edwin Mayall and many others prospered as the growing middle classes adopted the daguerreotype portrait as their own equivalent to the hand painted miniatures of their betters and whilst many professional photographers churned out an almost identical product some soon developed highly distinctive styles of their own. Daguerreotypes like paintings were regarded as individual works of art but the calotype negative which could be used to produce a number of identical prints was felt to be more akin to an etching from which many prints could be made.

Daguerreotypes are easily recognized by collectors. Because of their mirror like surface they can only be viewed if held at the correct angle as if they are tilted even slightly a negative effect is produced in the image. Calotypes are salted paper prints usually with a dull matt appearance and the surface has the roughness of the fine writing paper used at that time and if you are fortunate you may find a trace of the paper makers watermark to help in their positive identification. Calotype negatives are easier to identify, being negatives the black and white shading is reversed and the paper has often been waxed to assist in the printing giving the paper a translucent appearance.

The negative and positive process discovered by Fox Talbot changed the history of photography and became the basis of most modern methods of photography. Sir John Herschel the astronomer and scientist was the first to name Fox Talbot's original reversed pictures negatives and the re-reversed copy prints positives. In 1819 Herschel discovered that hyposulphite of soda, now called sodium thiosulphate, dissolved the salts of silver and later hearing of Fox Talbot and Daguerre's still secret discoveries began taking paper photographs using hyposulphate of soda to arrest the further action of light by washing away the chloride of silver or other silver salts used. Both Daguerre and Fox Talbot soon adopted it in their work.

Photographs by these or any of the other pioneers of photography are highly prized by collectors and being a direct link with the earliest days of photography are a delightful contrast to almost every other aspect of collecting photographic antiques.

In almost every other case an item in less than perfect condition should

'The Gamekeeper', a calotype by Fox Talbot, 1842. (Courtesy of the Fox Talbot Museum.)

A calotype of Oxford High Street, 9½ in by 7½ in, taken by Fox Talbot in September 1843. Sold at Sotheby's Belgravia on 29 October 1982 for £2,200.

not be considered for inclusion in your collection. If a camera or stereoscope is damaged or discoloured or an old photograph is creased or heavily marked or stained it should be rejected and even a low price should not tempt the would be collector. This may seem a very harsh attitude to adopt, but unless it is a great rarity such an item is not only almost worthless but it will also spoil the appearance of your collection. However anything which gives us a direct link with the fathers of photography should be treasured

Label of a talbotype (or calotype) photogenic drawing by Fox Talbot in 1843. Sold at Sotheby's Belgravia on 3 March 1982 for £80.

however unhappy we are with its condition, although naturally the nicer the item the more desirable it becomes.

Miniature painter Henry Collen, one of Queen Victoria's painting masters, became the first professional calotypist, opening a studio in the early summer of 1841, but David Octavius Hill of Edinburgh was probably the first painter to realise the artistic possibilities inherent in the talbotype process. In 1843, impressed with the drama of the occasion, he decided to paint a giant picture of all the 474 ministers who participated in the first General Assembly of the newly formed Free Church of Scotland. Acting on the advice of Sir David Brewster he began working with Robert Adamson, a professional calotypist, in what was to become a famous photographic partnership and the photographs that they took together, which were labelled 'Calotype portrait executed by R. Adamson, under the artistic direction of D.O. Hill', are now world renowned.

This collaboration of Hill arranging the artistic effects of the sitters and backgrounds and Adamson attending to the cameras and the processing of the photographs lasted for four and a half years. About 1,400 of their paper negatives are known although it is possible that more than twice that number were made during the time that they worked together as other examples are still being found by collectors today.

Most of the Hill and Adamson negatives were whole plate 8½ in by 6½ in photographs although a few smaller and several larger ones have been discovered and the subject matter varies from their portraits of Scottish Free Church ministers and distinguished members of Scottish society to the old stone cottages, their inhabitants, the sailors and fishing boats of local seaside villages and a few architectural views and landscapes. Hill often expressed his interest in the work of Rembrandt and some of the Hill and Adamson calotypes are indeed reminiscent of the powerful close-ups of Rembrandt's self portraits. In a letter to Brewster, Hill wrote 'The rough and unequal texture throughout of the paper is the main cause of the calotype failing in details before the daguerreotype—and this is the very life of it. They look like the imperfect work of man—and not the perfect work of God'.

Hill and Adamson's artistry was not surpassed by any other calotype photographer and was probably only equalled by the outstanding photographers of a later generation like Julia Margaret Cameron and Gaspard Felix Tournachon 'Nadar' who used the much better wet plate process.

The daguerreotype process was mainly used by portrait photographers but most of the calotypes that are found today are outdoor scenes. Fox Talbot's calotypes feature architecture and landscape pictures from all over Great Britain and even a few that he took in France. Reverend George Bridges and Reverend Calvert Jones who were friends of Fox Talbot used his calotype process during their Mediterranean travels in the 1840s and James Mudd of Manchester and Samuel Smith of Wisbech were amongst many other early photographers whose paper negatives and prints are very collectable today, whilst the work of previously unknown and unrecognised calotypists such as Dr Thomas Keith of Scotland and others is constantly being discovered or rediscovered.

Many variations and improvements to both the daguerreotype and calotype processes were made which helped to shorten exposure times and improved the images but the first major improvement was one made to Fox Talbot's paper process by the Frenchman Louis-Désiré Blanquart-Evrard in January 1847. Fox Talbot had coated the surface of the paper with the light sensitive salts of silver but Blanquart-Evrard, by putting his paper into successive baths of iodode of potassium and nitrate of silver soaked the

A late portrait of David Octavius Hill.

'Dumbarton Presbytery'. The group includes Rev Alexander of Duntocher, Rev Smith, Rev Pollock and Rev McMillan and is a calotype, 7¾ in by 5¾ in, inscribed and dated 29 March 1845 by David Octavius Hill and Robert Adamson. This group was transferred virtually intact to the 'Disruption' painting for which it was a study. Sold at Sotheby's Belgravia on 11 June 1976 for £480.

paper with the light sensitive substances.

Paper prepared in this way could be kept for months. It was moistened in an acid solution of nitrate of silver immediately before use and had to be exposed whilst still wet, usually being held between two thin glass plates, and was developed in gallic acid. Paper negatives prepared in this way were much more sensitive to light than any of the previous processes, needing only a quarter of the exposure time given to a calotype or daguerreotype, and they had the additional advantage of recording much greater graduation of tone and detail than any earlier paper process.

During the early 1840s many other paper processes were also described, the variations mostly using the salts or solutions of different metals in the preparation or developing of the photographs but the only one that proved to be practical was the cyanotype. This process was first described by Sir John Herschel in June 1842 and was named for the cyanogen used in combination with iron in the sensitive coating. It is the cheapest, easiest and most permanent way of making photographic prints, the print only needing to be washed in cold water after exposure. Although an extremely slow process the cyanotype proved ideal for making contact copies. Herschel used cyanotypes to make exact copies of complex calculations and notes which are the earliest known forerunners of the modern photo-copying process.

Mrs Anna Atkins used the cyanotype to record the plants in her comprehensive collection of British seaweeds. Her three volume work *Photographs of British Algae: Cyanotype Impressions*, which was issued in parts from 1843 to

1853, contained 411 plates of British seaweeds made by the cyanotype process with the descriptions, preface and even the title reproduced in the same way. Collectors can expect to pay prices of up to £200 or so, depending of course on the condition of the print and quality of the image, when single examples of Mrs Atkins cyanotypes are purchased at the larger sale rooms. Of course as always one should keep a sharp eye open for them elsewhere as, like many other types of early photographs, they can be found at much more reasonable prices by the collector who is prepared to spend his or her time searching through piles of engravings, ephemera and prints etc in out of the way places.

The cyanotype appears to have been little used until it was reintroduced by Marion & Co as the ferro-prussiate or blue process in the early 1880s, but it has been in common use for blue prints since then. The most interesting and collectable items produced by this process are probably those produced during the Boer War when the British defenders of Mafeking ran out of money and postage stamps and Lieutenant-Colonel Baden-Powell authorized the production of five hundred copies of a drawing of a one pound note, and a run of two different types of postage stamps a one penny and a three penny, all produced photographically using Sir John Herschel's process.

The waxed paper process initiated in 1851 by another Frenchman, Gustave Le Gray, was the finest paper negative process of them all and the beautiful photographs that they produced are highly valued by collectors today. Unlike the calotype which was waxed after exposure to make it easier to print, in this new process the paper was waxed before being iodised in an entirely new set of substances, rice water, sugar of milk, iodide of

'The Fishergirl' by David Octavius Hill and Robert Adamson 8¼ in by 6¼ in. Sold at Sotheby's Belgravia on 24 October 1975 for £150.

potassium, cyanide of potassium and fluoride of potassium. Waxed paper negatives made by Le Gray's process could be prepared up to two weeks before being used, needed approximately the same exposure time, about three or four minutes in brilliant sunshine, as the calotype, and had the added advantage that development could be delayed until three or four days after exposure.

Gustave Le Gray also claimed to have invented the collodion process on the basis of an 1850 publication. He had begun his artistic career as a painter and produced extraordinary work in all fields throughout the 1850s. His famous seascapes were large albumen prints made by combining separate wet collodion glass plate negatives of dramatically lighted seas with those of beautifully detailed skies. They caused a great sensation when they were first exhibited in London in 1856, but in 1859 Le Gray sold his photographic establishment to the painter Alophe and shortly thereafter he disappeared from history. The wet collodion process that he had laid claim to had been introduced by an Englishman, Frederick Scott Archer, in March 1851 and had become an instant success.

Niepce de Saint Victor, a nephew of Nicéphore Niepce, had published an albumen, the white of eggs, on glass process on 12 June 1848 but it was too slow to be used for portraiture. Scott Archer's process, in which a glass plate coated with a film of collodion made from gun cotton, alcohol and ether was sensitized with a solution of silver nitrate, was much faster with exposures of five seconds to about two minutes depending on conditions.

Scott Archer published his process without patent restrictions so that

A plate from 'Cyanotypes of British and foreign flowering plants and ferns', a series of 160 cyanotype plates of sizes varying between 13¼ in by 9¾ in and 7½ in by 4¾ in taken by Anna Atkins in 1854. The work was sold at Sotheby's Belgravia on 28 October 1981 for £2,800.

Waxed paper negative (right) and contact print (centre) of a group portrait of the family of P.W. Fry taken in the 1850s. Sold at Sotheby's Belgravia on 14 March 1979 for £380.

Below *'An Effet de Soleil'. An albumen print from a collodion on glass negative, 12¾ in by 16¼ in, printed in red ink with the facsimile signature 'Gustave Le Gray'. It is mounted on card with a blind stamped photographer's credit 'Gustave Le Gray & Co, Paris 1856'. Sold at Sotheby's Belgravia on 28 June 1978 for £4,200.*

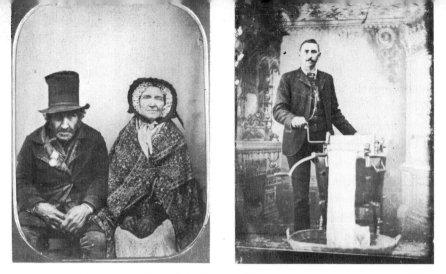

anyone could use it without hindrance. However a subsequent modification, consisting of a collodion positive on glass made by bleaching an under-exposed wet collodion negative and viewing it against a dark background by reflected light discovered by Scott Archer and two friends Peter W. Fry and Fallon Horne was patented in England by an American James Cutting in July 1854. Cutting called these collodion positives ambrotypes and the name became generally used for this process. Ambrotypes being similar to, but cheaper and easier to produce than, daguerreotypes soon replaced them for portraiture and were the fashionable photograph from 1853 to about 1860 when the carte de visite became the popular form of photography.

In 1853 a French amateur photographer Adolphe Alexandre Martin published a variant collodion positive process which used black enamelled tinplate instead of glass. This process was patented by William Kloen and Daniel Jones in Great Britain in 1856 and by Professor Hamilton Smith in the United States of America that same year and became very popular in the United States. Originally called melainotypes or ferrotypes they were soon popularly referred to as tintypes and came into general use by street photographers in the United States about 1860.

The American Civil War gave the tintype a quick boost as a cheap photograph that could be safely kept in a uniform pocket or posted home and they were soon being fitted into inexpensive items of jewellery and collected in special albums that were made to house them. Tintypes did not become popular in Great Britain or Europe until well into the 1870s when they were introduced as 'American' novelty photographs by itinerant photographers.

Collectors should seek out the unusual images and examples like those made on brown tinplate or those made on leather and paper which are both extremely rare, even though the tintype process was used by beach fairground and street photographers until well after World War 2. Like the daguerreotype, collodion positives were each a unique photographic image and were sold in a protective case or at the very least in the cheapest

Far left *A half plate ambrotype portrait of an elderly couple, tinted, 1860. Sold with two quarter plate ambrotype portraits at Christie's South Kensington on 27 June 1978 for £175.*

Left *A quarter plate tintype showing a new washing machine.* (Courtesy of Bill Rodgers.)

Right *The earliest extant photograph on leather. A rubber stamp impresion on the back shows that it was exhibited at Munich in 1854.* (Courtesy of the Bensusan Museum of Photography, Johannesburg.)

examples in a protective card folder.

Glass collodion negatives could be printed on the salted paper used in Fox Talbot's calotype process but an improved paper process was described by Louis-Désiré Blanquart-Evrard in 1850 in which a smooth slightly glossy surface was obtained by coating the paper with albumen treated with ammonium chloride before sensitizing with silver nitrate. This proved ideal for printing the glass collodion negatives and was used by most photographers right up to the end of the nineteenth century. Most of the early photographs found by collectors today will be these albumen prints.

Men of great endurance used the glass wet collodion process to create photographs that are highly valued by collectors today. Carrying their cumbersome equipment across deserts, up mountains and over the seas, these photographers were men like Francis Frith who in 1856 travelled more than 800 miles up the Nile recording the mysteries of Egypt often in temperatures of more than 110°F with the collodion on his plates drying almost as he coated them; the brothers Louise-Auguste Bisson and Auguste-Rosalie Bisson who accompanied Emperor Napoleon III and Empress Eugénie on a mountain climbing exhibition to Switzerland in 1860 and photographed Mont Blanc and its glaciers in the sub zero temperatures of the Alps washing the plates with melted snow after developing them; and Roger Fenton who sailed to the Crimean War in 1855 and took more than 300 negatives of the fortifications, guns, ships, troops and the canteen operators who also tended the wounded as Florence Nightingale's nurses, although the intense heat often almost boiled the emulsion on the plates as he prepared them in his 'photographic van'.

Fenton had used Le Gray's waxed paper process with great success during his photographic tour of Russia in the summer of 1852 and the photographs that he produced there were typical of those produced by many of the great early French photographers who used Le Gray's process. His concentration on the qualities and angles of the light and his sensitive use of figures to give life and humanity to his landscape studies is highly reminiscent of the work of Le Gray, Baldus, Le Secq, Regnault and many others.

Collectors of these exciting early photographs will also look for examples of the work of Felice Beato who used the collodion wet plate process to record the Indian Mutiny of 1857, James Robertson the official photographer to the British army who worked with him and who had photographed the fall of Sebastopol, William Notman photographer of the Canadian Pioneers in the 1860s and Mathew B. Brady the famed recorder of the American Civil War.

Brady, like so many early photographers, was originally a portrait painter. He was taught the daguerreotype process by the pioneer American daguerreotypists Samuel F.B. Morse and John William Draper and opened a glass roofed studio in New York in 1844. He was soon winning exhibition prizes and gold medals for his daguerreotypes and began a collection of photographs of prominent people and politicians which he gradually built up over the following fifty years. Like many others Brady switched to the wet collodion plate process in the early 1850s and by 1856 when be brought Alexander Gardner, an experienced photographer from Scotland, to New York Brady had opened several studios and was employing a number of assistants to work in them.

The photograph that Brady took of Abraham Lincoln on 27 February 1860 was the most important one of his entire career and possibly changed the course of history. Abraham Lincoln said of this photograph, 'Brady and the Cooper Union speech made me President of the United States.' When the Civil War broke out Brady obtained a pass from President Lincoln and set about documenting the entire war. His photographic van became a common sight to the soldiers and he photographed almost every aspect of

An albumen print, 15¼ in by 19in, from 'Egypt', Saini and Jerusalem', a bound set of seventeen large photographs by Francis Frith, 1857. Sold at Sotheby's Belgravia on 29 October 1976 for £7,500.

Above *An advertisement for Francis Frith's photographs.*

Below *Balaclava, General Bosquet and his aides du camp, 1855. An albumen print, 6½ in by 6¼ in, by Roger Fenton. Sold at Sotheby's Belgravia on 14 March 1979 for £120.*

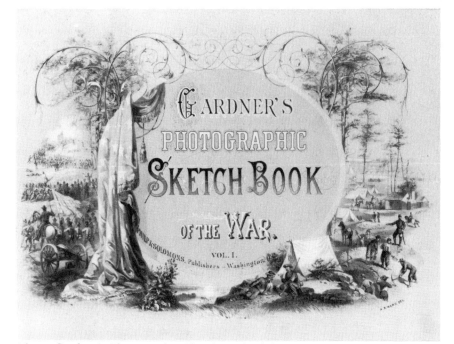

Above Gardner's Photographic Sketch Book of the War Volume I *containing fifty photographs, 6¾ in by 8¾ in, the mounts printed with title, date of exposure, details of photographer, printer and publisher. The negatives were by W.R. Pywell, T.H. O'Sullivan, Barnard & Gibson, Wood & Gibson, D.B. Woodbury, J. Gardner and Alexander Gardner and were exposed between August 1862 and May 1864. It was published by Philip & Solomons, Washington in 1866. Sold at Sotheby's Belgravia on 21 June 1974 for £3,200.*

Below *A photograph from* Gardner's Photographic Sketch Book of the War Volume I. (Courtesy of Sotheby's Belgravia.)

the war spending more than $100,000 and employing twenty photographers, amongst them Alexander Gardner who had been running Brady's Washington studio since 1858. Brady took the first photographs of the war at the Battle of Bull Run where he was almost killed. But he registered the photographs taken by all his photographers in his own name and in 1863 Gardner and many other cameramen who felt that they were entitled to the credit and profit for their own work left and formed their own photographic corps.

In all, more than 300 cameramen were issued passes by the Army of the Potomac, although not all of them were directly concerned in photographing the scenes of battles. They included men like Timothy H. O'Sullivan famed photographer of America's Far West and William Henry Jackson a gifted photographer who later travelled the length and breadth of America recording previously uncharted sights but although all their photographs are avidly sought after by collectors of the Civil War items as well as by collectors of old photographs it is Brady who will always be remembered as the photographer of Abraham Lincoln and the American Civil War.

The flamboyance of the French photographers at this time is perhaps exemplified by the work of Nadar whose real name was Gaspard Félix Tournachon. Nadar, a cartoonist who became a famous portrait photographer, had a large circle of prominent and artistic friends. They made his studio in the Boulevard des Capucines in Paris their meeting place and gave him the opportunity of producing some of the outstanding photographic portraits of the day. Posing his subjects naturally against plain backgrounds he produced fascinating photographs of the intelligentsia of Paris. An avid experimenter he became the leading French microphotographer and took the first aerial photographs in Paris in 1858 and continued his balloon experiments for several years. His efforts were the subject of many caricatures in the French press and his own production of carte de visite self portraits in his balloon shows his good humoured acceptance of this and his agreement with the old adage 'Providing that you spell the name correctly any publicity is good publicity'.

Nadar also began experimenting with artificial light at this time. In 1860 he installed a fifty element Bunsen battery in his Boulevard des Capucines studio and continued his experimenting with supplementary light sources to alleviate the problem of harsh and excessive shadows in portraits until he obtained satisfactory results in 1863. He began using artificial light to take photographs in the sewers and catacombs and produced a hundred photographs, using mannequins and exposures of up to eighteen minutes in some of them and they caused a sensation when they were shown at the International Exhibition in London in 1862.

In the 1870 siege of Paris during the Franco-Prussian war, Nadar was in charge of the balloon service from Paris and suggested using microphotography to convey messages into and out of the beleaguerred city, although

Left *The famous French portrait photographer Nadar (Gaspard Felix Tournachon) was the first man to take an aerial photograph.*

Below right *Portrait of Queen Victoria, an albumen print, 10¾ in by 8¾ in, mounted on card, by Charles Clifford Brown. Sold at Sotheby's Belgravia on 29 October 1976 for £190.*

in the event the messages were printed onto 1¾ in by 2⅜ in collodion pellicules which when they arrived in Paris were projected by magic lantern and then copied from the screen by a band of clerks. Towards the end of the seige a small number were successfully printed by being projected directly onto photographic paper and collectors should look for examples of both types of message in order to have a comprehensive collection. The importance of Nadar's contribution to the history of photography is shown by the prices now being paid by collectors and art dealers for examples of his work.

If photography seems to have been male dominated in its early days this is a true reflection of the times when the demure upper class Victorian ladies who would have been the only ones with the knowledge, money and time to devote to the pursuit of photography were neither expected nor permitted to indulge in such masculine pastimes.

Although Queen Victoria had a private darkroom in her palace and Lady Hawarden had shown that she could take some beautiful photographs the only really outstanding female photographer of those early days was the renowned Mrs Julia Margaret Cameron who, taking up photography at the age of 48, created a style that was uniquely her own and produced photographs that were valued in her own time and are much sought after by collectors today. During the twelve years that she was interested in photography she took many hundreds of photographs and although a great many were figure studies and religious or allegorical compositions it is her remarkable large close-up portraits of famous men for which she is so renowned today.

All her photographs are contact prints made directly from the large sized wet plates that she used in her 8 in by 10 in and 12 in by 15 in cameras without any retouching or enlarging at all. They all seem to be slightly out of focus because her lenses were not quite sharp enough to record fine details but because of, or in spite of that, each unsmiling photograph filling face seems to capture a little of the essence of the soul of the sitter.

George Frederick Watts and Alfred Lord Tennyson were both close friends of Mrs Cameron and had a great influence on her religious and allegorical pictures which were in the style of the Pre-Raphaelite painters. This again was a reflection of the times in which she lived. With the advent of the wet collodion plate many artists had turned to photography and tried to express their artistic training in the new medium giving birth to a spate of 'artistic' photographs.

Allegorical photographs were nothing new, daguerreotypists and calotypists had made them since the earliest days of photography even Hill and Adamson had dressed friends in armour and medieval clothing and photographed them in pseudo historical settings, but until the introduction of the wet collodion plate process the integrity of the photograph had been respected. The new breed of artistic photographers had a different approach. In order to emulate the fashionable painters of the day they manipulated the image, retouched the negatives and combined several negatives to make one finished photograph.

William Lake Price, a water colour artist turned photographer, showed

composite photographs of this type in 1855 and in 1857. Oscar Gustave Rejlander a Swedish artist living in England submitted a combination photograph measuring 31 in by 16 in made from thirty negatives of individuals and groups of figures and a number of additional ones for the background to the Manchester Art Treasures Exhibition. This photograph was acclaimed a triumph, the final seal of approval being given by Queen Victoria who bought it and presented it to her husband Prince Albert.

A year later another artist turned photographer, Henry Peach Robinson, composed his famous photograph 'Fading Away' from five negatives and Prince Albert rewarded his efforts by ordering a copy of every pictorial photograph that he produced, which was to be one a year for many years. The most notable of these was probably 'Bring Home the May' in 1862 which Robinson printed from nine different negatives charging 20 guineas for the 40 in by 15 in exhibition print and one guinea for half size copy prints of it.

All these and examples of the many similar types of photographs that were being produced at that time are very collectable today and specialized collections of them or to fine it down even further specialized collections of the work of any one of the artist/photographers who were active then would make an ideal focal point for a collection of antique photographs.

Further interplay between art and photography came when Eadweard Muybridge showed by his series of photographs of a galloping horse that all four of the horses feet are lifted off the ground at the same time but close

Julia Margaret Cameron reading a book. An albumen print 6⅛ in by 4¼ in taken in the 1860s which has been attributed to Lewis Carroll in an article published in Lilliput *in 1940. It is known that Lewis Carroll did photograph Mrs Cameron on 15 September 1862 and this date accords with the age of the subject in the photograph which is in many ways characteristic of Carroll's work. Although positive corroboration was lacking it was sold at Christie's South Kensington on 27 October 1977 for £450.*

An albumen print, 11 in by 9 in, of Sir John Herschel. The print is mounted on card in a gilt window mount and is inscribed 'Nach dem Lebens Julia Margaret Cameron d'après nature'. The original frame back is inscribed 'For Vienna Exhibition Julia Margaret Cameron Nach dem leben Sir John Herschel The Great Astronomer Vienna Exhibition Julia Margaret Cameron Group 12 No 426'. Taken in April 1869. Sold Sotheby's Belgravia on 21 March 1980 for £2,800.

together and not stretched wide apart as painters had shown them. Muybridge's series of action photographs influenced the cubist, surrealist, and futurist schools of painting and in return many photographers tried to emulate the artistic blurred effects of Turner and Whistler by using soft focus lenses and wide open lenses and others tried to produce impressionistic painting like photographs by use of the gum-bichromate and bromoil processes.

Towards the end of the nineteenth century Robinson who had become one of the foremost exponents of 'art' photography in Victorian England launched into extended attacks on the introduction of these impressionistic ideas from painting into photography but the advent of dry plate photography in the early 1880s had led to a new influx of amateur photographers who although often confused themselves brought a wind of change into photography.

One of the leaders of these new photographers, Peter Henry Emerson an American doctor living in London, was at first a devotee of soft focus photography, holding in his book *Naturalistic Photography* that this was the best way of emulating natural vision. He later renounced this viewpoint in a black bordered pamphlet entitled *Death of Naturalistic Photography, a Renunciation,* but nevertheless produced a stream of beautiful photographs. In 1892, together with similarly minded enthusiasts, Emerson was one of the founders of the Linked Ring Brotherhood, an organization dedicated to producing artistic photographs. Its members included talented photographers such as Frederick H. Evans and Frank Sutcliffe whose prints were collected then and are still highly regarded by collectors today.

Sutcliffe lived in Whitby a small fishing port on the coast of Yorkshire and most of the photographs that he took between 1872 and 1910 are of the

'When the day's work is done'. A composite print on a porcelain plaque, 10¼ in by 15¼ in, by Henry Peach Robinson, first published in 1877. Sold at Sotheby's Belgravia on 29 October 1976 for £450.

everyday life of Whitby and the surrounding villages. Sutcliffe's own prints are difficult to find today, but the Sutcliffe Gallery in Whitby stages a permanent exhibition of his work and they sell modern sepia toned photographic prints made from Sutcliffe's original glass plate negatives at prices ranging from less than £7 for a 6 in by 8 in print from an unblemished negative to more than £50 for a retouched 10 in × 12 in print from a damaged or spotted negative.

Sutcliffe used collodion wet plates for his early photographs but changed to commercially produced dry plates when they became available in the 1880s. Although he varnished most of his negatives to protect them many have developed pinholes and scratches in the emulsion and show other signs of a hundred years of wear and tear and the work involved in retouching the negatives and prints accounts for the higher prices of prints from the less well preserved negatives.

The Linked Ring exhibited their photographs at the Salon held annually at the Dudley Gallery, Piccadilly, and reproduced them in their celebrated *Photograms of the Year* copies of which are now avidly sought by collectors.

The American equivalent of the Linked Ring was the Photo-Secession group which was formed in New York at the turn of the century. Great photographers like Alfred Steiglitz, whose photographs had been amongst the first to be exhibited at Linked Ring's Salons and reproduced in *Photogram of the Year,* Alvin Langdon Coburn, Edward Steichen and Clarence H. White, were early members and their publication *Camera Work* contains examples of their work along with that of many others.

Although they are not yet photographic 'antiques', photographs by the outstanding twentieth century photographers such as Paul Strand, Edward Weston, Ansel Adams, Man Ray, Dr Erich Salmon, Alfred Eisenstaedt, Lazlow Moholy-Nagy, Arnold Newman, Bill Brandt, Cartier-Bresson and New York newspaper photographer Arthur Fellig, known as 'Weegee the famous' whose photographs have become classic examples of the genre, are with many others now being collected and treasured.

Exhibitions including many sponsored by the Arts Council in Great

Above *'The Gallop' from* Animals in Motion *by Eadweard Muybridge taken between 1872 and 1885.*

Below *'Quanting the Marsh Hay'. A platinum print, 6 in by 9 in, by P.H. Emerson, mounted on a page as plate XVI from* Life and Landscape on the Norfolk Broads, *1886. Sold at Sotheby's Belgravia on 29 October 1980 for £260.*

Above From an album of 94 albumen prints approximately 5¾ in by 7¾ in by Frank Meadow Sutcliffe c 1870. The album was sold at Sotheby's Belgravia on 19 March 1976 for £1,600.

Left 'Study of a waterfall'. A toned silver print, 15¾ in by 11¼ in, signed and dated in pencil by Alvin Langdon Coburn, 1911. Sold at Sotheby's Belgravia on 28 October 1981 for £220.

Britain and others such as *Cubism and American Photography* which opened 30 October 1981 at the Stirling and Francine Clark Art Institute in Williamstown, Massachusetts and travelled to the International Museum of Photography at George Eastman House, Rochester, New York, 18 December to 14 February 1982, and to several other venues in the United States of America during the next year or two are ideal places for collectors to see examples of and learn more about these valuable photographs and the often beautifully illustrated catalogues of these exhibitions of photographs are very collectable in their own right. Collectors must however be prepared to take the lavish praise and sometimes over optimistic descriptions given in exhibition and salesroom catalogues with a pinch of salt, and must learn to rely on their own feelings about a photograph more than other people's opinions.

Auction houses can be a wonderful source of collectable items but we must always remember that the rule of *caveat emptor* (buyer beware) is the rule in an auction and you will soon find that the biggest danger that can befall a collector in a salesroom is catching 'auction fever'. To be penned in a room with other collectors and perhaps dealers all wishing to obtain the same camera or photograph brings out the worst in a collector. Rationality flies out of the window and bid follows bid almost without control until the desire to buy at almost any price is satisfied.

The major auction houses will freely give their opinions of lots to potential buyers before the sale. They will point out any known faults and give an estimate of the price that the item is likely to bring, however, they accept no responsibility for what are after all only their opinions. Sotheby's conditions of sale say 'All goods are sold with all faults and imperfections and errors of description . . . buyers should satisfy themselves prior to the sale as to the conditions of each lot and should exercise and rely on their own judgement as to whether the lot accords with the description'.

Most auctioneers will bid on behalf of clients without charge and many dealers will bid for clients usually charging about 5% of the hammer price for this service, but always remember that the hammer price is not the final amount that you pay as most auction houses now charge a buyers premium of 10% plus VAT and in some cases VAT may be payable on the item purchased also.

Buying anything at an auction can be a risky business but most responsible auction houses will reimburse the bidder if an item proves to be a deliberate forgery. Although fortunately few forgers have dabbled in the field of photographica collectors will remember the unhappy incident that occurred when a set of black and white photographs of child models dressed in rags and posed against 'Victorian' backgrounds which were rephotographed and reproduced as a series of calotypes and exhibited as the work of a fictitious Victorian photographer of the 1840s Francis Hetling. The investigations of Scotland Yard's antiques and art fraud squad into this and into fake Victorian photographs on sale in America underlines yet again the need for respecting the rule *caveat emptor*.

Seen in retrospect it is now obvious that the long exposure times necessary in the 1840s would have made it impossible to capture the action pose in one of these photographs and that some of the details such as an anachronistic head scarf, which was positively dated at twenty years after the photograph was supposedly taken, a girl who is much too full faced and obviously well fed to be a Victorian street urchin and another wearing a ring which she wouldn't have done then, all clearly point out that these calotypes are imitations and not original 1840s examples yet they fooled many experts when they were first brought to light and are a salutary reminder to collectors of the perils of photographic collecting.

On a much happier note however it is a pleasure to point out that a student has found two antique imperial size albumen photographs by Alexander Gardner in an old book store in Vienna and that one of them which is of President Abraham Lincoln with his son Tad is identical to a print sold at a Christie's East auction in New York in 1982 for $4,180, and that an antique imperial size albumen print by Gardner of President Lincoln with his two secretaries, John Nicolay and John Hay, reputedly found in an old log cabin in Vermont was sold at the same venue in 1978 for a gigantic $20,000.

So keep your eyes open collectors, there is hope for us yet!

'Le Valet de Coeur'. A bromide print, 8½ in by 6 in, by Man Ray. Inscribed on the back 'Pour Mon Amie Jacqueline Breton 11 Septembre 1934'. Sold at Sotheby's Belgravia on 11 June 1976 for £460.

Chapter 6

The first collectors of photographs

Collecting photographs was a great Victorian passion and although at first only the well to do could afford to buy them competition amongst photographers brought prices down and large numbers of photographs were soon being bought and collected by the general public.

Although the world's earliest surviving negative had been taken by Fox Talbot in 1835, because of the patent restrictions that he imposed and because the public had fallen in love with the wonderful detail that could be recorded by the daguerreotype very few photographers used Fox Talbot's calotype process until the middle 1840s. The early Victorian collectors of photographs were mainly collectors of daguerreotypes who displayed their collections in frames or cases, each photograph was cherished as a valuable individual image and these daguerreotypes could only be reproduced by re-photographing them. Copy daguerreotypes, if possible displayed with the original are interesting photographic curios and the display cases holding a number of daguerreotypes are also much sought after by modern collectors.

Some of the pioneer calotypists were amateurs who either kept their prints themselves or distributed them to a small circle of family and friends and knowledgeable collectors keep a constant look out for the small caches of these early photographs that still occasionally come to light. Albums of calotypes put together by these early collectors were sometimes augmented by those of the few early commercial users of the calotype process.

Henry Collen a miniature portraitist was one of the first of these professional calotypists opening a studio in London at 29 Somerset Street, and it is known that he took a pair of stereoscopic photographs of Charles Babbage in August 1841. Utilizing his painting skills Collen was the originator of the art of retouching photographs to correct any supposed imperfections or defects in the appearance of the sitter.

David Octavious Hill and Robert Adamson were the first outstanding calotype photographers and the large albums of calotypes that they produced between 1843 and 1847 which were sold at prices ranging from £40 to £50 each and the individual calotypes that were issued separately were avidly bought up by contemporary collectors and are greatly valued by photographic collectors today. Individual calotypes by Hill and Adamson

Left *John Benjamin Dancer was amongst the very first in England to use and experiment with the daguerreotype process. This early daguerreotype view with a 1½ in by 1¼ in exposed image area has a manuscript note 'No 5. A non reversed photograph taken from the roof of the Manchester Exchange in 1842. The lens belonged to an opera glass and the reflector was a polished daguerreotype plate.' This is one of the very few surviving early outdoor daguerreotype views taken in England. Sold at Sotheby's Belgravia on 24 October 1975 for £1,350.*

Below *Lovejoy's Shop, Reading. Fox Talbot's picture of the shop which sold his calotypes, taken in 1845. (Courtesy of the Fox Talbot Museum.)*

can usually be bought at prices ranging from £40 or £50 to £500 or £600 depending upon the quality and interest of the image but one outstanding example 'A study of Fishermen' brought £1,900 at Christie's South Kensington on 23 June 1983. The huge albums of a hundred or more calotypes are now very rare indeed and collectors will recall that an outstanding collection of 258 of their best calotypes contained in three albums was purchased by the National Portrait Gallery from the Royal Academy of Art on 26 January 1973 for £32,178.50 (donated by an anonymous benefactor).

In order to popularize the calotype process Fox Talbot sold examples of his photographs through art shops, print sellers and stationers, and published the first book to be illustrated by real photographs *The Pencil of Nature* which was sold in six parts containing between three and seven photographs each, the first part issued on 29 June 1844 and the others at irregular intervals until part six was issued on 23 April 1846.

In a previous book *Collecting Old Cameras* I gave details of the earliest publication illustrated with a real photograph. This was a slim volume published privately at the end of January 1844 as a memorial to the death of Catherine Mary Walter elder daughter of John Walter II who was then the chief proprietor of The Times newspaper in London. It was written by her brother and had a calotype print of a bust of Catherine Mary Walter taken by Fox Talbot's assistant Nicholas Henneman pasted on to the front page of each copy, but Fox Talbot's *The Pencil of Nature* was the first commercially published book to be illustrated with real photographs.

A copy of *The Pencil of Nature* in reasonable condition lacking three of the listed calotypes but with one extra calotype 'The Woodchoppers' sold at Sotheby's December 1971 for £2,500 but I would think that a similar copy might reach more than ten times that amount today as a single outstanding 1843 Fox Talbot calotype of Trafalgar Square showing the construction of Nelson's Column sold for £7,500 at Sotheby's on 29 October 1982.

Fox Talbot's second book *Sun Pictures in Scotland* published in the autumn of 1845 in between parts four and five of *The Pencil of Nature* contains 23 photographs varying in size between 4 in by 3¼ in to 6 in by 7½ in and has only two printed pages, the title page and a list of the photographs, but a slip of paper 'A notice to the reader—the plates in the present work are impressed by the agency of light alone, without any aid from the artist's pencil. They are the sun pictures themselves, and not, as some persons have imagined, engravings in imitation' was inserted into each copy of both books.

In a further effort to popularize his photographic process Fox Talbot presented a sample photograph in each copy of *The Art Union* for June 1846 to illustrate an article on the talbotype. We do not know exactly how many copies of his books were sold although they are very rare today, but it is known that in 1846 the circulation of *The Art Union* was more than 7,000 copies per month and a copy with one of Fox Talbot's calotype photographs still intact is a great find for a collector today.

Fox Talbot's book led to a fashion of keeping paper photographs pasted into books and this in turn gradually led to the production of special albums suitable for the purpose, but the next great fillip for photography came from the Great Exhibition of 1851. This the first great international exhibition included the world's first really large display of photography and showed that English photographers were sadly no longer the world leaders. The French proved themselves superior to all others in their use and development of the paper processes and only Scottish photographers submitted albumen on glass photographs that were anywhere near the quality of those of the French, whilst daguerreotypes by American photographers were vastly superior to all the others.

The first detailed description of the daguerreotype process had been brought to the United States on 20 September 1839 on the transatlantic steamship British Queen and by the beginning of October a D.W. Seager had begun to make daguerreotype photographs in New York. Although collectors have been searching for them for years no examples of his work have been identified and the earliest known American daguerreotype is one made by Joseph Saxton in Philadelphia on 16 October 1839 which is in the collection of the Historical Society of Pennsylvania.

The Americans adopted the daguerreotype with great enthusiasm. Dr John William Draper, a professor of chemistry at New York University, made some of the world's first daguerreotype portraits during October and November 1839 and during that same winter of 1839-40 Francois Gourard exhibited daguerreotypes from France, some taken by Daguerre and some of which he had taken himself in Boston, New York and Providence, Rhode Island. Gourard gave demonstrations and sold sets of daguerreotype

Portrait of a gentleman. A calotype, 7¾ in by 6 in, by Thomas Rodger. It is oval mounted on card with two blind stamped credits 'T. Rodger' and 'Thomas Rodger Calotypist, St Andrews'. Taken in the 1850s. Sold at Sotheby's Belgravia on 24 October 1979 for £60.

This calotype of a bust of
Catherine Mary Walter, taken
by Hernamen, is pasted in on
the first page of a book written
by her brother as a memorial to
her. It was the first book ever
to have been illustrated with a
real photograph. This copy
was sold at Sotheby's Belgravia on 9 March 1977 for
£2,200.

CATHERINE MARY WALTER
BORN DECEMBER 11ᵗ.ᵖ MDCCCXIX
DIED JANUARY XVIᵗ MDCCCXLIV

An illustration from Sun
Pictures in Scotland by Wil-
liam Henry Fox Talbot, 1845.
The book was sold at Sotheby's
Belgravia on 13 December
1972 for £1,000.

cameras and apparatus to the large numbers who thronged his exhibitions. Information about the daguerreotype process spread like wildfire and by the end of 1840 daguerreotypes were being made in towns and cities right across America.

As was the case elsewhere most of these daguerreotypes were miniature portraits and although many of them have a haunting beauty collectors will seek out the more unusual outdoor scenes and the genre daguerreotypes which show the ordinary artifacts of everyday life of those days. American daguerreotypes shown at the Great Exhibition included a set of eight beautiful whole plate 6½ in × 8½ in views of Cincinnati, Ohio, which had been taken by Charles Fontayne and William Southgate Porter in 1848. Framed side by side to form one continuous panorama they showed the riverfront crowded with steamboats of all kinds with the city ascending the hills into the background.

Panoramic sets of photographs such as these had been displayed before this in the United States. Frederick and William Langenheim had made up eight panoramic sets of five daguerreotypes each, the first photographs ever of the Niagara Falls which they had taken in 1845. They presented seven of these sets to famous and important people of the day, President James K. Polk of the United States, Queen Victoria, L.J.M. Daguerre, the Duke of Brunswick and the kings of Prussia, Saxony and Wurtemberg and more recently their eighth set was given pride of place at the opening on 10 December 1940 of the American Museum of Photography in Philadelphia, the first museum in the United States devoted entirely to photography.

The Langenheim brothers bought Fox Talbot's American calotype patent from him in 1848 hoping to sell licences for the use of the process to the large numbers of professional daguerreotypists who were then doing a thriving business all over the United States, but they were not able to sell even one of these licences and they became the only professional calotypists in America, so that except for the work of a few amateurs their calotypes are the only early American ones that can be found by collectors today.

The Langenheims had originated the use of positive photographs on albumen on glass plates, which they called hyalotypes, for magic lantern slides in 1849. They showed some of these at the Great Exhibition and later used the process to produce the glass stereoscopic transparencies which had been introduced by A. Ferrier in Paris in 1851. Examples of any of these early albumen on glass transparencies are getting harder to find today as they make fine additions to collections of early photographs, of magic lanterns, and of stereoscopes, and specialist collectors in all these fields are looking for them all the time. The only reason that some are still about is because the contemporary Victorians were themselves great collectors of these then intriguing new inventions.

Robert Hunt, author of the first history of photography *Researches on Light,* London 1844 when writing his *Synopsis of the Contents of the Great Exhibition* which was published as a companion to the official catalogue of the Exhibition in 1851 described several of the then latest improvements to the various photographic processes particularly observing that 'The most recent improvement is the introduction of the use of glass plates for the reception of the first *negative* image in the camera.'

This, the next great step forward in photography, was Frederick Scott Archer's wet collodion process. A glass plate was coated with a film of collodion made by dissolving gun cotton in ether, sensitized in a solution of silver nitrate, exposed in the camera, and then developed and fixed whilst still wet. The fastest photographic process yet, it was used almost universally for the next thirty years but although it was so very popular few of the untold millions of wet plate negatives that were made all around the world seem to have survived and few private collections can boast of any today. The partitioned wooden boxes in which they were supplied and stored are seldom offered in photographic sales and when they do crop up, particularly if they were associated with well known photographers they fetch very high prices indeed.

The wet collodion negatives were usually printed on to light sensitive paper which had been prepared by coating it with a thin film of the white of eggs, which gave a finer surface than calotype paper when sensitized in the same way. The albumen paper was contact printed by being exposed to sunlight under the glass negative and when it had darkened to the required density it was taken into the dark room, fixed and toned to give the characteristic rich sepia coloured image that collectors admire so much in these antique photographs.

The photographic visiting card became the next photographic fad to catch the public's fancy. Suggested by several people during the early 1850s, it was patented as the 'carte de visite', an albumen paper print pasted onto a

'Agricultural machinery shown by Messrs Hornsby & Son'. A positive print from a glass plate negative made by C.M. Ferrier of Paris to be printed by Henneman and Malone to illustrate the 130 presentation copies of the Reports of the Juries to the Royal Commissioners and Executive Committee of the Great Exhibition. *The prints were made between September and November 1851. The negative, which is amongst the earliest known glass plate negatives, was sold at Sotheby's Belgravia on 29 June 1979 for £130.*

2½ in by 4 in card mount by André Adolphe Disderi in Paris on 27 November 1854. In his patent he described his method of taking ten small photographs on one glass plate so that the cost of each was reduced.

He was soon doing a brisk business with these inexpensive little photographs but the great craze for collecting cartes de visite and their real popularity began in May 1859 when Napoleon III riding at the head of his troops en route to Italy halted his entire army outside Disderi's studio whilst he went in to have his photograph taken. The publicity that attended this made

An uncut carte de visite contact sheet from the studios of John Jabez Edwin Mayall. From a lot of thirty albumen prints taken in April 1863 which were sold at Sotheby's Belgravia on 29 June 1979 for £150.

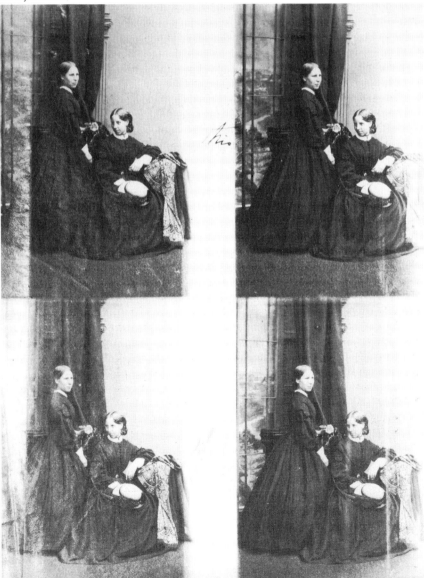

Disderi famous and everyone else in Paris from the Empress down followed the Emperor's lead and Disderi was soon booked up for weeks in advance. His cartes with his signature printed on the back were soon being collected all over Europe. *The Photographic News* of 4 October 1861 estimated that Disderi was taking 1,200,000 francs (£48,000) a year in his Paris studio alone and they said that the craze for cartes de visite became so overwhelming that in Paris alone some 33,000 people were engaged in the production of photographs and photographic supplies that summer.

In England cartes were introduced in 1857 by A. Marion & Co. These now rare early cartes had small photographs varying in size from about 1½ in by 1¾ in to 1½ in by 2¼ in pasted on to card with a plain back unlike later examples which almost invariably had the photographer's name or an artistic design printed on their back.

As had been the case in Paris it was the Royal Family that gave these new style photographs their big boost. In August 1860 J.E. Mayall published a 'Royal Album' of carte de visite photographs of the British Royal Family and the success of these little photographs was so great that London's photographers vied with Mayall and each other to take photographs of the other great personages of the day and put them on sale as cartes de visite. The final touch was added when Queen Victoria instructed one of her ladies-in-waiting to write to all the great ladies in London asking for copies of their cartes for Her Majesty's private collection and after that there was no holding back.

The carte de visite became the most popular form of photography in the world. With prices of an 8 in by 10 in portrait photograph ranging from £2 or £3 to as much as £10 or £12 at the more fashionable photographers, photography had been until now a rich man's pastime but suddenly the new fashionable carte de visite photographs were available for 10 or 12 shillings a dozen, and almost everyone could afford them.

Special cameras and sliding plate holders that could take a number of the small carte de visite photographs on a single plate were soon being produced and special albums to store them in were made in a great variety that ranged from inexpensive ones with card covers to beautiful examples containing decorated pages and music boxes which played when they were opened and with covers of carved wood, ivory, leather, mother of pearl, papier mâché, silver, velvet and almost every other expensive material that was then available. Albums with clocks, revolving albums, display cases, frames and fans of spreading cartes were all popular and modern collectors will delight in some of the more extravagant items that were produced and are now gracing collections.

People collected cartes of their family and friends and the cartes of famous people sold in tens and sometimes hundreds of thousands. Actors and actresses, Lords and Ladies, clergymen of all denominations and even ladies of little virtue were displayed side by side in shop windows and many photographers made fortunes from selling the ubiquitous cartes de visite.

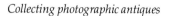

Cartes de visite can be collected showing famous photographic faces, on this page Sir John Herschel, Sir Charles Wheatstone and Sir David Brewster, or for the famous photographic names on the reverse, on the opposite page Elliott and Fry, Jabex Hughes and Mayall.

Far right *The first carte de visite in a Victorian album.*

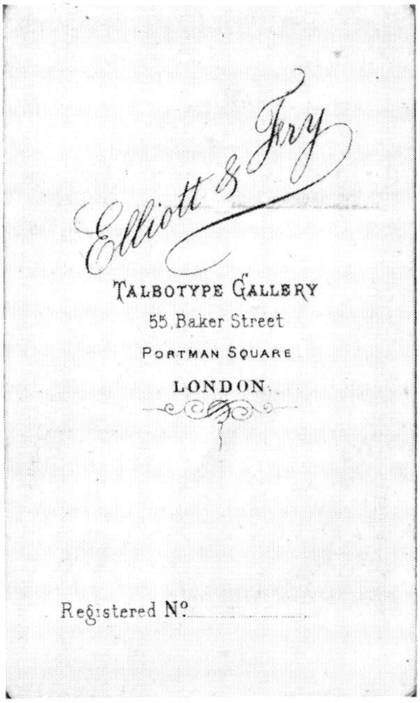
Elliott & Fry
Talbotype Gallery
55, Baker Street
Portman Square
LONDON.
Registered No.

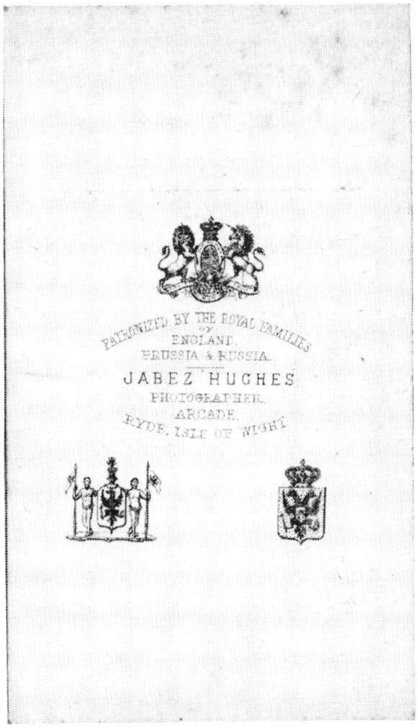
PATRONIZED BY THE ROYAL FAMILIES
OF
ENGLAND,
PRUSSIA & RUSSIA.
JABEZ HUGHES
PHOTOGRAPHER,
ARCADE,
RYDE, ISLE OF WIGHT

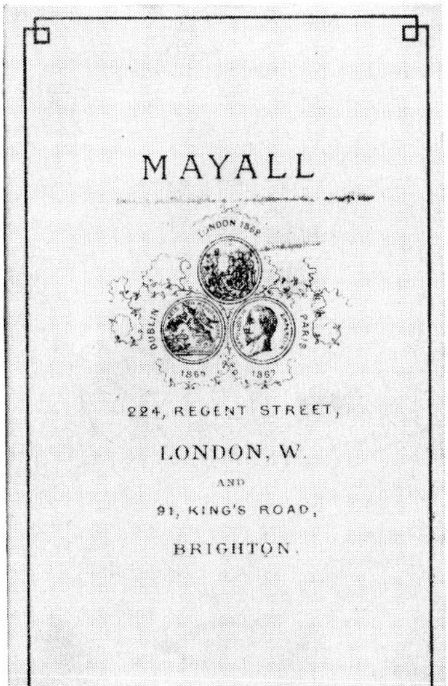
MAYALL
LONDON 1862
DUBLIN
PARIS
1865
1867
224, REGENT STREET,
LONDON, W.
AND
91, KING'S ROAD,
BRIGHTON.
Marion, Imp. Paris

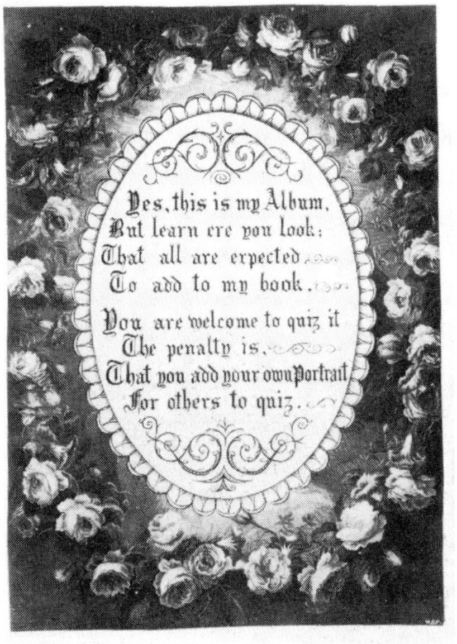
Yes, this is my Album,
But learn ere you look;
That all are expected
To add to my book.
You are welcome to quiz it
The penalty is,
That you add your own Portrait
For others to quiz.

A family scrap album containing sixty photographs, cut out carte de visite portraits of family, friends and members of the aristocracy. Albumen prints on pages with hand painted lithographic designs of fruit, flowers and insects. The book is bound in green leather and monogrammed 'HB', it dates from the 1860s. Sold at Sotheby's Belgravia on 17 June 1981 for £65.

Scott Archer's wet plate process was also used to produce many other novel types of photographs and the microphotograph was one of these.

John Benjamin Dancer, a Liverpool instrument maker, was amongst the very first to use the daguerreotype process in England. He was Great Britain's first photographer outside London and in 1839 took a three day stagecoach ride to see the first exhibition of Daguerre's own photographs in London, returning home happy in the knowledge that his own daguerreotypes were as fine as those of the inventor himself. Dancer soon added cameras to the list of instruments that he produced and before the end of 1839, using a microscope lens of 1½ in focal length in one of his own cameras, made a daguerreotype microphotograph. The resultant 1 in image of a document 20 in long is the earliest example of microphotography on record, but none of Dancer's early microphotographs are known to have survived.

The resolution of fine detail made possible by Scott Archer's wet plate process re-kindled Dancer's interest in this work. He made his first wet plate microphotograph in February 1852 and on 25 April 1853 made a microphotograph of William Sturgeon's memorial tablet. Whenever he made a perfect microphotograph during his early experiments Dancer signed the glass slide with a diamond and presented it to a friend or a scientific colleague. These diamond signed microphotographs do not carry the usual green or yellow Dancer label. All his microphotographs are scarce today but these few diamond signed ones are the rarest ones of all and few collectors can boast of having found one for their collections.

Interest in these microphotographic slides grew rapidly and Dancer was soon producing them commercially to satisfy the public's desire to collect these new novelties. Other photographers had begun to experiment with very small photographs. The text of one, a minute photograph of a page of the *Illustrated London News* taken by Alfred Rosling shown at a photographic exhibition in December 1852 could easily be read with a magnifying glass but the first real microphotographs taken on micoroscope slides to be viewed in a microscope were those taken by Dancer in 1852. They were collected avidly from 1853 until about 1900 and are still very collectable items today. Dancer sold his microphotograph slides until about 1885 when his daughters took on the business as E.E. Dancer & Co.

Dancer slides can be recognized by the green, yellow or white labels with the initials J.B.D. but a number have been found with retailers labels on them. In 1873 he published a catalogue from his 43 Cross Street, Manchester premises listing 277 microphotographs at one shilling each or 10/6d per dozen, a 1 in objective magnifying about 50 diameter to be used for viewing them.

In 1900 the business was purchased by a Mr. R. Suter of 10 Highweek Road, South Tottenham, Middlesex who published a list of the 512 slides then available 'All at 1/- each' but some of the later ones could not have been taken until 1887, the year that Dancer died. Dancer was the originator but several other photographers also produced microphotographs during the second half of the nineteenth century.

The Historical Group of the Royal Photographic Society, which all collectors should consider joining, have published a number of articles on early microphotography in their newsletters and we are all indebted to the members of the Historical Group in general and to Arthur T. Gill BSc Hon FRPS FRSA in particular for the interesting information therein.

Below left *'The tight garter'. A 'naughty but nice' carte de visite.*

Below right *The 'Graphotrope' carte de visite viewer. It is 9 in high, made of mahogany and takes fifty cartes de visite held in a metal frame which change automatically when the top is rotated on its base. American, 1866. It was sold, complete with 47 metal frames and ten cartes de visite, at Sotheby's Belgravia on 26 June 1981 for £220.*

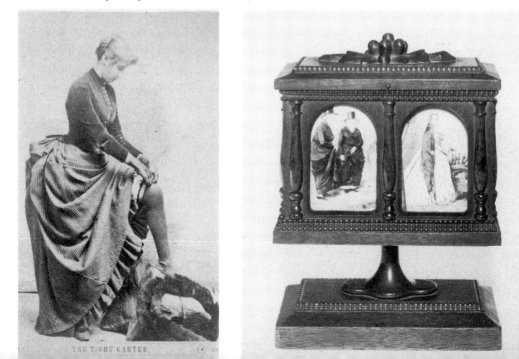

Photographs had been mounted in items of jewellery from the earliest days of photography and collectors can still find bracelets, earrings, lockets, rings and other personal items inset with daguerreotype and ambrotype portraits of loved ones. In 1857 Sir David Brewster had suggested using microphotographs mounted on small glass cylinders with the other spherical end to serve as the magnifier and mounting these stanhope lenses in jewellery. Queen Victoria who was addicted to photographic novelties proudly wore a signet ring containing a microphotograph of a group of five portraits of her family made by Dancer.

The mini mania for collecting microphotographs spread to Europe where it was publicized in 1859 by the Parisian optician Rene Prudent Patrice Dagron who caused a diamond ring containing microphotographs of several princes to be lost. It's loss and subsequent return to the police was widely reported in the newspapers and it proved to be a wonderful advertisement for microphotographs. Within a year most of the leading Paris opticians were making microphotograph slides and souvenirs with microphotographs on stanhope lenses set into them but after a few years bawdy photographs began to be exhibited in this way and the stanhopes fell into disrepute. Examples of early stanhopes are very rare today but collectors will find an ample supply of the more common souvenir item usually containing microphotographs of seaside resorts or tourist spots which date from the turn of the century.

By the end of 1866 the photographic trade in Great Britain was in the doldrums. Public demand for portraits was falling off and interest in cartes de visite and the other novelties that had been so popular was fading fast but the industry was saved by the introduction of a new larger size photograph.

This was the cabinet photograph, a 4 in by 5½ in photograph mounted on a 4¼ in by 6½ in card first suggested by F.R. Window, a London photographer, in May 1866. This new style photograph became very popular and within a couple of years it was being made all over the world. Collectors will find many examples still in mint condition today as once again photographs were being collected. Cartes de visite were still being made although in far smaller numbers and the new cabinet size was now being used not only for family portraits but also for everything and everyone from actors to clergymen, politicians and even spirit photographs. Pictures were produced for almost every aspect of photography that the collectors of the day were interested in and collections of cabinet photographs and the even larger sizes that were introduced in the 1870s still occasionally come to light and give great pleasure to the modern collector.

As we have seen our Victorian ancestors were great collectors and the invention of photography provided them with a wonderful new source of collectabilia, but although there have been collectors of photographs and photographic collections since the earliest days of photography the modern photographic collecting craze only came to the public's attention when the larger auction houses became involved at the end of the 1960s.

A few dedicated collectors had been quietly enjoying themselves for many years collecting photographic antiques and had happily ignored the scorn of friends and family who had laughed at their collections of photographic 'rubbish'. In London one small unofficial group of friendly collectors of photographic antiques included a collector of stereoscopes and stereograms, a collector of magic lanterns and early motion picture items and a collector of old cameras, and, in our happy way if we saw a collectable item that would be of interest to another collector we would pass the information on to him so that he could acquire it for his collection.

This happy dream-like bubble of collecting innocence was burst in 1967 when in the first major modern event of its kind the Park-Bernet Galleries in New York auctioned off the Will Weissberg collection of rare photographs, cameras and other items of photographica. The unexpectedly high interest in the history of photography at that time is shown by the $17,865 which the 205 lots brought, much of it in postal bids from around the United States and a few from Europe.

Groups of collectors began to get together and a sense of nostalgia amongst Americans together with a revival of interest in the American Civil War led to a marked increase in the prices of early photographs there which was further fuelled by the sale of the Sidney R. Strober collection which was held at the Parke-Bernet Galleries on 7 February 1970.

The first large sale of early photographic images and related equipment in Great Britain held at Sotheby's in Belgravia on 21 December 1971 was also a great success and the numbers of collectors and dealers increased rapidly as more and more jumped on to the bandwagon and were soon joined by investors and even by 'improvers' who bought up broken bits of old

These items of daguerreotype jewellery were sold at Christie's South Kensington on 30 October 1978 for prices that ranged from £30 to £45.

cameras and equipment and cannibalised them to produce saleable photographic 'antiques'.

Collectors in the early days had little to guide them and few books to refer to. My own library included such classics as *Nicéphore Niepce* by Victor Fouque translated by Edward Epstein 1935, Beaumont Newhall's *History of Photography* 1937, *The Catalogue of the Kodak Museum* 1947, *The History of Photography* by Helmut and Alison Gernsheim 1955, *Stereo Views* by William Culp Darrah 1964, and *The Picture History of Photography* by Peter Pollack 1969, and the acquisition of each of these was an event in itself.

Books for collectors have of course proliferated since then. My own *Collecting Old Cameras, Victorian Photographs* by B.E.C. Howarth-Loomes and a series of books on early photography by Brian Coe, Curator of the Kodak Museum all offer advice and guidance to both established and novice collectors. Reading as much as you can about the subject will add both pleasure and profit to your collecting.

Below left *A cabinet size portrait of Benjamin Disraeli, late 1860s.* (Courtesy of Kodak Museum, Harrow.)

Below right *A cabinet size photograph of my father as a baby, New York, 1893.*

Chapter 7

Stereoscopic photography

Stereoscopes and stereoscopic views were probably the most popular parlour entertainment of the Victorian era achieving then the popularity that television has today. An enormous range of stereoscopes ranging from cheap hand held models to elaborate and expensive pieces of furniture were available and the slogan of the London Stereoscopic Company founded by George Swan Nottage in 1854 'No home without a stereoscope' almost became a reality.

A stereo card sold at Christie's in South Kensington on 29 October 1981 showed an interesting selection of early stereoscopes and stereographs topped by three wet plate cameras. Catalogued as being taken at the Crystal Palace, the date is uncertain. It was possibly taken at the Great Exhibition of 1851 but may have been at a later exhibition after the Palace had been re-elected in Sydenham. Most of the stereoscopes shown are Brewster pattern viewers but a number are on elaborate table stands and the scene vividly demonstrates the large selection of stereoscopes that were available in those early days.

Stereoscopic photography, the use of two photographs of the same subject taken from slightly different positions so that when viewed correctly they are combined by the brain to give an impression of depth, was another of the inventions brought to life at the Great Exhibition. Jules Duboscq, a French optician, showed several examples of Sir David Brewster's stereoscope and it lit the fuse of yet another photographic collecting craze that swept the world.

Sir David Brewster's stereoscope, a modification of a design originally suggested by Sir Charles Wheatstone, and subsequent improvements made by Claudet and others helped to popularize the stereoscope and within a short while no home was complete without a parlour stereoscope and a collection of stereocards.

Wheatstone's first stereoscopes, one using mirrors and the other prisms to present the appropriate image to the each eye, were made in 1832 although it was not until 1838 that his paper describing the reflecting stereoscope in detail was published by the Royal Society. An example of this reflecting stereoscope is on display in the Science Museum in London, but

Top *Display of stereographs and stereograms at the Crystal Palace, possibly 1851.* (Courtesy of Christie's South Kensington.)

Centre *A stereoscopic daguerreotype recording the official visit of Queen Victoria, Prince Albert, Napoleon III and the Empress Eugenie to the Crystal Palace on 20 April 1855. Sold at Sotheby's Belgravia on 11 June 1976 for £360.*

Left *Sir David Brewster seated beside a table supporting a stereoscopic viewer of his own design, holding a photograph of Prince Albert. The original of this portrait, taken in 1854 by B.E. Dupper, is a waxed albumen print, 8¾ in by 6¾ in.* (Courtesy of Sotheby's Belgravia.)

although reflecting stereoscopes and the pairs of pictures made for them were still being offered in Horne & Thornthwaite's catalogue for 1857 only few could have been sold and I have not been able to find one in the thirty years or so that I have been collecting photographic antiques.

The invention of photography should have given a wonderful boost to the stereoscope but because of their mirror like surface daguerreotypes were not suitable for viewing in the reflecting stereoscope and although pairs of calotypes were made by Fox Talbot, Henry Collen, Roger Fenton, and other leading photographers of the day the stereoscope did not catch the public's interest until Jules Duboscq's display of Brewster type stereoscopes and stereoscopic daguerreotypes delighted Queen Victoria and Prince Albert at the opening of the Great Exhibition.

Duboscq presented the Queen with a highly finished stereoscope and a matching set of stereoscopic daguerreotypes and her interest in this latest curiosity led to a torrent of orders so great that many of his English competitors began to manufacture their own stereoscopes and within a few months nearly 25,000 stereoscopes a week were being sold in London and Paris.

Large numbers of stereoscopic photographs of the Great Exhibition were soon being made and the foremost photographers of the day vied with each other in their efforts to produce more varied and unusual results. Antoine Claudet even managing to take stereoscopic portraits and groups. Sets of stereoscopic cards and stereoscopic daguerreotypes were soon available on a wide range of subjects, foreign travel and strange native wonders being the most popular. The stereoscope opened a window on the world for the Victorians in the way that television does for us today and it was just as popular.

Ghost pictures were suggested by Brewster after seeing a calotype of York Minster made by Hill and Adamson in 1844 in which a boy seated on a step, who had left halfway through the exposure, appeared transparent on the print and became popular subjects for the stereoscope. Nudes, 'naughty but nice' scenes showing slightly dishevelled young ladies in their undergarments, scenes of married bliss, love, discord and even risque jokes were all portrayed in the stereoscope, indeed the list of subjects was to be almost endless.

The success of the London Stereoscopic Company illustrates the excitement that the public felt about stereoscopic photography at that time. Founded in 1854 by George Swan Nottage, a man of plebian background and little education who started by making and selling a few Brewster type stereoscopes and the stereoscopic photographs for them, it is reported that within two years his company had sold over 500,000 stereoscopes and their catalogue listing a choice of more than 10,000 different stereoscopic slides was distributed throughout the world.

Collecting stereographs became a great passion and the initial excitement lasted for more than a decade. In 1862 The London Stereoscopic Company sold almost a million stereocards and in America where the craze took off a little later and lasted longer Edward Anthony who had overtaken the Langenheim Brothers as the largest producer sold many hundreds of thousands of stereocards in 1861 and 1862. In Paris A. Ferrier was almost matching Nottage's London output and thousand upon thousands of other professional photographers joined in the outpouring of stereoscopic photographs.

Stereoscopes for viewing these stereographs were made in large numbers and great variety and many collectors concentrate on collecting stereoscopes although putting together a really comprehensive collection of all the different selections, sizes and styles offered by the Victorian manufacturers is a lifetime's work and few collectors have so far been successful in their efforts.

Antoine Claudet was an early advocate of stereoscopic photography whose stereoscopes and stereoscopic daguerreotypes are now much sought after. He introduced several improvements to the stereoscope. In March 1853 he patented his own version of the folding pocket stereoscope, a small morocco case usually holding a single stereoscopic daguerreotype, which had a flap holding two lenses so that when opened it became a box stereoscope. In March 1855 he patented an improved Brewster type box

Stereoscopic photography

Right *A Smith, Beck & Beck achromatic stereoscope mounted on a matching burr walnut cabinet containing 200 stereograms. The piece is 18½ in high and was made in 1870. Sold at Sotheby's Chester on 6 July 1983 for £260.*

Below left *Sir Walter Scott's Monument, Edinburgh—a stereocard by G. W. Wilson of Aberdeen.*

Bottom left *A stereocard from a series of 'Welsh Costumes' by Francis Bedford. This is No 4, Market Women.*

stereoscope with adjustable eye pieces and lenses and in April 1858 he described his stereomonoscope which combined two stereophotographs into a single image on a large ground screen so that several people could see the picture simultaneously. Claudet also introduced a cabinet stereoscope which used knobs on the sides to move an endless band on which a number of stereo slides were mounted so that each picture could be moved into position for viewing, and a later version with two facing eyepieces for use by two people at the same time.

These and many of the other stereoscopic improvements and inventions like the folding combination stereographascopes were copied or sometimes just pirated all over the world. The most popular stereoscope of all was the simple Holmes American skeletal type hand viewer designed by Oliver Wendell Holmes and first produced by his friend Joseph L. Bates in Boston, USA in 1861 and variations of it were produced by very many manufacturers right through to the early part of the twentieth century.

Collectors today are indebted to those early enthusiasts and innovators. Although, as is the nature of things, many and perhaps even most of the early collections of stereoscopic photographs and the great variety of stereoscopes that went with them have now gone with the wind large numbers of interesting examples can still be found at relatively reasonable prices, although as with all collectabilia remarkable stereographs and stereoscopes bring remarkably high prices.

The approximately 3½ by 7 in stereoscopic daguerreotype slides for the early Brewster type stereoscopes sold for between 8s 6d and 12s 6d each and became the standard size for stereographs. Because each slide needed two separate exposures most of these stereoscopic daguerreotypes were

Above left *A Burfield & Rouch walnut stereoscopic viewer on a brass stand. It stands 16 in high when unextended and is dated 15 September 1854. Sold at Sotheby's Belgravia on 30 November 1979 for £240.*

Above right *An unusual carved oak gothic style stereoscope, 18½ in high and made in the 1850s. Sold at Sotheby's Belgravia on 29 October 1980 for £450.*

Opposite left *A automatic coin operated stereoscope. Sold at Sotheby's Chester on 10 November 1982 for £200.*

Opposite right *A walnut floor standing pedestal stereoscopic viewer 48 in high. Made in England in 1870. Sold at Sotheby's Belgravia on 15 June 1979 for £380.*

Left *W.E. Kilburn's folding pocket stereoscope of 1853 with a daguerreotype portrait. Sold at Sotheby's Belgravia on 17 June 1981 for £200.*

portraits, sculptures, still life studies or views of exhibitions. Collectors will find that few exterior scenes were taken and that these rare examples almost invariably fetch high prices today.

Very few calotypes were made for the stereoscope. Transparencies on glass sold well for about 7s 6d each the process giving particularly fine detail and quality, paper transparencies printed on translucent paper and sometimes hand painted in colours on the back and perforated so that they gave different effects when illuminated from the front or rear were produced and a small number of stereoscopic ambrotypes and tintypes were also sold but by far the largest numbers were the albumen prints from glass negatives made by the then revolutionary new wet collodion process first introduced in 1851, the year that Daguerre died.

Sets of stereoscopic photographs were available covering almost every imaginable subject from astronomy to zoology and few late Victorian homes were complete without a viewer and a selection of stereo cards. Wealthier homes often had a several viewers and small libraries of cards neatly stacked in boxes, book form containers, or in specially made cabinets or bookcases.

Stereoscopic photographs were made using almost every photographic process then known. The earliest were stereoscopic daguerreotypes and these are now the most scarce bringing anything from £30 to £1,500 each depending on their quality and subject matter.

Portraits were the most popular subjects and outdoor scenes and photographs of photographers or scientists and their equipment are now very rare and expensive. A stereoscopic daguerreotype of photographic and optical equipment including a daguerreotype camera, a box for holding plates, a mercury developing box, a sensitizing box, a Culpepper micro-scope, a telescope and a solar microscope, with the printed label of Chad-burn Brothers, Opticians & Co, Sheffield on the reverse was sold at Christie's in South Kensington on 30 June 1977 for £340 and would bring much more than that today.

Nude stereo daguerreotypes which were a profitable side line for photo-graphers in the 1850s are also scarce and valuable today and a fine tinted study of two nude young women seated on a sofa was sold by Christie's at that same sale for £580 and another of a nude young woman standing beside a harp was sold at Sotheby's on 25 March 1983 for £858. Although they seem innocuous enough to us today nude stereodaguerreotypes were considered naughty erotica by the Victorian gentlemen at whom they were aimed and many cabinets designed to hold stereoscopes and stereograms had secret compartments in which to conceal them. These cabinets can still be found today but most of them have long since been emptied and now only serve to remind us of the foibles of the Victorian middle classes.

In the United States William and Frederick Langenheim who patented their 'hyalotype' process, the first photographic positives on glass lantern slides, in 1848 purchased Fox Talbot's American calotype patent for $6,000 in that same year and one of their rare pairs of stereoscopic pictures made by the calotype process c 1850 which is said to be the earliest American stereograph extant is preserved in the Franklin Institute. The Langenheims produced stereoscopic glass transparencies at the end of 1853 in an attempt to compete with the European imports which come chiefly from France but they only sold in small numbers and are now extremely rare.

J.F. Mascher, another Philadelphian daguerreotypist, followed the Lang-enheim's lead in stereoscopic photography but continued to use the daguerreotype process for this purpose and in March 1853 he patented a folding stereoscopic daguerreotype case similar to those patented by W.E. Kilburn and Antoine Claudet in England and by John Stull in Philadelphia earlier that year. These folding stereoscopic daguerreotype cases were copied by many other manufacturers and pirated copies without a maker's name on them can also be found but they are all extremely rare and one or better still a selection of them will make a fine addition to any collection.

Most of the photographers who recorded the American frontiers and accompanied the exploration trips took stereoscopic pictures as well as the large views that ranged in size from the standard 6½ in by 8½ in whole plates up to the extra large 20 in by 24 in mammoth plates.

One of these early photographers Solomon Nunes Carvalho was the first native born American photographer known to be of Jewish origin. An artist, early photographer and inventor born in Charleston, South Carolina in 1815, he served as the official artist/photographer with General John Charles Fremont's Fifth Survey of the Far West of 1853-54 which was sent to

Above left *A stereoscopic viewer on a cast metal stand with fluted column and an open scroll work base, made in the 1860s. Sold at Sotheby's Belgravia on 14 March 1979 for £540.*

Above right *An unusual carved wood stereoscopic viewer 27 in high. It was probably made in France in about 1870. Sold at Sotheby's Belgravia on 7 September 1979 for £650.*

map out the most desirable transcontinental railway route.

Carvalho's original photographs and sketches of the trip are now lost but his book *Incidents of Travel and Adventure in the Far West* has been reprinted many times and one edition in 1954 included a biography of Carvalho by B.W. Korn and reproductions of many of his photographs and sketches. The photographs record scenes of outstanding beauty and a serious search for the originals or any of Carvalho's other photographs or memorabilia would be a worthwhile research project for collectors of photographic antiques.

In 1855 the Langenheims took a similar series of views along a route from Philadelphia to Niagara Falls which included stereoscopic pictures that they reproduced on porcelain, glass, and albumenised paper. The examples on porcelain are amongst the most rare of American stereo graphs. They later opened 'Langenheims Stereoscopic Cosmorama Exhibition' at 188 Chestnut Street, Philadelphia. This exhibition consisted of a number of cabinet stereoscopes each containing 25 glass stereoscopic pictures of 'the splendid Niagara Falls as seen in winter, and many other interesting views in Europe'. This was the first photographic peep show and with admission priced at 25 cents per person was the forerunner of the penny arcades that came fifty years later.

A stereoscopic daguerreotype of a cook preparing vegetables taken by Antoine Claudet c 1850. Sold at Sotheby's Belgravia on 25 March 1983 for £572.

Oliver Wendell Holmes who claimed that he had examined 'perhaps a hundred thousand stereographs' invented the hand stereoscope that is named after him in 1859, but his friend Joseph L. Bates, a professional photographer, was the first to manufacture it. Collectors will find the Holmes-Bates label that is seen on the back of many American stereocards made in the 1860s an interesting item of ephemera for their collections of stereoscopic memorabilia.

Another most unusual item for the collector of stereoscopic antiques is Swan's stereoscopic casket. Invented by Henry Swan and patented by him in 1862 this self contained portrait and viewer achieved its effect by mounting two collodion positive photographs, one of them tinted, on two right angled prisms placed together with their hypotenuse faces touching.

Although it is now 125 years since the first flush of enthusiasm for stereoscopic photographs swept the world there is still almost unlimited scope for collectors. By 1862 the London Stereoscopic Company was selling almost a million stereographs a year.

In the 1870s over a hundred American photographers published lists of more than 1,000 different stereographs and there were thousands of smaller local photographers offering views of their own areas. It has been said that by the turn of the century between three and four million different stereographs were produced in the United States alone, the more popular of them selling in tens of thousands, and the picture was the same in Great Britain and on the Continent with the major producers sending photographers around the globe for the avid stereograph buying public.

Rare stereographs such as those made by the ferrotype or tintype process and those made by mounting tissue albumen prints between two glass plates are collectable in their own right but most collectors only collect the more common stereocards which reflect their own special interests. Those

Above 'The Stereoscopic Treasury', 1860s, with a group of 34 stereoscopic cards including genre subjects and posed groups. They are all albumen prints on yellow card mounts and have been hand coloured. Sold at Sotheby's Belgravia on 12 March 1982 for £400.

Right A stereocard and envelope from 'The Stereoscopic Cabinet', a series of fourteen monthly parts of three stereocards each, all taken by prominent photographers including Roger Fenton, R. Howlett and E. Moxham and published between November 1859 and December 1860. The complete set was sold at Christie's South Kensington on 27 October 1983 for £400.

No. I. November, 1859.

Either Stereograph separately, 1s.
The Packet of Three Stereographs, 2s. 6d.

THE STEREOSCOPIC CABINET:
or,
Monthly Packet of Pictures for the Stereoscope.

EDITED AND PUBLISHED BY
LOVELL REEVE, 5, HENRIETTA STREET, COVENT GARDEN.

CONTENTS.

1. Church of St. Ouen, Rouen, the finest example known of Flamboyant Gothic. Photographed by R. Howlett.
2. Group of Mummies, in the Greco-Roman Saloon, British Museum. Photographed by R. Fenton.
3. On board the Yacht 'Maraquita.' Photographed by Captain Henry at sea, during a cruise to Iceland.

The Packets will pass through the Post for a penny, and may be ordered of any Bookseller in town or country.

showing photographers and their equipment are of course always highly prized for giving us a glimpse of the contemporary scene and collectors have specialized in the stereographs of a single photographer, special area, special era, or those whose subject matter has some special appeal for them personally and wonderful collections of subjects such as horses, railways and shipping have been made by devotees of those subjects.

Many first class series of scenic views of the British Isles were issued. The best known were probably Francis Bedford's regional series which included thousands of views covering almost all of England and Wales and those of G.W. Wilson of Aberdeen whose views of Scottish scenery and townscapes often achieve a remarkable beauty but many other photographers were producing stereo views of equal brilliance and clarity at that time.

Negretti and Zambra who led the field with their stereoscopic daguerreotypes of the Crystal Palace in 1851 photographed it again when it was reconstructed in Sydenham and issued a series of stereo cards with grey mounts in 1856, and their series of stereo cards showing such exotic foreign subjects as 'Our Indian Empire' photographed 'by permission of the Honorable East India Company' and the series photographed for them by Francis Frith showing Egypt issued in 1857 and the Holy Land issued in 1858 received universal acclaim. Neither Frith nor Negretti and Zambra are named on these stereo cards but many were signed and numbered on the negatives by Frith himself and collectors will find his signature on the prints.

In 1858 Negretti and Zambra published an eighteen page catalogue *Egypt and Nubia: Descriptive Catalogue of One Hundred Stereoscopic Views of the Pyramids, the Nile, Karnak, Thebes, Aboo-Simbel and All the Most Interesting Objects of Egypt and Nubia,* which gave an eighteen page detailed description of Frith's photographs together with a summary of testimonials and editorial comments and is now greatly valued both as a collector's item itself and also for the insight that it gives to the work of an outstanding early stereoscopic photographer.

Although Negretti and Zambra issued the Frith stereocards in Great Britain for more than twenty years and many more were distributed in the United States by major firms such as the Langenheim Brothers and the New York Stereoscopic Company, who both put their own named labels on the backs of the cards, these Frith stereographs are very scarce today and collectors especially treasure those that show Frith's signature.

The square corners of these early stereocards were often damaged in use and cards with rounded corners, first introduced in 1868, were rapidly adopted by most photographers although many continued to use up the old square cornered cards until their stocks were exhausted. This provides another convenient cut off point in the history of stereoscopic photography and a number of collectors of photographic antiques concentrate on the earlier square cornered stereocards.

Interest in stereoscopic photography gradually declined as time passed

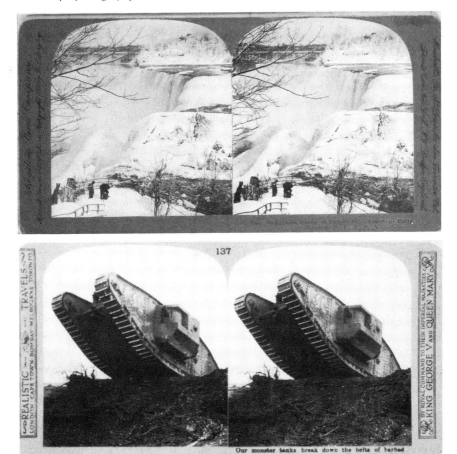

Top *Niagara Falls in winter, a curved stereocard by the Keystone View Company c 1900. A group of photographers can be seen on Luna Island at the bottom left of the picture.*

Above *A stereocard from 'The Great War', a 'Realistic Travels' series of 300 silver prints mounted on grey cards. Two hundred and ninety-nine cards (No 170 was missing) were sold, with a metal Holmes type viewer, at Sotheby's Belgravia on 28 October 1981 for £90.*

until a new competitor to the standard 3½ in by 7 in stereocard was introduced in 1873. This was the deluxe or artistic size stereocard which measured a nominal 4½ in by 7 in but which in practice varied from 4 in to 5 in by 7 in depending on the whim of the manufacturer or photographer. The larger size card was popular for several years but sold in rapidly decreasing numbers after 1880. This may have been due to the introduction of the curved or warped stereocards in 1879. Developed to give added impact to

Left *J.B. Dancer of Manchester made the first twin lens stereoscopic camera in 1853. This camera, his improved model patented in 1856, was sold at Christie's South Kensington on 21 October 1977 for £21,000 which was a world record for any camera.*

the three dimensional effect of the image these curved cards came into almost universal use by the early 1890s and it is these that are most easily found by collectors today.

In Great Britain and Europe interest in stereoscopic photography had almost completely vanished by the early 1880s, but in the United States two young brothers Ben and Elmer Underwood who had commenced selling stereo cards as door to door salesmen in 1882 were so successful that by 1891 they were covering the entire United States from a head office in New York and were employing a staff of photographers to produce their own stereo negatives. The Spanish-American War and the Boer War in South Africa gave added impetus to their sales drives and by 1901 they were producing more than seven million stereo cards a year most of them sold as boxed sets usually of one hundred cards with an accompanying descriptive guidebook and they were also selling hundreds of thousands of lightweight Holmes type stereoscopic viewers with aluminium hoods for viewing them with.

By the early part of the twentieth century Griffith and Griffith, the Keystone View Company, and the H.C. White Company had joined Underwood and Underwood in this enormous outpouring of stereocards and as other companies gradually gave up the business the Keystone View Company bought them out one by one becoming the only important manufacturer of stereocards and eventually accumulating more than two million negatives some going back to the 1860s.

Collectors will also find large numbers of stereocards with curved mounts that were published separately by innumerable smaller photographers from the 1880s until well after World War 1 and a selection of these to show how widespread the art had become will add interest to any collection. To take advantage of this renewed flood of interest in stereoscopic cards enormous numbers of non-photographic cards were reproduced by half tone lithoprint processes, they were often coloured and almost always sold very cheaply or given away as premium cards or trade cards in packets of

Right *One of the earliest surviving binocular stereoscopic daguerreotype/wet plate cameras complete with original negative plates and chemicals, made in 1854. Sold at Sotheby's Belgravia on 19 March 1976 for £1,800.*

cigarettes and breakfast foods etc. The stereo pictures that were printed in magazines and newspapers which the readers were invited to cut out and mount for themselves were a variant of these. These lithoprints have little or no value today. Most collectors will not bother with them and the most interesting and rare examples in the finest mint condition are seldom worth more than a few pence each.

Collections of stereocards should be carefully cross indexed under type, date, photographer, subject matter and any other heading of relevant interest. Great collections can still be put together at a reasonable cost but although stereocards were made in vast numbers the supply will eventually dry up and today's collectors will have had the advantage of being the early birds who have caught the worms.

The earliest pairs of stereoscopic photographs were made by taking the first photograph and then moving the entire camera sideways to take the second one, the distance that the camera was moved varying from two or three inches to several feet depending upon the distance of the subject and the inclination of the photographer. Sir David Brewster who had first suggested the use of a binocular stereoscopic camera in 1847, had produced one before the end of 1849 and an 1850 lithograph of a stereo photograph made with his binocular camera that has recently been rediscovered by Arthur T. Gill is probably the earliest stereo photograph taken with a binocular camera extant.

The earliest British patent for a binocular stereoscopic camera was taken out by Jacob Brett on 8 July 1853 but the earliest surviving example of a binocular stereoscopic camera was until recently the one made by J.B. Dancer in 1853. This camera was preserved in the collection of the Manchester Library and Philosophical Society until their premises were completely destroyed by German bombs during one of the Luftwaffe's raids on Manchester in 1940.

Dancer patented an improved binocular stereoscopic camera in 1856 and

A Horne and Thornthwaite folding stereo camera sold at Sotheby's Belgravia on 2 March 1979 for £3,800.

what was thought to be the only surviving example is preserved in the Science Museum Collection in London, but another has recently come to light and has been purchased by an American collector which shows what wonderful opportunities for discoveries still exist for collectors of photographic antiques.

Single lens stereoscopic cameras such as Lattimer Clarke's 1853 camera which was fixed to a parallel bar linkage that allowed the camera to slide across to fixed positions, Ross' camera of 1856 in which the lens could slide across the front of the camera and in which the entire camera could also slide from side to side along a folding two foot base, and Powell's lovely single lens stereoscopic camera of 1858 were made in small numbers right through the 1860s but by that time most stereoscopic cameras were of the typical wet plate sliding box construction and an increasing number of bellows cameras were also being made. All of these types are still occasionally offered to collectors and although they are expensive they make well worthwhile additions to any collection, and will eventually prove to have been sound investments too.

The introduction of commercial dry plates and then roll film cameras in the 1880s brought in its train many new stereoscopic cameras which made it easy for everyone from the merest novice to the experienced amateur photographer to take their own stereoscopic photographs and a new style of all metal cameras, stereo 'jumelles' (binoculars) was introduced in France in two sizes, 2⅝ in by 5⅛ in and 1¾ in by 4¼ in.

The Verascope cameras made from the mid 1890s by Jules Richard of Paris produced negatives from which prints and glass and later celluloid positives were made. Most people preferred the glass positives for viewing and many viewers were made ranging from simple box form hand held ones to the elaborate Taxiphote magazine viewers that were introduced by Jules

A rare sliding box combined stereo/panoramic camera. The mahogany grooved track on the top of the carrying case allows the camera to rotate through a 60° arc or to slide along the 23¼ in track to form a composite panorama. It was made in England in 1870. Sold at Sotheby's Belgravia on 7 July 1978 for £2,000.

An Ottewill stereoscopic wet plate camera outfit for 3 in by 3 in pairs of photographs on 3¼ in by 6¾ in plates. The mahogany sliding box camera is fitted with an A. Ross lens, a rising front, brass fittings and a grooved base. The folding rail is 23 in long and slots into a turntable on the top of the mahogany carrying case which is 13½ in long with hinged doors at the sides. It was made in England in 1858. Sold at Sotheby's Belgravia on 20 March 1981 for £3,800.

A stereoscopic sliding wet plate camera outfit made by T.H. Croughton of London in 1860. It has an f8 lens and takes 2¾ in by 2¾ in pairs of photographs on 3¼ in by 6¾ in plates. Sold at Sotheby's Belgravia on 20 March 1981 for £750.

Richard in 1900. These Taxiphote viewers held slotted boxes of fifty unmounted glass positives that could be brought into position for viewing by merely pressing a lever. They were very successful and were made in great variety and copied by many other manufacturers.

Louis Ducos Du Hauron who had invented one of the first practical processes for colour photography in 1869 patented the Anaglyph process of

Below *A Block 'Le Physiographe' stereoscopic binocular camera 5 cm by 12 cm made in France in 1896 and inscribed W. Watson & Sons Opticians, 313 High Holborn, London. It has twin lenses in the side with a right angle viewfinder in one eyepiece and an exposure counter in the other and has a three speed shutter. Sold at Sotheby's Belgravia on 20 March 1981 for £680.*

Bottom *A very rare Ives Komscop magic lantern attachment made of mahogany with brass fittings by Newton & Co in 1895. Attached to a magic lantern it projects through a series of glass reflectors and mirrors three glass separation positives through red, green and blue filters to three lenses which form a projected image in full colour. Sold at Sotheby's Belgravia on 28 October 1980 for £800.*

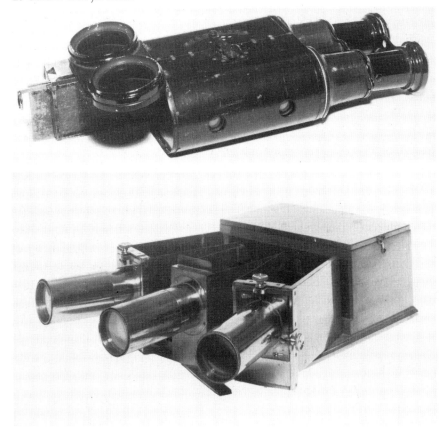

stereoscopic photography on 15 September 1891. Based on the earlier inventions of W. Rollman in 1853 and J.C. d'Almeida in 1858, the pair of stereoscopic photographs in an anaglyph are printed on top of each other, one in red and the other in blue/green and when viewed through a pair of spectacles with lenses of those colours in reversed positions the photographs combine to give a three dimensional image.

Examples of the equipment of the projection method using polarized filters on the projector and polarized glasses to view the image on the screen patented by J. Anderson in 1891 are now extremely rare and I do not know of any in a private collection. Frederic Eugene Ive's famous Kromscop stereoscope of 1892 which produces the original three dimensional image in full colour, and his parallax stereogram first made in 1903 which does not need a viewer are also amongst the great rarities of stereoscopic photographic antiques and highly prized by collectors today.

Ive's parallax stereogram was the precursor of the modern lenticular print, the latest version of which is produced by the Nimslo system. The four lens Nimslo camera was mainly designed by Jerry Nims and Allan Lo for whom it was named. It takes four approximately half frame pictures side by side each time that the shutter release button is pressed making eighteen stereo photographs on a standard 36 exposure 35 mm film. A special printing machine which optically slices very thin strips of each negative produces a colour print with a thin lenticular plastic overlay which gives a three dimensional effect without the use of any special viewing aids.

Earlier examples of lenticular stereoscopic prints and multi lens stereo cameras such as the K.B. Lentic camera which had six lenses spaced 2¼ in apart are perhaps more exciting finds for collectors but the several different versions of the Nimslo camera which have now been produced are well worth looking for and they too will one day become valuable collectors items.

Many hundreds of two and sometimes three lens stereoscopic cameras, beamsplitters, viewers, and other more esoteric items of stereoscopic equipment that range from the Wheatstone viewers made for pairs of large stereoscopic X-ray photographs to parallax bars and transposing printing frames can still be found by collectors today so look for them whilst they are still around and put together your own collection of stereoscopic photographic antiques.

Chapter 8

Moving pictures

Three different discoveries led to moving pictures, the magic lantern, the phenomenon of persistence of vision, and photography, and each has left a wealth of collectable antiques for us to find.

The magic lantern was first described in 1659 by the Dutchman Christian Huygens. In a diagram attached to his notes Huygens showed the arrangement of a concave mirror behind the light source, a biconvex condensing lens, the slide, and a biconvex objective lens, that became the standard optical system for magic lanterns, and before the end of the 1870s they were being made in most European countries.

Richard Reeves, a friend of Huygens, introduced the magic lantern to England in the early 1660s. Balthasar de Monconys reported that he had seen one when visiting Reeves in May 1663 and Samuel Pepys recorded in his diary for 19 August 1666 'Comes by agreement Mr Reeves . . . . He did also bring a lanthorn with pictures in glasse, to make strange things to appear on a wall, very pretty.' Pepys was so enthralled by the magic lantern that he bought it from Reeves and noted in his diary for 22 August that he had settled his account for '. . . the lanthorn that shows tricks.'

Several manufacturers were producing magic lanterns in Great Britain at the end of the seventeenth century and these early examples are highly prized by collectors today. The Magic Lantern Society of Great Britain stages exhibitions at its conventions and before spending large sums on old magic lanterns collectors of motion picture antiques would be well advised to attend these and to visit museums like the Barnes Museum of Cinematography in St Ives, Cornwall in order to get some idea of how lovely perfect and pristine examples of these early magic lanterns can be.

The earliest magic lanterns used sunlight or candlelight for illumination. Oil burners gradually replaced candles, the level of illumination was further improved by placing a concave mirror behind the oil burner so as to reflect and concentrate the light on to the lenses and in the late 1770s by the introduction of the Argand pot lamp which used a circular wick to supply oxygen to the centre of the flame, a chimney to provide extra upwards draught and a pre-heated thick oil or tallow for fuel, which gave far better illumination than any preceding type. Early magic lanterns complete with their means of

A triple mahogany and metal magic lantern, 32¾ in high, c 1890. Sold at Sotheby's Belgravia on 1 August 1972 for £200.

illumination are scarce and hard to find today but this of course makes them all the more desirable to a collector.

Larger magic lanterns were soon being built and used for public exhibitions and for the next hundred years or so the favourite exhibits were mainly slides of ghosts and demons. Robertson's Phantasmagoria is a late eighteenth century example of this forerunner of today's horror films and video nasties. The invention of oxy-hydrogen limelight and later the electric arc light during the nineteenth century led to the much greater use of the magic lantern for both education and entertainment which developed in Victorian times and it is examples of these later slides and magic lanterns which are usually found by collectors today.

Although outstanding examples of double and triple magic lanterns are sometimes offered for sale these larger examples are perhaps more suitable for museums than for the average private collector living in a flat or small suburban house for whom storage space can become a problem. The answer to this is to form a collection of the smaller or toy magic lanterns. A collection of these amazingly attractive little items can be just as interesting as a collection of their larger brothers and will not only take up less space but will also be correspondingly less expensive to collect, a small elaborately painted late eighteenth century or early nineteenth century lamposcope in good condition for instance can still occasionally be found for between £80 and £100. Magic lanterns often come complete with boxes of slides and again smaller magic lanterns have smaller slides and a collection of small lanterns is eventually far more manageable than one composed of the giant size triurnialls.

Left *A toy magic lantern, complete with slides, in a wooden box 13¼ in wide. Made in Germany in 1905. Sold at Sotheby's Belgravia on 14 November 1980 for £75.*

Below *A hand painted magic lantern slide, 16 in by 2½ in, early nineteenth century. (Courtesy of Sotheby's Belgravia.)*

Slide collectors soon learn to concentrate on slides of subjects that interest them personally although as always it is hard to resist outstanding examples or tempting bargains of any kind and we all buy groups of items because we badly want one of them in the hope that one day we will be able to exchange the unwanted balance of the lot with another collector. Sets of slides for both home and professional use were sold covering almost every conceivable field of interest from architecture to zoology and collectors will find further ranges and subdivisions within each subject itself.

Collectors of spirit and ghost slides for instance have formed collections that range from the earliest seventeenth and eighteenth century slides of gruesome ghostly apparitions to slides of ghosts spirits and haunted buildings made by nineteenth and twentieth century spiritualists, psychic researchers and spirit photographers. Sir Arthur Conan Doyle, the originator of Sherlock Holmes who was himself an ardent Spiritualist, built up an impressive collection of ghost and spirit photographs many of which were shown as lantern slides, and there are still many more slides of this kind to be found.

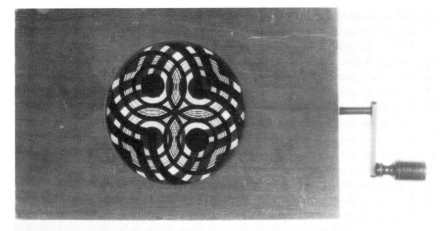

Above *A revolving mechanical magic lantern slide which gives a kaleidoscopic effect on the screen when the handle is turned. Made in England in 1900. (Courtesy of Sotheby's Belgravia.)*

Right *A 'spirit' photograph from the collection of Sir Arthur Conan Doyle. Miss E. M. Bubb, the sitter in this psychic photograph by William Hope brought her own packet of plates with her, signed one, placed it in the dark slide and developed it herself, obtaining this spirit extra.*

In an early attempt to produce motion on the screen Étienne Gaspard Robert, known as Robertson, a Belgian showman, patented the Phantasmagoria in which he used a mobile magic lantern placed behind a thin translucent screen which was set up between the lantern and the audience. By moving the lantern up to or away from the screen he made the images seem larger or smaller apparently rushing up to or away from the awe struck audience.

Another macabre effect was produced by John Henry Pepper, the inventor of the famous Pepper's Ghost Illusion, which combined a projected ghostly figure reflected onto a sloping glass screen with living actors on a stage and although the apparatus is no longer with us the ephemera associated with these shows is very collectable and will help to round out and give an extra dimension to a collection of early moving picture items. As techniques improved two, three and sometimes even more lanterns were used to produce dissolving views by fading one slide into another so as to turn a daylight scene into a moonlit one or make figures appear or disappear on the screen.

The panoramic slide was perhaps the earliest method of creating movement on the screen that can still be found by collectors today. The long thin slide, which usually measured between 14 in to 20 in by 4 in, was painted with a series of images and when passed slowly in front of the lens the images appeared to flow across the screen. These panoramic slides were among the first methods used to produce movement on the screen but collectors should know that they were still being produced at the end of the nineteenth century and should be careful because the later examples were often crude imitations of the early ones.

The earliest mechanical slides were slipping slides in which a slipping glass or glasses with black patches were slipped over a fixed glass painted with two or more stages of some simple action alternately covering and uncovering the different stages of the action. Examples of these are not too

A pair of Carpenter & Wesley No 2 Phantasmagoria dissolving view magic lanterns, 26½ in high. Sold with forty slides at Sotheby's Belgravia on 20 March 1981 for £580.

difficult to find today but many collectors prefer the rotary slides in which the illusion of movement is produced by rotating a circular glass over a fixed one. In the simplest of these rotary slides the moving circular glass is worked up and down by a lever at the side of the slide and in a more unusual version of the lever slide a square glass was made to move up and down over a fixed image. In other early versions of these slides the moving glass was rotated by a belt and pulley drive and in more elaborate examples the glass discs were framed in brass rims and turned in opposite directions by twin bands. A rare example of this is the Eidotrope which used two pierced metal discs revolving in opposite directions to produce moving patterns on the screen and the same idea was used in Chromatrope slides which when revolved projected rapidly expanding and contracting designs in brilliant colours.

Rackwork slides also used circular glasses, one being fixed in the wooden slide and the other set in a toothed brass frame which was rotated by a pinion wheel turned by a handle at the side of the frame. Collectors will find elaborate examples of rackwork slides which have two rotating or sometimes counter rotating glasses in addition to the fixed glass and these could provide remarkable effects on the screen.

The Choreutoscope slide invented by L.S. Beale in 1866 was in a more direct line to the moving pictures that we know today. A handle on the front of the slide turned a circular disc with a protruding pin which engaged a notch on the slide moving it on one picture and opening the shutter at the same time.

The Ross Wheel of Life patented in 1871 was another step forward. It had two circular glasses, one bearing a sequence of figures and the other was blacked out except for a small segment which rotated each time the figured glass moved forward one part of the sequence. It was derived from the Phenakistiscope and this leads us into the persistence of vision and the fertile field of optical toys demonstrating this remarkable fact, which is the basis of modern moving pictures.

The first optical toy to make use of movement was the Kaleidoscope invented by Sir David Brewster in 1816 and his *Treatise on the Kaleidoscope* published in 1819 is a valuable collector's item today. Early examples of the Kaleidoscope are hard to find. Although they are not in the direct line they make interesting additions to a collection of early motion picture items and many collectors have put together highly regarded specialized collections of them.

Shadow entertainments, with their use of images shown on a screen, will have an obvious attraction for collectors in this field and although they too have no direct connection with modern moving pictures they were a similar kind of public entertainment. Originating in the Far East with the Chinese shadow plays which used the shadows thrown on to a screen by articulated puppets that were usually made from sheepskin or the belly skin of donkeys, shadow shows customarily depicted legendary or historical

Left *A London Stereoscopic Co 'Jewel' kaleidoscope on a cast iron fluted column and leaf-cast base. It is 17 in high and was made in 1890. Sold at Sotheby's Belgravia on 29 June 1977 for £320.*

Below right *A toy Ombres Chinoises Transformations Instantanees theatre set comprising a lithographed stage front with white cloth screen and 25 figures in their original box. Made in France in 1880. Although some of the figures were damaged this was sold at Sotheby's Belgravia on 26 June 1981 for £100.*

themes. Puppets from Java used in similar entertainments were made of thicker buffalo hide and collectors will readily recognise their long thin jointed arms that were manipulated by rods attached to the hands.

Shadow shows spread through Turkey and North Africa, developing local characters and characteristics on their way, and these in their turn influenced the European shadow shows which became known as Ombres Chinoises. Collectors will delight in the many toy shadow shows, lantern slides and instruction books for making hand shadows that proliferated in the Victorian period.

Chinese perforated metal balls containing a candle which remained upright as the ball rolled along casting its changing shadows on the background and Japanese magic mirrors which displayed the image on their back when the sun or a strong light was reflected from their shiny slightly convex face were popular shadow entertainments and anamorphic images which were reflected in a polished metal cylinder were another nineteenth century optical toy that collectors look for today.

Peepshows, dioramas and panoramas although again not in the direct line of descent to moving pictures are also of great interest to collectors and once again it is the ephemera and toy versions that have come down to us today. Much like the popular camera obscura, seventeenth century peepshows or perspective boxes had flat pictures painted on the inside of the walls and on the floor of the box. By tricks of perspective, lighting and in later ones mirrors, a life like three dimensional effect was achieved.

One of the my favourite portable camera obscuras was indeed dressed up as a child's toy peep show when I first found it in an old antique shop. It was only after I had taken it home cleaned it up and carefully removed the penny plain and twopenny coloured cut-out characters that had been pasted inside it that it turned out to be as I had hoped an early nineteenth century hand crafted camera obscura made for early experimental photography.

Some peepshows were made by setting models against a perspective background. By the middle of the eighteenth century they were being made of scenes painted on several panes of glass set one behind the other viewed through a lens at the front and lit from the top, back or sides. Toy concertina like peepshows were popular during the nineteenth century and collectors will find that those depicting contemporary subjects such as *The opening of the Thames Tunnel* or *The Great Exhibition of 1851* which were both very popular, can be found at reasonable prices.

Large peepshows were exhibited by itinerate showmen in streets and fairs all over the world and collectors have found engravings showing them almost everywhere from China to Chelsea. In his novel *Our Mutual Friend* Charles Dickens describes a peepshow at a village fair which had first been shown as a scene from the Battle of Waterloo but which the showman had kept fresh and up to date after each subsequent great battle by altering the shape of the Duke of Wellington's nose so that he took on the appearance of the latest triumphant general.

Peep-eggs were miniature alabaster egg shaped peepshows each containing two scenes which were displayed alternately by turning two small knobs at the sides of the egg and viewed through a double convex lens fixed into a hole at the top of the egg.

In 1781 Philip Jacob de Loutherbourg announced his brilliant idea of creating a walk-in room sized peepshow which would hold the spectators as well as the images to be viewed. Calling it the Eidophusikon he opened the first one in a room in his home in February of that year. Loutherbourg who was a well-known artist and scenic designer painted his life-like scenes

A Polyrama Panoptique day or night viewer—a 13¾ in long wooden box covered in brown paper with a hinged lid at the top and a flap at the back—with eight views 7½ in by 9 in. Made in France in 1850. Sold at Sotheby's Belgravia on 26 June 1981 for £300.

Frith's 'Cosmoscope' unfolds to construct a viewer with a folding shade. It is 16¾ in long and was made in 1870. Sold at Sotheby's Belgravia on 18 July 1980 for £220.

Lane's Telescopic View of the Great Exhibition, designed by Rawlins and published by C.A. Lane in England in 1851. The folded paper 'peep show' expands to provide a glimpse inside the Great Exhibition. Contained within its printed cardboard envelope, it was sold at Sotheby's Belgravia on 18 September 1981 for £200.

on to fine materials and illuminated them with both projected and reflected light. This idea of containing the audience in a darkened auditorium was a great success and was incorporated into all subsequent public entertainments of this kind although it was not used in the theatre until introduced by Sir Henry Irving at the end of the nineteenth century.

The Panorama, invented by Robert Barker and patented by him as *La nature à coup d'oeil* on 19 June 1787, developed into a canvas 16 ft high and 45 ft in diameter attached to the inside of a circular building which was slowly revolved around the audience seated in the darkened centre of the circle.

In the Diorama, another variation of this effective entertainment that was invented by Louis Jacques Mandé Daguerre and Charles Marie Bouton, the audience were revolved inside the scenery which was made of large opaque and transparent paintings that could be illuminated from the front or the back by a series of complicated coloured screens and shutters which would completely transform the scene being viewed.

Although panoramas and dioramas were very popular through most of the nineteenth century they were almost all illuminated by lamps and gas lights and many of them were eventually destroyed by fire. The only surviving building is that of Daguerre's London Diorama in Park Square East, Regents Park. The facade of the building remains exactly as it was when it was opened on 29 September 1823 except that the name has been painted out.

Here again all that collectors can hope to find today are the ephemera associated with these popular entertainments and examples of the many toy panoramas and dioramas that were sold in those days, but these should be treasured as milestones in the development of modern cinemas.

It is with toys too that the fact of the persistence of vision was first demonstrated at the beginning of the nineteenth century. The simplest of these was a length of wire with the centre part bent into a semi-circle, so that when the ends of the wire were twirled between the fingers and thumbs it gave the appearance of a complete globe.

The Thaumotrope, invented by Dr John Ayrton Paris in 1825 and first sold by William Phillips in London on 2 April 1825, was a paper disc with different images on each face and strings attached to either side. When the strings were twirled the images merged so that a parrot on one side entered the cage on the other, a rider mounted his horse or a sentry entered his sentry box. As happened with many of these inventions several scientists conceived the idea simultaneously and Sir John Herschel who also illustrated this principle at the same time is indeed credited with its invention by some authorities.

This was also the case with the invention of the Phenakistoscope another collectable item in the history of motion picture. The Phenakistoscope was a cardboard disc with sixteen progressive figures representing phases of a movement and sixteen slots in the edge. When rotated on a spindle and held in front of a mirror the figures seen reflected through the slots in the

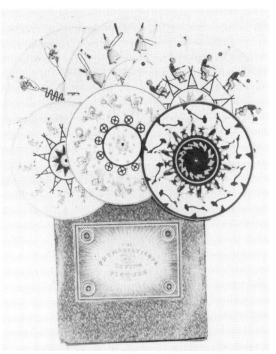

Left *A set of seventeen early nineteenth century English Phenakistiscope hand discs, each of which gives an illusion of movement when revolved and viewed through slits, contained in their original 9½ in square envelope. Sold at Sotheby's Belgravia on 2 March 1979 for £320.*

Below *A Zoetrope and its original cardboard box, made in England in 1870. Sold at Sotheby's Belgravia on 7 September 1979 for £320.*

edge seem to move. It was first described by a Belgian scientist, Joseph Antoine Ferdinand Plateau, in January 1833 and published quite independently by an Austrian scientist, Simon Stampfer, as the Stroboscope in February 1833. Collectors should look out for Stampfer's first set of six double sided Stroboscope discs which can be distinguished by the round holes around the edge, later ones using the slots which were to become the standard in this type of device.

Stampfer also suggested the idea of printing the sets of progressive figures used on the Stroboscope discs onto a strip of paper to be placed inside a revolving cylinder with the viewing slots pierced through its wall. William George Horner suggested a similar improvement on the Phenakistoscope disc, which he called the Daedalum in January 1844. A Frenchman, Peter Désvignes, patented this and several similar devices in England on 27 February 1860 but nothing seems to have come of it until the idea was resurrected in 1867 and patented under different names by M. Bradley in England on 6 March and by William E. Lincoln in the United States on 23 April. Lincoln called his appliance the Zoetrope. It became very popular under this name and sold widely throughout Europe and America which has left some delightful designs about for collectors to look for today. Both the original apparatus and the strips of picture can be found in a great variety and they make colourful additions to any collection.

The Praxinoscope patented by Emile Reynaud in Paris on 30 August 1877 was a further advance. The images were reflected by a series of small rectangular mirrors set one for each picture around a central drum, doing away with the need for the slotted drum and its consequent dark intervals between the pictures. On 6 January 1879 Reynaud added an improvement, the Praxinoscope Theatre, to his patent. In this the Praxinoscope was set in a box fitted with a wooden panel where the images move about as if they are on a stage with a glass fronted proscenium.

Although these delightful optical toys were as popular then as they are with collectors today it was Reynauds Projection Praxinoscope, in which the strips of moving figures were illuminated by an oil lamp and projected by a lens on to a screen, and his Theatre Optique, patented on 1 December 1888 in which a long strip of images perforated between the pictures was looped around the device in the centre of which a toothed mirror drum reflected each image in turn through a lens and on to a screen, which gives him the credit of being the first to give public performances of moving pictures projected on to a screen by means of transparent strips of individual images.

It was the invention of photography that ultimately gave life to the figures projected on to the screen. In 1849 photographers William and Frederick Langenheim of Philadelphia used the albumen on glass process to produce the first photographic lantern slides. Actors were soon being employed in series of posed pictures for narrative lantern slides which were projected sequentially. On 5 February 1870 the American Henry R. Heyl presented

the first public exhibition of his Phasmatrope, a series of such photographs fitted around a large disc which was rotated intermittently by a ratchet and pawl with an oscillating shutter covering the pictures as the disc was turned, so that when projected by a magic lantern the flickering figures on the screen reproduced their original motions.

The Phantascope lantern invented by John Arthur Roebuck Rudge in 1875 used an intermittent motion device similar to that on many modern cinema projectors to project a series of seven slides that revolved around the lamp house to give the smoothest illusion of motion yet seen and there were many even earlier inventors and inventions.

Jules Duboscq had patented the Stereo Phenakistoscope, a device for viewing a series of stereoscopic photographs in 1852, and other suggestions for producing moving pictures were made by Antoine Francois Jean Claudet in 1853, Henri du Mont in 1859, William Thomas Shaw in 1861, Louis Ducos du Hauron in 1864, Sir Charles Wheatstone in 1870 and by several other innovative photographers. In many cases it is doubtful if their apparatus was ever produced and almost everything that has survived is safely preserved in museums but the odd chance that something exciting will turn up keeps collectors awake and on their toes.

Eadweard Muybridge an Englishman who was born Edward James Muggeridge and changed his name to the Saxon version before emigrating to California in the wake of the 1849 gold rush was the first to take a series of photographs of an action and use them to reproduce the original motion. Muybridge, whose other claim to fame was that he shot and killed his wife's lover and was acquitted, became a well-known photographer and early in 1872 was asked by Leland Stanford, a former governor of California and president of the Central Pacific Railroad, to try and photograph a trotting horse.

In May 1872 Muybridge managed to take several photographs of Stanford's horse Occident at the Sacramento race course but because of the slowness of the wet plate process none were very successful. At another attempt in April 1873, however, several of the negatives were sharp enough to give a recognisable silhouette of the horse and driver and some of them clearly showed the trotting horse with all four feet lifted off the ground at the same time.

Muybridge's personal problems and other engagements kept him busy for the next few years but in 1878 Stanford again engaged him to photograph his horses in motion. Financed by the very wealthy Leland Stanford, Muybridge went to Stanford's Californian home Palo Alto, constructed a set of twelve Scovill plate cameras in a shed facing a whitened race track and set up a white screen marked with a few horizontal lines at the bottom and numbered vertical lines 21 in apart on the other side of the track. A thin thread was stretched across the track from the special double drop shutter of each camera so that as the horse trotted along the track it broke the threads and released the shutters of the cameras in close sequence. Although Muybridge was still using wet plates by June 1878 he succesfully photographed a series of successive photographs of horses in motion.

Improving his shutter mechanism and increasing the number of cameras first to 24 and later to forty Muybridge photographed many other animals, birds and athletes in action. After printing some of these series of photographs in strips for viewing in a Zoetrope in 1879 he designed the Zoogyroscope, a projector based on the Phenakistoscope, which he renamed the Zoopraxiscope in 1881.

Above left *An 8¾ in diameter Praxinoscope made in 1880. Sold with nine pictorial strips at Phillips on 17 March 1982 for £380.*

Right *The title slide of the set 'Johnny Todd's Extraordinary Adventures in Dreamland'.* (Courtesy of Sotheby's Belgravia.)

Muybridge returned to his home town of Kingston upon Thames in England and when he died there on 8 May 1904 he left his Zoopraxiscope, slides, scrapbook and his *Animal Locomotion* to the Kingston Public Library together with the income from £3,000 for the purchase of reference books. Many of his slides have been loaned to the Science Museum in London but his Zoopraxiscope and many other interesting items of Muybridge memorabilia can still be seen in the Kingston Museum.

Copies of Muybridge's original works *The Horse in Motion,* Boston, 1882, with text by J.B.D. Stillman, *Animal Locomotion,* Philadelphia, 1887, and *Descriptive Zoopraxography,* Philadelphia, 1893 are now extremely rare but *Animals in Motion,* London, 1899, and *The Human Figure in Motion,* London, 1901, which are extracted from *Animal Locomotion* and single plates from all of his books are still occasionally offered at both photographic and book sales.

Animal Locomotion, sub-titled *An electro-photographic investigation of consecutive phases of animal movement,* consisted of 781 photo-engravings bound in eleven folio volumes. The plates printed by the Photogravure Company of New York vary in size from 12 in high by 9 in wide to 6 in by 18 in wide and contain over 20,000 illustrations of men, women, children, animals and

A plate from 'Animal Locomotion' which is a group of 42 photogravure plates of human subjects. Each plate is 18¾ in by 23¾ in and is printed with a number and the inscription 'Copyright 1887, by Eadweard Muybridge. All rights reserved.' These plates were sold at Sotheby's Belgravia on 29 October 1976 for £1,500.

birds in motion. Only 37 complete sets of eleven volumes were sold for $600 a set but several hundred selections of one hundred plates were sold for $100 each and their prices today are correspondingly high. The Dover Press rephotographed the original calotype prints and reprinted *Animals in Motion* in 1955 and *The Human Figure in Motion* in 1957. Examples of these are easier to locate and also fetch respectable prices today.

Dr Etienne Jules Marey, who had been investigating the flight of birds since the early 1870s, designed a photographic gun to take sequences of pictures of birds in flight. By February 1882 he had built a camera taking twelve photographs around the edge of a circular glass plate. This was based on earlier camera designs suggested by Alfred A. Pollock in 1867 and Pierre Jules César Janssen, a French astronomer, in 1874. In 1888 Marey improved on his camera gun design with a new chronophotographic camera which used rolls of paper film instead of glass plates.

Ottomar Anschütz, a Prussian photographer, began taking instantaneous photographs of animals in 1882 using the prototype of what was to become the Goerz-Anschutz focal plane shutter in a small hand camera. By 1887 he had adopted Muybridge's system and using a set of 24 of these small cameras in rapid sequence recomposed the original movements in his Tachyscope, an instrument resembling a Zoetrope with the cylinder

Illustration of Marey's photographic gun from La Nature, *Paris 1882.* (Courtesy of the Deutches Museum.)

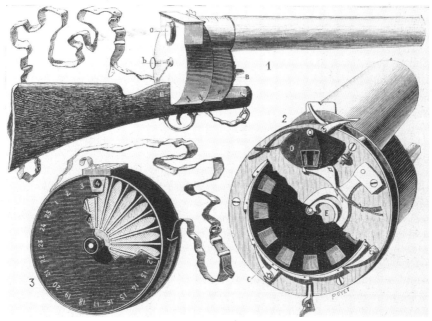

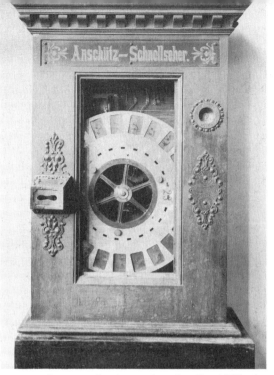

Anschütz's penny in the slot 'Schnellseher' (Tachyscope), 1877. (Courtesy of the Deutches Museum.)

mounted on a horizontal axle. In 1889 Anschütz built his Electrical Tachyscope, a viewing device in which the series of 24 photographs were illuminated successively by a spiral Geissler tube. Any of these devices would be a wonderful find today.

As has been seen there were many stepping stones along the way to the invention of moving photography but successful motion pictures were only finally made possible by the introduction of thin flexible transparent roll film. In 1885 George Eastman introduced the Eastman-Walker roll holder which he had designed with William H. Walker and a paper based stripping film to use with it. The paper base of the film was coated with a thin layer of soluble gelatin topped with a sensitized gelatine emulsion and after exposure and processing the thin gelatin emulsion with the image was stripped from the paper and transferred to glass or sheets of a heavier gelatin.

Eastman-Walker roll holders were produced to fit almost every camera that was sold in those days. Over the years they were produced in four metric sizes and eleven imperial sizes ranging from quarter plate to 11 in by 14 in and the wide flange could be adapted to fit most sizes in between but nevertheless they are not easy to come by today and I know of no private collector with a complete set of them.

Eastman also produced a detective camera with a built in roll holder in 1886 and this has now become a much sought after collector's item as only fifty were made because they proved to be too expensive. In 1888 he patented and produced the first Kodak camera, a small box camera with a built in roll holder which became an instant success. The Kodak camera was sold loaded with a roll of negative paper based stripping film sufficient for one hundred exposures and after the last exposure had been made the camera was returned to Eastman's factory where it was reloaded with a fresh film and returned to the customer. The exposed film was developed and printed and sent back to the customer, usually in about ten days.

Meanwhile Eastman had been experimenting with a transparent film base. Frederick Scott Archer first mentioned the advantage of stripping the sensitive layer of film from its support in March 1851 and in August 1855 patented a method of coating a finished glass plate negative with transparent gutta-percha and then immersing it in water so as to separate the image from the glass backing and produce a tough and flexible negative.

Alexander Parkes obtained the first patent for a flexible film in 1856 and although the idea was taken up by other photographers it was celluloid, invented by Alexander Parkes in 1861 and first called Parkesine, that became the base for the earliest successful transparent roll film.

The Reverend Hannibal Goodwin of Newark applied for a patent for a transparent roll film made of nitrocellulose and camphor on 2 May 1887. John Carbutt, another English photographer who had emigrated to the United States, introduced the first commercial emulsion coated celluloid films 'Carbutt's flexible negative films' in 1888. However it was the thin transparent celluloid roll film introduced by George Eastman in 1889 and popularized by him as an improved replacement for the paper roll film in his first Kodak cameras that swept the field and provided just the material needed by the pioneers of the motion picture.

Examples of all these early roll films and the cameras that they were used in are very rare today but as always it is the knowledgeable collector, who recognizes their importance in both the history of the camera and the history of the cinema, who will pick out these valuable photographic antiques when others have passed them by. Collectors should also be aware of the importance of several of the early experimental motion picture cameras and projectors which seem to have disappeared leaving little or no trace.

Wordsworth Donisthorpe patented a moving picture camera using dry plates in 1876 and together with W.C. Crofts patented another using flexible film in August 1889 but to date all that has been found of their work are a few frames of film that are now in the Kodak Museum. Louise-Aimé Augustine Le Prince, a Frenchman living in Leeds, built a camera/projector with sixteen lenses which recorded alternate sequences of eight photographs on each of two rolls of paper film in 1887. On 10 January 1888 he applied for a patent which included a single lens version of his motion picture camera using coated gelatine or Eastman paper film and in 1889 he designed a projector with a Maltese Cross mechanism and another fitted with an arc lamp. However, during a visit to his brother in France in September 1890 he boarded the train from Dijon to Paris and then disappeared. No trace of him or his luggage has ever been found.

Many other early motion picture pioneers both recorded and unrecorded were experimenting with new ideas for cameras and projectors before success came in the 1890s. They must have left many collectable examples of their apparatus for us to find today.

William Friese-Green, a professional photographer, became interested in motion pictures when he produced a series of photographic lantern slides showing seven stages of some simple movement for Rudge's Phantascope lantern. Working with civil engineer Mortimer Evans he had, by 1888, built a camera taking four or five quarter plate photographs on a roll of paper film and an improved twin lantern projector to show them with. The Friese-Green and Evans British Patent No 10131 dated 21 June 1889 is generally accepted as one of the germinal motion picture camera patents. A stereoscopic film camera was patented by Frederick H. Varley, an associate of Freise-Green, on 26 March 1890 and another very similar one by Friese-Green on 29 November 1893. A further patent for a motion picture camera granted to Friese-Green and J.A. Prestwick in August 1896 was for the famous Prestwich motion picture camera which was used by professional film makers all over the world for many years.

Freise-Green's claim to be the inventor of the cinema is however contested by the supporters of many other researchers in this field. The first successful commercial application of these ideas was made by Thomas Alva Edison together with his research assistant William Kennedy Laurie Dickson, a Scotsman who had emigrated to the United States in 1879. After many experiments, one of which used a series of microphotographs placed on the cylinder of an Edison Phonograph, they perfected a method using Eastman's celluloid film and in April 1891 Edison applied for patents for his Kinetograph camera and Kinetoscope viewing apparatus which introduced the use of perforated film strips. With slight variations the four rectangular perforations per frame that he used became the standard 35 mm film perforation for the entire world. The Kinetoscope first shown in America in 1893 and in London in October 1894 became an almost instant world-wide success. The films were shown at 46 frames per second and lasted about fifteen seconds each and the coin in the slot mechanism could be coupled to an Edison Phonograph to give talking pictures.

The success of the Kinetoscope brought many other inventors into the field. Jean Aimé LeRoy, another American, claimed to have built a film projector in 1893 but the first evidence of its existence are theatrical playbills for 'LeRoy's Marvellous Cinematographe' dated early in 1895. On 14 June 1894 Grey and Otway Latham with their father Major Woodville Latham filmed a prize fight staged in Edison's 'Black Maria' the first purpose built film studio. They displayed the film in enlarged Kinetoscopes in Manhattan in July 1894 and in April 1895, together with W.K.L. Dickson who had by then left Edison, they built a projecting Kinetoscope and gave their first public showing of projected films in May 1895.

On 12 January 1894 C. Francis Jenkins patented a 'Phantascope' camera which used a continuously moving film exposed through a ring of lenses on a disc rotated to match the speed of the film. He joined forces with Thomas Armat and on 19 February 1896 they patented their Vitascope projector which was successfully demonstrated to Edison and bought by him to be sold under his own name. The first public showing of twelve Kinetoscope films by the Vitascope, which included two English films purchased from Robert W. Paul, was at Kostler and Bial's Music Hall in New York on 23 April 1896. It was a great success and Vitascope projectors were soon being sold to theatres all over the United States where some of them must still be waiting to be discovered by enthusiastic collectors.

During the 1890s the race to provide projected motion pictures hotted up in Europe too. In France Marey's chief assistant George Demeny patented a version of the Phenakistoscope that he called the Phonoscope on 3 March 1892 and a film camera for photographs to use in it on 10 October 1893, but he did not produce a really successful camera and projector until 1896.

Leon-Guillaume Bouly patented a motion picture camera on 12 February 1892 and an improved camera/projector on 27 December 1893. Bouly called his apparatus the Cinematographe and apparently produced a number of them although only two examples have been unearthed to date, leaving another treasure trove for the enterprising collector.

Louis Jean Lumière and his older brother Auguste Marie Louis Nicolas Lumière must have the credit for putting on the first public exhibition of projected moving pictures to a paying audience and so launching the modern cinema industry. Their family business in Lyons was one of the largest suppliers of photographic materials in France and in August 1894, following the success of Edison's Kinetoscope, they decided to produce their own motion pictures. They built a combined camera/projector that used the same 35 mm film used by Edison but with only one round perforation per frame instead of the four rectangular perforations per frame used by Edison. The 35 mm film width used was half the width of the film produced by Eastman for his Kodak cameras and was probably made by slitting the 2¾ in Kodak film down the centre and joining the ends to give a strip of about 50 ft of 35 mm film.

The Lumière brothers patented their machine which they called the Cinématographe on 13 February 1895. They gave their first public exhibition, a one minute film 'La Sortie des Ouvriers de l'Usine Lumière' (Workers leaving the Lumière Factory), in Paris on 22 March 1895 and on 28 December 1895 they hired the Salon Indien at the Grand Cafe, Boulevard des Capucines 14, Paris, and charging one franc admission gave the world's first cinema show to a fee paying public.

The Lumière Cinématographe was introduced to London by showman Felicien Trewey on 20 February 1896 and from 9 March 1896 it was included in the programmes of the Empire Theatre of Varieties in Leicester Square where it ran successfully for more than a year, but the cinématographe

A Lumiére Cinématographe camera/projector of 1895. (Courtesy of the Deutches Museum.)

show was not the first film show to be exhibited in England.

In the autumn of 1894 Robert William Paul, a scientific instrument maker of Hatton Garden, London, found that Edison's Kinetoscope was patented in every country in the world except England and at the instigation of the two Greek owners of a Kinetoscope Parlour in Old Broad Street he started producing copies of it. However Edison's films were only supplied to purchasers of his own machine so together with photographer Birt Acres, Paul developed a camera based on Marey's Chronophotographic film camera of 1890 and on 29 March 1895 sent a sample of a test film that they had made to Edison offering to supply English films for the Kinetoscope.

Paul and Acres soon went their separate ways. Acres filmed the Oxford and Cambridge boat race on 30 March 1895 and after patenting the Kinetic camera on 27 May used it to film the Derby at Epsom. He developed a film projector 'The Kinetic Lantern' and used it to show films at the Royal Photographic Society on 14 January 1896. Paul, who was selling his Kinetoscopes to Charles Pathé and many other exhibitors, designed a new camera and a projector which he demonstrated at the Finsbury Technical College on 20 February 1896 and then before an audience of 320 at the Royal Institution on 28 February. The Paul Theatrograph was first shown to a paying public at the Egyptian Hall on 19 March 1896, at Olympia from 21 March, and one of his projectors renamed the Animatograph was used for the nightly film shows at the Alhambra, Leicester Square, that commenced on 25 March and ran for more than four years.

In Germany Carl Skladanowsky built a sequence camera using the 3½ in film produced by George Eastman for his No 2 Kodak camera. Skladanowsky patented his Bioscop projector in November 1895 and his two sons Max and Emil gave their first public show with it at the Berlin Wintergarten that same day.

Oscar Messter who worked in his father's small optical business in Berlin saw the first cinematograph show there in April 1896, sent to London for some strips of Edison Kinetograph film, and by 15 June 1896 had built a projector that was the first to incorporate the Maltese Cross mechanism to provide the intermittent film movement that is still being used today.

The commercial success of these early cinema entertainments led to an upsurge of new ideas and by the end of 1896 dozens of new cameras and projectors were being produced. In his book *Living Pictures,* published by the Optician and Photographic Trades Review in 1899, Henry V. Hopwood gave this list of motion picture cameras, projectors and viewers of the 1890s that he had noted in his somewhat extensive research: Anarithmoscope, Artograph, Badizograph, Centograph, Chronophotographoscope, Cinagraphoscope, Cinograph, Cinomograph, Cinoscope, Cosmonograph, Cosmoscope, Diaramiscope, Electroscope, Hypnoscope, Kathoscope, Kinematoterm, Kaptopticum, Kinebleposcope, Kinesetograph, Kinesterograph, Kinetinephone, Kinevitagraph, Luminograph, Magniscope, Movendoscope, Movemendoscope, Motorscope, Mutoscope, Pictorialograph, Pantobiograph, Pantomamiograph, Phantograph, Phonomendoscope, Photomotoscope, Photokinematograph, Phototrope, Rayoscope, Scenamatograph, Stereopticon, Stinetiscope, Taumatograph, Thromotrope, Variscope, Venotrope, Viroscope, Vitograph, Viviograph, Virtescope, Visionoscope, Vitelitiscope, Vitamotograph, Vivendograph, Vitopticon, Vivrescope, Waterscope, Wonderscope, X-ograph, Zoetrope, Zinematograph.

Add these to the ones that have been mentioned earlier in this chapter and if we include odd items of equipment such as Short's Filoscope 1898, Birt Acre's Kineoptican 1896, C. Goodwin Norton's Photochromoscope 1898, E.G. Lauster's Eidoloscope, Georges Méliés' Star film camera, and all those

Messter's Kinetograph using a five arm Maltese Cross was the first German film projector and, was made in 1896. (Courtesy of the Deutches Museum.)

weird and wonderful cameras and projectors that were advertised in the British Journal of Photography and the various trade magazines of those days you will get some idea of the marvellous assortment of items waiting to be found by collectors.

Many have completely disappeared with the passage of time. Whilst the projectors grew too large for most collectors the brass and mahogany, and sometimes all metal, cameras that gradually replaced these earliest ones during the first decade or two of the twentieth century are just as appealing. They include many famous names some of which are still with us today. A selection is listed below.

Aeroscope	1911	Movietone-Wall	1924
Akeley	1918	Moy (Moyer)	1905
Bell & Howell	1912	Moy and Castle	1909
Cinex	1926	Newman & Sinclair	1911
Chronique	1910	Pathe	1890
Darling	1904	Prestwich	1898
Debrie	1908	Prevost	1905
Eracam	1910	Schustek	1908
Eclair (Gillon)	1913	Technicolor	1915
Gaumont	1896	Urban	1905
Jenkins	1895	Warwick	1906
Lubin	1901	Willart	1922
Mitchell	1920	Williamson	1902

The importance of some standardization for motion picture films was recognized by the Lumière brothers as early as 1895 when they modified the design of their Cinématographe combined moving picture camera/projector to accept the four perforation per frame 35 mm film used by Edison instead of the single round perforation per frame that they had originally used. This meant that they could show Edison's films on their own projectors. It was not however until the Motion Picture Patents Agreement of 1907 that the original Edison 35 mm width with four rectangular perforations per frame became the standard for professional motion picture film.

Meanwhile, much to the delight of collectors today, variations of film width, frame size and the number, position, shape and size of perforations multiplied almost beyond belief. Everything has been tried from the 2⅞ in width of Mutoscope and Biograph films of 1895 to the 3 mm wide 'bootlace' film used by Eric Berndt in America in 1960. Films with round, square or oblong perforations, with perforations on one side, both sides or in the centre, perforations on the frame line or at the film's edge, open sided perforations, closed perforations or both were all used. Other wonderful ideas ranged from the glass plates of the British Kammatograph of 1897, the circular film disc of the Canadian Baker Kinematograph for home talking pictures of 1904, and the flat circular 11 in disc, photographed outwards from the centre, of the American Spirograph of 1915.

The proliferation of professional film sizes was added to in 1898 when Birt Acres patented his Birtac camera/projector which used a half width 17.5 mm film made by splitting 35 mm film down the centre and was the first sub-standard home movie outfit designed for amateur use. Cecil T. Hepworth also used 17.5 mm film in the Biocam which he first showed in March 1899, but with central narrow slot perforations on the frame line. Another machine 'The Junior Prestwich' produced for amateurs by J.A. Prestwich that same year took 13 mm film.

Gaumont's 'Chrono de Poche' used 15 mm film with a centre perforation, the Kinora camera of 1908 used 25.4 mm film, Edison's Home Kinetoscope

Pathe 'Kok' home cinemato-graph, 1912. (Courtesy of Christie's South Kensing-ton.)

The 16 mm Model 'A' Cine Kodak Camera and the Koda-scope Model 'A' projector introduced with Kodak 16 mm reversal film in 1923. (Courtesy of the Kodak Museum, Harrow.)

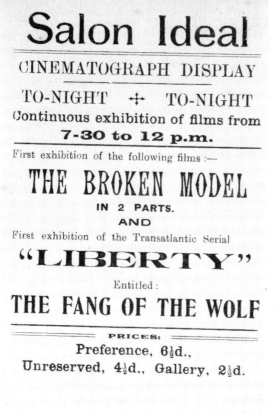

Salon Ideal

CINEMATOGRAPH DISPLAY

TO-NIGHT ✢ TO-NIGHT

Continuous exhibition of films from
7-30 to 12 p.m.

First exhibition of the following films :—

THE BROKEN MODEL

IN 2 PARTS.

AND

First exhibition of the Transatlantic Serial

"LIBERTY"

Entitled :

THE FANG OF THE WOLF

PRICES:

Preference, 6½d.,
Unreserved, 4½d., Gallery, 2½d.

Left *Advertising leaflet of 1918 for the 'Salon Ideal' cinema.*

Below right *A scene from the festival film 'The Magic Box', based on the life of the British inventor of the moving picture, William Friese-Greene. Robert Donat plays the role of the inventor and guest star Bernard Miles appears in the cameo role of Cousin Alfred.* (Courtesy of THORN EMI Screen Entertainment.)

of 1912 used 22 mm film which had three rows of 6 mm by 4 mm pictures with two rows of perforations between them, the Pathe 'Kok' home cinematograph of 1912 used 28 mm film with three perforations on one side and one perforation on the other side of each frame and many manufacturers produced other novel ideas at that time.

The first really successful home movie outfit was that produced by Pathe in France in 1922 which used 9.5 mm film with a slotted single frameline perforation but it was rapidly followed in January 1923 by the Eastman Kodak Company's Cine-Kodak camera and Kodascope projector which used a reversal safety 16 mm film with one perforation on either side of the frame line.

In 1929 the American Kodel Electric and Manufacturing Company attempted to capture the amateur movie market by introducing their Homovie system which used 16 mm film and produced four quarter size pictures in each normal 16 mm frame but they were swept aside when Eastman Kodak introduced their Cine-Kodak Eight-20 Camera which used a 25 ft roll of 16 mm film taking quarter sized pictures down one half of the film and then with the roll turned over another quarter size picture sequence down the other half of the film. The film was slit down the centre after reversal processing and the two halves joined together to make a 50 ft length of 8 mm film.

Bell & Howell's Filmo Straight Eight Camera introduced in September 1935, the Universal Camera Company's Univex Straight 8 Camera of 1936 and several other cameras took a 50 ft length of single run 8 mm film and for many years 8 mm, 9.5 mm, and 16 mm cameras and projectors competed for a share of the home movie market whilst oddities such as the Campro and the Midas 9.5 mm combined camera/projectors added to the lists of motion picture cameras and projectors many of which seem to have been made for collectors rather than for the users.

There are excellent collections of professional motion picture memorabilia which include advertising material, film star photographs, posters, stills from films and the myriads of other collectable items produced by the cinema industry and it has become a popular field for collectors, but except for a few major collections interest in motion picture cameras has not yet taken off to any great degree and aside from the classical historical items of the nineteenth century which every collector is or should be looking for prices are still very reasonable and provide an excellent opportunity for collectors to build a master collection at comparatively small cost.

As always happens with collectors, my only regrets after many years of collecting photographic antiques are the ones that got away and for me that is particularly poignant in the field of early motion pictures. I have handled and for one reason or another been unable to acquire a Praxinoscope Theatre, a Lumière Cinématographe in pristine condition, the mechanism of one of Edison's earliest film projectors and last but not least a quarter size 35 mm wood and brass Edwardian cine camera in mint condition which had been used by a cinema manager to film local events for splicing into the national newsreels. There are still countless items of similar quality and interest out there waiting to be found, so good hunting, and if I do not find it first, good luck to you!

Chapter 9

Collecting photographic bonds and shares

Collecting the bonds and share certificates of companies associated with photography adds another new and adventurous dimension to collecting photographic antiques. Scripophily, the recently coined name for the collecting of old bond and share certificates, is taken from 'scrip' the commonly used word for share certificates and 'ophily' from a Greek stem meaning 'for love of'. It first gained prominence in the early 1970s at the same time that collecting photographica achieved its first great burst of popularity and provides yet another field of great interest for collectors of photographic antiques.

Fortunately for us photographic bonds and shares are as yet not included in the 'objects de art' category that has been bidded up by antique dealers who are more concerned with bonds from pre-revolutionary Russia, Imperial China and other such esoteric times and places than our, in their eyes, more mundane items of photographic interest. Many of the certificates were printed by the leading printing houses in Great Britain, the United States and the major European countries and they produced wonderful examples of the engraver's art which added to their value in the boom years of 1979-80 when dealers and investors spent heavily to build up portfolios of outstanding examples and prices rocketed.

German dealers led the field in the race to higher and higher prices and in 1978 the price of one outstanding Chinese bond leaped from £500 to £14,000 in less than a year, but the price of that same bond has now dropped to £5,000 and the prices of other similar highly priced bonds has also dropped enormously. Since then the market has stabilized at a much lower and more sensible level with much of the demand now coming from genuine collectors rather than from dealers and speculators, and as a result of this and of the accidental loss, destruction and discarding that inevitably happens in the course of time the value of certificates is once again gradually rising.

Compared with philately, scripophily is still in its infancy and indeed the name still has a strange ring to some ears but the number of collectors of bonds and shares is constantly growing as more and more people realize the wonderful addition to their collections that photographic bond and share certificates can make.

Collectors of photographic antiques are just beginning to appreciate the interest and value of these old certificates and with photographic items still in the category of 'junk' shares to most of the larger dealers they are still quite inexpensive to buy. I have even rescued one or two that would have finished up as waste paper but for my timely arrival which shows the excellent opportunities that still exist for collectors of photographic scripophily.

Most of the collectable bonds and shares of early companies in the photographic, motion picture and allied industries are no longer traded by stockbrokers in the world's stock exchanges and they are considered to be obsolete and worthless securities, but to collectors they are relics of the early days of the industry and their value lies in the history that they illustrate as well as in their scarcity and in many cases visual beauty.

The growing worldwide interest that has developed in the 1980s has seen the number of collectors rise from about 300 when the first German catalogues were published in 1976 to a present estimated 30,000 and this is even more impressive when seen in conjunction with the societies, specialist dealers and the publications that have sprung into being to cater for the ever growing demand that has been built up by collectors hungry both for certificates and for information about them.

The Concise Oxford Dictionary gives the following definitions for the items of collectabilia in which we are interested:

Bond government's or public company's documentary promise to pay borrowed money, debenture.

Debenture sealed bond of corporation or company acknowledging sum on which interest is due till principle is repaid.

Share one of the equal parts into which a company's capital is divided entitling holder to proportion of profits.

Stock capital of corporation or company contributed by individuals for prosecution of some undertaking and divided into shares entitling holders to proportion of profits.

Bonds and shares reflect the two main methods of financing a company. The share certificates are issued to the shareholders who are the owners of the Company and provide the risk capital involved which entitles them to benefit most if the company is successful but also means that they may have little or no guaranteed return if things go wrong. Companies can raise additional money in several different ways but it is mainly done by means of bank overdrafts and the issue of bonds. The bonds that we collect were the evidence of an individual's loan to a company and guaranteed both his funds and the agreed rate of interest for the period of the loan. The period of the loan and the date of commencement of repayments are stated on the bond and this helps us to determine how many of an issue have been redeemed and how many are still outstanding and this of course affects the rarity and the value of the bond to collectors.

Debentures are similar to bonds but are usually issued in limited numbers to borrow money for a specific purpose. About the same size as bonds but usually less elaborate they were most popular with British companies because of the way in which our tax system worked.

Bonds and share certificates are original documents issued by companies and provide a fascinating background to a collection of photographic antiques. Most collectors of photographica come across items of ephemera associated with photography in the course of their searches for collectabilia but bonds and shares add a new and so far almost untouched area to our collecting.

Early shares and bonds were mostly issued 'To Bearer' which meant that physical possession of the bond was the important factor, and the company kept only the smallest number of records possible. In Switzerland and a few other countries this is still usually the case but most countries now require the registration of shares and their re-registration when they are sold so that a record is readily available. There is no limit to the number of times that a share may be bought and sold and as the original certificate must be cancelled or destroyed and a new one issued each time there is no limit to the number of certificates that may be around.

Bearer shares on the other hand are not issued to any particular investor and they do not have to be cancelled and re-issued each time that they are sold so that the number of bearer shares is limited to the authorized capital

The Automatic Photograph Company Limited. Debenture for £25, No 1, dated 1892. Red print certificate, price £12.

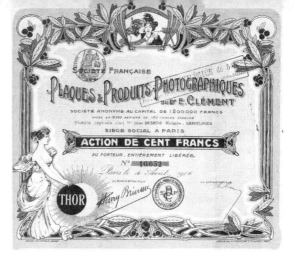

Plaques & Produits Photo-graphique du Dr E. Clément. 100 francs, issued in France in 1906. Price £42.

of the company which is usually shown on the certificate. In order to minimize the amount of record keeping necessary almost all bonds are bearer bonds and the owner is personally responsible for claiming the interest and ultimate repayment of the principle.

In order to attract investors many bonds and shares bore beautiful and elaborate designs and for security reasons they were mostly engraved by printers used in the production of bank notes, such as the American Bank Note Company, Bradbury Wilkinson, de la Rue and Waterlow. The fancy borders and vignettes that adorn bonds and shares add much to their visual attraction. In a few examples that I have seen the vignettes were engraved from photographs and in other they show examples of the cameras and projectors that the company produced which all adds to their interest and value to the collector of photographic antiques.

Groups of people joining together to finance private enterprises are not a modern phenomena. The earliest British chartered company was the Muscovy Company formed in 1553 to discover 'the unknown lands in the North' and trade with Russia and the Baltic countries, and other historical examples of this method of raising capital include those used during the reigns of Henry VIII and Elizabeth I to provide ships and provisions for the merchant adventurers who sailed forth to find new lands establish new colonies and provide new trading opportunities for their backers.

The modern stock exchange originated in 1657 when the East India Company began to allow public subscriptions to its capital to be fully transferable to third parties and in 1720 during the South Sea Fever parliament passed the Bubble Act which made a royal charter of incorporation necessary for the formation of any joint stock company.

Until 1839, that magical date for collectors of photographic antiques, most businesses were partnerships but a new Company Act was passed in Great Britain in the 1840s, and with the progress of the industrial revolution which commenced in Great Britain in the early part of the nineteenth century and in a short while spread throughout the civilized world, modern stock market methods were developed.

Photo-Machine. Fifty $100 shares issued in the USA in 1913. Black print with vignette green border, price £30.

Joint stock companies obtain their capital by selling shares to the public and by issuing bonds. In Great Britain the name of the holder of the share or shares is entered both on the certificate and on the company's register of shareholders. European and some other overseas shares can either be registered or issued to bearer. Bearer bonds are issued for fixed sums of capital but a share certificate can be for any number of shares.

The company will send any dividends or interest due directly to all shareholders on its register but each certificate of bearer stock has a sheet of numbered and dated coupons which the holder must produce to the paying agents in order to receive any interest due. The talon, a detachable slip at the side of some sheets of coupons, is exchanged for a fresh sheet of coupons when those attached to the bond have been used. Many collectors and dealers place little value on bearer certificates with their coupons missing or with incomplete sheets of coupons but this of course ultimately depends on the interest and rarity of the certificate and is after all their natural state.

Collectable bonds and shares have been cancelled in many different ways. Early Victorian certificates were usually cancelled by ink lines drawn across the face or through the signatures but later examples were often cancelled by punch holes, perforations, or slits and some were cancelled by rubber stamps or by having the word cancelled written across them. Collectors should choose certificates with as few cancellation marks as possible and should avoid any that are badly disfigured by unsightly or over heavy cancellation marks. Some American certificates will be found stamped with document, revenue, or transfer stamps which were used to pay the appropriate tax when they were cancelled or transferred. They usually enhance the appearance of the document and will usually enhance its value too.

From 1807 until 1863 French businesses were controlled by the Code de Commerce which came into force in 1807. This legalized three forms of business organizations, Societies en Nom Collectif which were simple partnerships, Societies en Commandite which had both active partners and silent partners who had only limited liability, and Societies Anonymes which limited liability for all the shareholders. The first two simply had to register with the authorities but the Societies Anonymes had each to obtain a special authorization from the Conseil d'Etat which was a government department. There were two different kinds of Societes en Commandite one in which the partnership was concluded upon the death of one of the partners and the other which was allowed to carry on after the death of a partner. The partnership agreement for their photographic experiments signed by Niepce and Daguerre on 14 December 1829 was of this second kind and after Niepce's death on 5 July 1832 he was succeeded by his son Isadore Niepce as laid down in their contract.

A vast number of companies have issued bonds and shares in the last 150 years and as a result of this many collections have become unwieldy and without a focus of attention but collectors of photographic antiques are spared this fate as we specialize in our own interest and indeed some of us specialize even further by subdividing the field into different areas such as camera manufacturers, still photography or motion pictures whilst others collect only nineteenth century or pre-World War 1 items or items from before some other significant date in the history of that section of photography in which they are personally interested. Smaller areas of specialization make it more difficult to find examples of collectabilia but makes it possible for collectors of even modest means to put together satisfying collections providing of course that they do not specialize in esoteria such as the Niepce-Daguerre partnership agreements or similar documents of great historic importance.

All collectors are magpies and when we start collecting we tend to pick up anything that is of the remotest photographic interest but sooner or later we all learn to discriminate and to discard the junk that accumulates in the course of time. Hard though it may be to believe when we are starting to collect, a small collection of rare and important items in first class condition

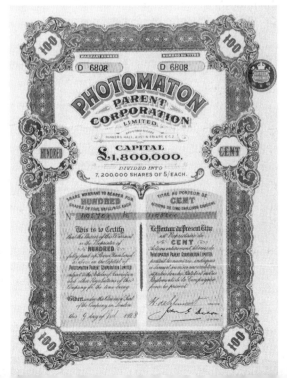

Photomaton Parent Corporation Limited. One hundred 5s shares issued in 1928. Purple print certificate, price £5. (Photomaton companies proliferated in the 1920s until they were all finally bankrupted!)

will always be better, more impressive and eventually more valuable than a much larger collection of unimportant and low value items in poor condition and although no collectors should be unduly influenced by financial reward or monetary considerations it is nevertheless nice to know that your judgement is sound and that the value of your collection is steadily increasing.

This applies to every aspect of collecting photographic antiques but perhaps especially to collecting the bonds and share certificates of photographic companies. By the very nature of things they are fragile and ephemeral and although we are all guilty of accepting an item of poor quality in order to fill a gap in our collection in the hope of eventually exchanging or even selling it when we find a better example we almost invariably discover that because of its condition no one is interested in it at all and that we have thrown our money away. As is the case with most collectors, I have seldom regretted extending my resources in order to obtain a rare and outstanding example of photographic collectabilia. What appears to be much too expensive to afford today will without a doubt become a choice item in your collection tomorrow and provide a pivot that will help to bring everything else into focus. If it is that good the only advice that one can offer is pay for it now and afford it later!

Remember that the important thing in determining the value and therefore the price of any object are condition, demand and rarity. No matter how good its condition is or how rare it is if no one else wants it there should be no need to pay an excessive price, so when buying never appear too eager or enthusiastic or up will go the cost. If there are two collectors and only one item then the one who is prepared to pay most will usually be the buyer and if they are both wealthy the sky may be the limit. However if there are two items and only one collector. . . .

The storage of a collection of photographic bonds and shares is always important even if they are not of the rarest and most valuable kind. They are usually printed on good quality paper and the advice of perfection is to store them in covers of cellophane rather than PVC, but as a matter of practical availability the albums sold for the purpose by various specialists are quite satisfactory provided that they are kept in stable conditions of heat and humidity and a cool dry cupboard at home will provide a safe environment for them. As with all collecting buy the best that you can afford. A good album with removable black protectors in the slip in pages will allow you to show two certificates to a page or by removing the black insert will display both the front and back of one that is printed or signed on both sides. It will provide good protection, last longer and will eventually prove to be good value.

A filing card system of your collection or even just a notebook containing details of your collection entered up as you acquire each item and with additional information entered as your research continues will also prove of great value and associated material will always add greatly to the interest and ultimate value of a collection. Wherever possible I complement my collection of photographic bonds and shares with other associated ephemera, advertisements bill heads, business cards, envelopes, labels, letter headings and examples of the films or photographs that the company produced and this helps to round out the collection and attracts the attention of even non-collectors.

One so far unresearched aspect of collecting photographic bonds and shares is the autographs of the signatories. Although most have been signed by comparatively unknown people many of the certificates issued by early photographic and motion picture companies must bear the signatures of pioneers of these industries and will become very valuable indeed so that once again the knowledgeable collector will be able to score over those who do not recognize an outstanding autograph on a photographic company's bond or share certificate.

Collecting the bonds and share certificates issued by companies of photographic interest is still in its infancy. At the time of writing prices in Great Britain range from £1 or £2 up to £25 for most of the examples that I have seen with very few priced at more than £12 or £15 which would be about the price for decorative nineteenth century examples in mint condition but collectors should be warned that some European dealers seem to have very inflated ideas of prices and often ask much higher prices for very similar items. The condition of a certificate depends on several factors including the quality of the paper, the amount of handling that it has received and the circumstances in which it has been stored. This all helps to determine its value and should be reflected in its price. Other factors that should be taken into account are its relative rarity, attractiveness and age.

Many companies held a reserve stock of certificates. Those that were numbered and kept as a reserve to cover the registration of new share holders are referred to as unissued and those without numbers which were used to replace lost or destroyed certificates are called reserve stock. These latter are often still found in mint condition but being without the company seals, revenue stamps or signatures are not highly regarded by collectors.

Certificates are issued for a registered number of shares which is recorded on the document. Collectors will find that most are for a few hundred shares or less and although the number of shares is mostly irrelevant those that were for large number of shares, five thousand, ten thousand or more are relatively rare and desirable as are the certificate number one of companies which was often issued to the company's chairman, president or principle stockholder. A low certificate number has no great significance but if the certificate number runs into the thousands or tens of thousands it shows that considerable number of the certificates were issued so collectors should beware of dealers who describe certificates numbered in the tens of thousands as 'rare'.

The condition of issued certificates is defined in fairly general terms ranging from:

Uncirculated	Mint, clean and crisp as issued.
Extremely Fine	Clean, almost as issued, but may have traces of folds.
Very Fine	Showing slight signs of wear with minor folds or creases.
Fine	Well handled, creased and worn but with only minor damage.
Fair	Very creased and worn, much circulated but still perfectly clear.
Poor	Extremely creased, damaged or stained.

However, one man's very fine is another man's very poor, so make sure that you agree with the seller's description and if possible inspect the item yourself before buying it. Although most reputable dealers will send their offerings to known buyers on approval, certificates at auctions are almost always sold as seen and so are not returnable because of their condition. In circumstances such as these or when buying through the post from a private party *caveat emptor,* let the buyer beware.

At this early stage in this new area of collecting photographic antiques the question of rarity does not often arise. Dealers will naturally quote higher prices for nineteenth century material than for twentieth century items and they will ask more for highly decorative and so more desirable certificates than for plain ones printed on poor quality paper but photographic collectors can use their knowledge of the field to great advantage when it comes to the historic importance of any company or certificate.

Regardless of the seller's feelings about the rarity and value of any certificate it pays to shop around and if necessary wait for the right dealer to offer the certificates that you want. I have for instance been offered examples of the same attractively bordered and vignetted certificates of a pre-World War 1 photographic manufacturer by three different dealers, two in England and one abroad, at £3, £22, and £145! I was offered the highest price first and hastily refused it, almost bought the middle one and was happy that I had not done so when about three weeks later I received the third one from a friendly dealer. Mentioning this gives me the opportunity to thank all my friends amongst collectors and dealers of bonds and shares for the help and information that they have so generously extended to me. Starting a collection of bond and share certificates now will give you the opportunity to get on the ground floor of this important new field of collecting and providing that you are careful and only buy good quality material you will have a collection that can only increase in value as time goes by.

As your collection of photographic bonds and shares grows you should consider insuring what will become a valuable asset. Your insurance broker will be able to tell you what cover you have under your household contents policy and may indeed be able to put you on the trail of bond and stock certificates that you can acquire to help build up your collection, but as your collection grows he will soon advise you to take out supplementary insurance to cover it in case of burglary or damage by fire or flood.

In your interest as much as in the interest of the insurance company you should store your certificates carefully. If you have purchased very expensive and exotic bonds and shares as an investment you will of course keep them carefully locked away in a safe or bank vault or you may have one or two framed and hung as wall decorations but most collectors will keep their certificates at home where they can go through them occasionally and have the enjoyment of showing them to fellow collectors and interested friends.

Most bonds and shares were folded before they were put away and have been kept folded and well creased if nothing worse until they reach us so that the first thing to do is to gently unfold them and straighten them out. Some of these original documents are now more than fifty or a hundred years old and should be handled with the greatest of care. They should be stored flat and if they have arrived in a folded or creased condition pressing them between two clean sheets of heavy paper or fine linen with a cool iron will help to restore their appearance. If they are very badly creased using damp sheets of heavy paper or fine cloth will help and in extreme cases running a dampened finger along the crease before ironing will sometimes work wonders, but do exercise the utmost care and use only a very cool iron and the least possible amount of moisture and be sure to air them well so that they are completely dry before putting them away.

As with all paper collectables gently rubbing with a very soft artist's eraser will freshen up grubby examples and even remove slight surface stains. The ideal of course is to only collect examples in perfect condition. We all occasionally accept a substandard item because of its rarity but items in poor condition will spoil, not enhance, a collection so please do be fussy about the quality of your collection, as quality will eventually prove to be more important to you than quantity. One should only collect for pleasure and not for investment or the hope of a quick profit but whether we like to admit it or not we all feel an extra glow when our expertise pays off and the value of our collection steadily increases.

Below left *Gnome Photographic Products Limited. 1,300 ordinary 2s shares issued in 1960. Black and blue print certificates with vignette of factory, price £3.*

Below right *The Rank Organisation Limited. 81 'A' non voting ordinary 5s shares issued in 1962. Brown and green print certificate, price £2.*

Eastman Kodak Company. 8¼ per cent convertible debenture due 2007 for $25,000, issued in the USA in 1983. Orange and black print certificate with eagle vignette, price £1.

Both new and established collectors will benefit from membership of the Bond and Share Society which has branches in the United States of America, South Africa and Canada. The Society's journal is full of interesting information and advertisements and the society organizes fairs and auctions especially for members. It will be able to put you in touch with collectors and dealers who can help you with your collection which makes membership, which still only costs £5 a year, very worth while. The Society currently has some 450 members and more than 22,000 people visited the exhibition of bond and share certificates arranged by the Society in conjunction with Herzog Hollender Phillips and Co of Bond Street at the Visitors Gallery in the London Stock Exchange in March 1984 which shows how rapidly interest in scripophily is spreading in what are still the early days of collecting bonds and share certificates.

The numbers of collectors now seems to be almost doubling year by year and this will undoubtedly mean that the value of obsolete bond and share certificates will increase as time goes by. Most early bond and stock certificates were disposed of when they were cancelled or when the companies closed down or were taken over and this applies as much to the certificates of photographic companies as to any others and their scarcity should ensure that their prices will rise. In fact a stockbroker who is also a collector has assured me that many of his antique certificates have proved to be better investments than the current ones he recommends to his clients!

An almost unlimited amount of research is needed into the history of photographic firms. We have as yet not ascertained which is the earliest surviving bond or share certificate of photographic interest and newcomers to this field will have wonderful opportunities in what is still an almost uncharted territory. Whilst nineteenth century examples of bonds and shares of photographic interest and items from the earliest days of the motion picture industry at the turn of the century can still be found fairly easily this is the time to join in and become a founder member of a new field of photographic collecting.

Chapter 10

Photographic philately

The happy coincidence of the announcements of both photography and countrywide uniform prepaid postage in 1839 has created yet another unusual range of collectabilia for collectors of photographic antiques. The modern approach to collecting stamps and postal history is thematic collecting, that is collecting world-wide adhesive stamps and other philatelic material to illustrate a chosen theme and collectors of photographic antiques have their own ideal theme pre-chosen for them. There is practically no limit to the scope of a thematic collection of photographic interest and it can include a large variety of different items ranging from the designs shown on the stamps themselves to letters, envelopes, postal documents and other philatelic material from all over the world.

Thematic collecting, called topical collecting in the United States is not a new phenomena although it is an important part of stamp collecting. The first recorded mention seems to have been in an article in the *Stamp Collector's Magazine* of 1 June 1863 by the Reverend Henry H. Higgins, in which he suggests arranging a collection of postage stamps in groups of the families, genera, species and varieties etc as one would in a zoological or botanical collection. Interest in thematic collecting spread from Great Britain to collectors around the world and articles such as 'A Collection of Heads' published in the 1 July issue of the *Stamp Collectors Magazine* describing the anonymous author's stamp collection comprised 'solely of those which are ornamented with portraits' began to be published in many philatelic magazines. The French philatelic magazine *Le Collectioneur de Timbres-Poste* published a number of articles on thematic collecting during the 1890s and by the turn of the century thematic collecting became an acceptable part of the philatelic spectrum and articles describing various themes and aspects of thematic collecting were being published fairly regularly in prestigious philatelic magazines such as *Gibbons Stamp Weekly* in Great Britain and *Mekeels Weekly Stamp News*, *The Philatelic West* and *Weekly Philatelic Era* in the United States.

The early pioneers of photography must have communicated their ideas to each other by post and their letters, complete with the covers, would make a wonderful starting point for a thematic collection of photographic postal history. The letter sent by James Watt to Thomas Wedgwood one Thursday in the 1790s in which he thanked Wedgwood for his 'instructions as to the Silver Pictures, about which, when at home, I will make some experiments' may have been the very first letter ever written about photography, but when Joseph Nicéphore Niepce began his first photographic experiments with a camera obscura in April 1816 he kept in constant communication with his brother Claude who had moved to Paris in March of that year. In a letter sent to Claude on 9 May 1816, he noted that when he recorded the image in the camera obscura on paper sensitized to light with chloride of silver the movement of the sun during the lengthy exposure did not cause any change in the image.

The Niepce brother's correspondence was published by Victor Fouque in *La Verite sur l'invention de la photographie*, Paris, 1867, but other letters by Nicéphore Niepce still occasionally come to light although if they pass through the larger auction houses they may be too expensive for many collectors today. During a visit to London in the winter of 1827 Nicéphore Niepce sent a record of his photographic experiments and several examples of his heliographic photographs to the Royal Society and these Niepce relics are now in the Gernsheim Collection. Niepce and Daguerre were corres-

An autographed manuscript letter from Joseph Nicéphore Niepce to his cousin. It is a single folded sheet, the letter taking up one full side, bearing a Chalons sur Socône postmark. Sold at Sotheby's Belgravia on 17 June 1981 for £1,300.

ponding with each other from early in 1826 but Fox Talbot first wrote about photography during a trip to Lake Como near Bellagio during October 1833, and as he mentioned in the *The Pencil of Nature,* this was in the nature of a note to himself rather than a letter.

All this was before the introduction of the Uniform Fourpenny Post on 5 December 1839 and the Uniform Penny Post in January 1840 and it is from this latter date that the great tidal wave of posting began and it is from then onwards that items of photographic postal interest really became available to collectors.

Photographers advertising envelopes are one interesting subject for collectors of philatelic photographic antiques. They became available from almost the earliest days of the new postal services. The artist William Mulready, RA prepared the design that is printed around the address portion of both the One Penny and the Two Penny letter sheets and envelopes which are named after him. These were the world's first prepaid postal stationery, and their potential as advertising sheets was realized almost as soon as they appeared. Like the penny black adhesive stamp, Mulreadys were sold to the public on 1 May 1840 but they were not available for postage until 6 May, those posted before 6 May were delivered but they were surcharged 2d each. Postal instructions and announcements of the prices at the Post Office, which were 1¼d and 2¼d, were printed at the sides of the letter sheet but not on the envelopes. A charge of 3d per dozen over the face value was made to cover the cost of the paper and printing but advertisers soon took advantage of this and provided the public with covers bearing their own advertisements at cut prices.

Large advertisers such as the Anti-Slave Trade Society sold Mulreadys with their own appeals and announcements printed inside, at one shilling and two shillings per dozen. The Clerical, Medical and General Life Assurance Company offered them to their agents with their Assurance Meeting Notices and the Agent's name printed on them for 10d per dozen, and private traders offered the penny ones printed with their advertisements at 9d per dozen. Mulreadys printed with an assortment of small advertisements first appeared on 30 May, 1840. Each edition had a guaranteed circulation of 5,000 copies and the publishers sold them at well under the cost price, 6d per dozen to the advertisers and 9d per dozen to the public, making up the difference and taking their profits from the charges made for the advertisements.

The adhesive stamp proved more popular with the public and as the postal authorities began to object to both the advertisements and price cutting, the use of Mulreadys as an advertising medium was stopped after the first year. In that short time it is estimated that nearly 400 different organizations and merchants sold their own advertising Mulreadys and there were some thirty different issues printed with an assortment of small advertisements, some bearing up to thirty individual advertisements.

I have examined the advertisements on about half of this number personally but to date I have found no camera or photography related advertisements on any of them although *The Athenaeum* had carried advertisments for 'Photogenic drawing paper' prepared by J.T. Cooper resident chemist of the Polytechnic Institution, on 16 March, 1839 and for 'Ackerman's Photogenic Drawing Box for copying objects by means of the sun' on 6 April, 1839 and the first photographic camera made for sale had been advertised by Francis West, a Fleet Street optician in *The Mirror of Literature, Amusement and Instruction* volume xxxiii in June 1839. One of the Mulreadys bearing printed small advertisements does include one for a W. English offering 'superior spectacles' and 'a choice of telescopes, thermometers, mathematical instruments and measuring tapes, etc. in great variety', and there is one Mulready printed by Tucker of Southampton bearing a large single advertisement for J.R. Stebbing 'By Appointment to her Royal Highness The Duchess of Kent, Resident Opticians, and Manufacturer of Mathematical, Optical, and Philosophical Instruments' a description which later often included the manufacture of cameras.

Caricatures of the Mulready design were produced by many of the leading artists of the day, those of John Leech and 'Phiz' Hablo Brown being particularly notable, and although stocks of unsold envelopes were withdrawn from post offices early in 1841 the Mulready envelopes had demonstrated the value of the illustrated envelope. Professional photographers soon recognized the publicity value of such illustrated envelopes and used them for both correspondence and for the sending of photographs, the latter in stiff board envelopes often marked 'Book Post—Photographs only'. These all make wonderful additions to a collection of philatelic photographic antiques.

My search for early photographic philatelic items has unearthed a letter written in French that was commenced in New York on 10 November, 1849 finished in Vera Cruz, Mexico and posted to France via an English ship on 14 December 1849 which contains a detailed order for a complete daguerreotype outfit giving details and prices to be paid for each item. Another find was a beautiful printed pictorial envelope by Bemrose of

A card cover for cabinet size photographs from the 'Van Der Weyde Light' studios of Regent Street, 1878.

Derby dated 1861 advertising Poulton's Stereoscopes together with a copy of Poulton's 1860 Catalogue listing over 1,800 Stereographs of 'English and other Scenery'. This catalogue was printed by Thomas Gough Gutch who was probably related to John Wheeley Gough Gutch, the famous pioneer photographer, whose letter dated 21 October 1858 describing his photographic activities including how he took 'a capital view of a serpentine rock thanks to Ponting's Collodion it took 3 minutes & ½ exposure, we have been doing them in 5 & 10 seconds, & if I had had Taylor's as last year ½ an hour would not have done . . . .' together with a few of his photographs makes another fine display.

Cartoon envelopes of photographic interest and the advertising covers of prominent photographers such as one from Jabez Hughes dated 1877 which I display together with one of the photographs taken by him and his shopping list for photographic chemicals written in his own hand, and another dated 1868 from William Notman the noted photographer of the Canadian West again accompanied by one of his photographs also make attention drawing display pieces.

Right *Cover used by Jabez Hughes to post completed carte de visite photographs to clients, 1877.*

Below *Thornton-Pickard parcel label, 1899.*

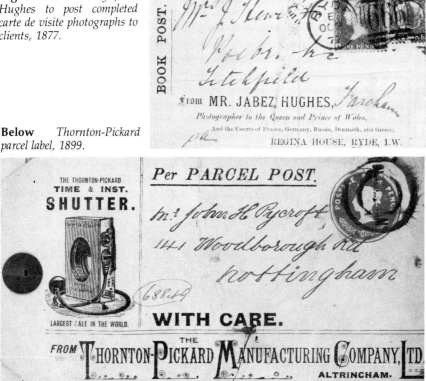

Left *A hand drawn Victorian cartoon cover sent in 1879. Cartoon covers showing cameras are rarely found today.*

Below *An advertising envelope of Poulton, photographic printer and publisher, 1861.*

    Another interesting aspect of photographic postal history is shown by the adhesive stamps found on the backs of photographs taken in the United States of America at the end of the Civil War. From September 1864 to August 1866 a tax on photographs of all kinds was levied in the North to provide additional funds to prosecute the Civil War. The tax on photographs and stereographs was 2 cents on those retailing for 25 cents or less, 3 cents on these retailing at 26 cents to 50 cents and 5 cents on those costing from 51 cents to $1.00. Revenue stamps were usually fixed to the photograph or stereograph to pay this tax. The 'USIR' 2 cents orange is the one that is found most often but almost any other type can be found on American photographs of the period especially on those from the summer

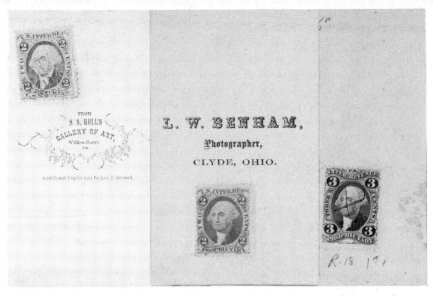

United States internal revenue adhesive stamps were fixed to the reverse of photographs to pay the tax levied from September 1864 to August 1866.

of 1866 when stocks of available stamps were used up in anticipation of the expiration of the levy.

The first direct use of photography in postal communications was during the siege of Paris 1870-71 during the Franco-Prussian War. Napoleon III declared war on Prussia on 19 July 1870 but barely six weeks later Bismark had completely defeated the French Army at Sedan forcing the Emperor to surrender there on 2 September 1870 and the Prussian army soon encircled Paris. After the last mail train left Paris on 18 September the Prussians held the city completely in their grasp and it seemed that the two million inhabitants of Paris would be starved into submission.

Gaspard Felix Tournachon better known to collectors of photographic antiques by his nom de plume 'Nadar' had suggested the use of captive balloons for observing enemy positions and was in charge of the 'Compagnie d'Aerostiers Militaires' (Company of Military Balloonists) when it was decided to take carrier pigeons out of Paris by balloon so that they could bring despatches back into the besieged city. The first of these pigeons to return carried despatches dated 27 September which reached Paris on 1 October and from September 1870 until February 1871 302 pigeons carrying despatches were released and 59 of them returned safely to Paris. They carried many important official despatches and some 95,000 private messages to the encircled Parisians.

The first pigeons each carried one single despatch which was rolled tightly, tied with thread and attached to a tail feather of the pigeon. From 19 October despatches were sent rolled in goose or crow quills for protection. The despatches were at first hand-written using minute characters on very thin paper, but following the suggestion made by Barreswil, a chemist of Tours, early in October the messages were written full size on large cards, reduced photographically and finally printed on both sides of photographic paper.

Despatches produced in this manner were sent to Paris from 8 November to 18 December 1870 and clearer letterpress then replaced the handwriting on many of these despatches. Dagron, a leading French microphotographer, had also suggested reducing messages photographically for transmission by pigeon post and although microphotographs were already arriving in Paris the authorities arranged for Dagron and two colleagues, his son-in-law Poisot and Ferrique, to take their equipment out of the city by balloon to establish another pigeon post depot at Clermont Ferrand.

They left on 12 November in the well-named balloons Daguerre and Niepce, but the Daguerre was shot down by the Prussians and lost with its precious load of equipment and pigeons and although the Niepce was also shot down into Prussian territory Dagron and his companions escaped but became separated and lost still more of their equipment. Dagron reached the original pigeon post depot at Tours on 18 November but without his specialized equipment was unable to produce the microdots he had suggested. The depot moved to Bordeaux and Dagron, working with inferior equipment, finally produced messages with a reduction of more than forty diameters on microfilm weighing 0.05 gm so that a pigeon could carry as many as twenty of them on each journey.

Le Daguerre manned balloon wrapper to Les Herbiers bearing a vertical pair of 1870-71 Seige 10c stamps finely cancelled by Paris stars '29' of Rue Pascal, the rarest of the star cancels in use during the Siege. There is no arrival circular date stamp as the mail was captured. The estimated value of this label in November 1984 was £280. (Courtesy of David Patterson, Stanley Gibbons International Limited.)

Dagron's souvenir of the Paris pigeon post of 1870-71. It carried a microfilm similar in size and make up to the last ones carried into Paris by pigeon.

Until early in November when the service was made available to the public most of the despatches were official correspondence and to increase their chances of reaching Paris the same despatches were often sent by several pigeons, one important official despatch being repeated 35 times in an effort to ensure that it reached its destination. When the despatches reached Paris they were unpacked at the Central Telegraph Office and placed between two thin sheets of glass. The earliest despatches on photographic paper were read through microscopes but the microfilms were projected on to a screen by a magic lantern and copied on to forms by a team of clerks who used telegram forms for the private messages.

A collection of items of photographic interest from the Siege of Paris pigeon post can commence with letters or despatches carried by the balloons Daguerre and Niepce, if only to display their names, and could include the early photographic despatches, the later microphotographic pellicles and the telegram forms and other items of associated ephemera including the souvenir carte de visite produced by the London Stereoscopic and Photograph Company which carried a microfilm of the front page of The Times of 19 January 1871 which The Times of 30 January 1871 reported had been sent to Paris by pigeon post. This has been disputed by photographic historians and although 99 years later on 4 February 1970 The Times finally admitted that its report of 30 January 1871 was probably not true this does not affect the carte's value as a collector's item.

Dagron produced a similar souvenir of the war carrying in this case a microfilm similar to the last ones carried by pigeon in to Paris with the page numbers printed at the top. He used page numbers 627 and 642 which were fictitious and contained a title page stating that it was a simulacrum and fifteen pages of fictitious letterpress private messages. The cartes de visite were sold individually or could be purchased bound between the centre pages of Dagron's booklet *La Poste par Pigeons Voyageurs—Notice sur le voyage du ballon Le Niepce emportant M. Dagron et ses collaborateurs et details sur la mission qu'ils avaient a remplir,* printed by Typographie Lahure in Paris.

A souvenir sheet measuring 24 cm by 16 cm with the inscription *La poste par pigeons voyageurs—specimen indentique aux pellicles du siege contenant la valeur d'une page de journal* and a copy of Dagron's replica microfilm reproduced in the centre was produced by the Aero Club and given to all who donated towards the fund for their Bartholdi monument, and several other souvenir 'pigeongrams' were also produced after the war. M. Maury, a well known stamp dealer in Paris, offered microfilms for 1 franc 25 centimes each in his 1894 catalogue and it is thought that he too produced his own war souvenir but all these microfilms, whether authentic pigeongrams produced during the war or post-war souvenir reproductions, are scarce and much sought after by collectors today. They are occasionally seen in the larger philatelic or photographic sales and in good condition have brought prices in excess of £150 each.

Collectors will find that *The pigeon post into Paris 1870-71* a monograph by J.D. Hayhurst, OBE, which gives details of the pigeon post, the souvenirs and medals associated with it and much other interesting information, is most helpful and a mine of information about this important part of photographic philately.

The official commemorative medals associated with the Paris pigeon post includes some fourteen 30 mm diameter medals struck in copper which are listed by John Hayhurst and several other types of medals both official and unofficial which were issued to commemorate the pigeon post. These medals can form an introduction to another important aspect of collecting photographic antiques, the collection of awards, medals, plaques and tokens of photographic interest.

Photographers tokens were issued for advertisement purposes but like all tradesmen's tokens they were sometimes circulated unofficially as currency. The earliest tradesmen's tokens of photographic interest were issued in the United States by Scovill and Feuchtwanger, manufacturers of brass plates, in the 1830s. Scovill and Feuchtwanger became manufacturers and suppliers of daguerreotype cameras and equipment in the 1840s and as the Scovill Manufacturing Company became one of the larger photographic supply houses in America.

Tokens were issued by many photographers in Europe and Great Britain. One interesting copper token issued by Thomas Johnson of Leicester in 1864 reads JOHNSON PHOTOGRAPHER and has a bearded portrait, possibly of Johnson himself, on the face and GALLOWTREE GATE LEICESTER and a shield bearing a floral pattern surmounted by a dragon on the reverse. Photographers tokens are scarce but I have two modern 'wooden Nickels' presented by William K. Rodgers, an American friend with a great collection of photographic medals and tokens whose collection commences with the Mungo Punton silver award presented by the Royal Scottish Society .in June 1845 when he presented his paper on *The Photographic Register Thermometer* and comes right up to date with many modern examples.

Many camera clubs and photographic societies awarded medals and plaques to honoured members and prizewinners at their various competitions and exhibitions in the nineteenth century and the early part of the

Obverse (above) and reverse (below) of two photographer's tokens by Lane of Brighton. (Courtesy of Bill Rodgers.)

twentieth century and collectors will find many other interesting and collectable awards that were made by learned societies and at industrial exhibitions for photographic exhibits, innovation and inventions. Medals have been issued to commemorate the anniversaries of camera companies, film manufacturers and photographic societies all over the world and many plaques and sculptured likenesses of the famous inventors of photography have been made in their honour. One of these, the famous George Eastman medal awarded to employees of the Eastman Kodak Company after 25 years of service is still fairly easy to find and should be in every collection.

Another direct and very collectable connection between photography and medallions is made by the Cameograph invented by Captain Howard M. Edmunds. The Cameograph mentioned in the Royal Mint Report for 1923 produced a bas-relief medallion from two special negatives of the sitter. They were produced commercially by the Cameograph Studios in London and are now very rare. The only example that I have located is in the Bill Rodgers collection in the United States but there must still be some around waiting for lucky and knowledgeable collectors to find.

The backs of Victorian carte de visite and cabinet size photographs are often illustrated with the different awards and medals that have been bestowed upon the photographer and a large frame filled with these would make a lovely showpiece for a collection.

Another direct use of photography in postal communications occurred at the Siege of Mafeking during the Boer War 1899-1902. Although photographing the defences of the town was banned photographic processes were used to alleviate some of the consequences of the siege. The first of these was the shortage of currency in Mafeking which made it difficult to provide for military payments and led to Lieutenant-Colonel R.S.S. Baden-Powell, commander of the Frontier Force defending the town to authorize the issue of garrison siege notes repayable on the resumption of civilian law.

The paper currency issued in the smaller denominations of 3d, 6d, 9d, 1s, 2s and 3s was not produced photographically and they are of no special interest to us, but the £1 note, designed by Baden-Powell personally, was produced photographically by Mr E.J. Ross, an enthusiastic local amateur photographer who had a Thornton-Pickard Ruby reflex camera in which he used Ilford plates. Ross was the only official photographer of the Siege having been given special permission by Major Lord Edward Cecil, Baden-Powell's Chief Staff Officer, to visit the outposts to take photographs.

Having discussed the feasibility of the project Baden-Powell sketched a currency note which Ross photographed and reproduced successfully. Baden-Powell then drew the detailed design for the £1 note and Ross made six negatives of the final sketch, although as one became damaged by shell fire only five of them were eventually used. Owing to the shortage of the usual photographic materials they were eventually printed using the cyanotype blueprint process invented by Sir John Herschel and first described by him in June 1842. The notes vary in colour from pale to medium blue, are each individually numbered, embossed with the One Penny Bechuanaland Protectorate revenue die and signed by both Mr R. Urry, manager of the Standard Bank at Mafeking, and Captain Greener, the Paymaster. 683 of these notes were printed but only 44 were ever redeemed and the other 639 remain in circulation to provide a rare find for collectors today.

Obverse and reverse of a solid copper, silver plated medal awarded in Frankfurt, Germany in 1884. (Courtesy of Bill Rodgers.)

The George Eastman Medal, awarded to Kodak employees after 25 years of service to the company.

A similar situation occurred with the official adhesive postage stamps. Because of the difficulty of communicating through the enemy lines the supply of 6d and 1s stamps used for external postage were more than adequate, but stocks of the 1d and 3d denominations used for the local postage which was 1d per ½ oz soon ran out. Following on the success of the photographic £1 notes Baden-Powell authorized the production of a supply of 1d and 3d stamps in the same manner.

In order to free as many able-bodied men as possible for the defence of the town, on the instructions of Baden-Powell, Major Lord Edward Cecil had formed a cadet corps of the boys from nine years old upwards. Most of these acted as messengers or delivered the local mail and a photograph of one of these, Cadet Sergeant-Major Warner Goodyear, on his bicycle taken by Dr D. Taylor, another Mafeking amateur photographer, was used for the central design of the 1d bicycle stamp. The photograph of Baden-Powell used for the 3d stamp was taken by E.B. Ross who produced the Mafeking £1 note, but although printed by the same blueprint process the colour of both stamps varies enormously and examples ranging from a very pale grey to a dark blue can be found, the lighter and darker ones being the most rare.

The width of the 1d bicycle stamp varies between 18 mm and 19.75 mm and the height between 23 mm and 23.5 mm. These 1d bicycle stamps were printed in sheets of twelve and a total of 9,476 were produced. The initials W and H of the stamp's designer Dr W.A. Hayes can be seen in the space separating the 'One Penny' value tablet at the bottom of the stamp from the part representing the original photograph. The Baden-Powell 3d stamp was also printed in sheets of twelve arranged in three horizontal rows of four

Left *Reverse of a carte de visite, showing medals awarded for photography.*

Below right *E.B. Ross producing the Mafeking £1 note in his underground dark room, with a reproduction of one of the notes in the bottom left hand corner.* (Courtesy of Robert Goldblatt.)

stamps each. There are two distinct formats, a narrow one of between 18 mm and 18½ mm wide which was first issued on either 7 April or 9 April 1900 of which 6,072 were printed, and a wide one 22 mm wide first issued on 11 April of which 3,036 were printed. Details of several different varieties of each of them are given in an extensive article by Robert Goldblatt published in the *South African Philatelist* for May 1978.

Many photographic essays of postage stamp designs have been made and these too are very collectable items but the next main postal items of photographic interest are the photographic airgraphs made using an apparatus developed by Kodak in the 1930s which photographed the original letters on 16 mm motion picture film so that in a manner reminiscent of the Paris Pigeon Post the negatives could be flown abroad and upon arrival enlarged and despatched to their destination. During the difficulties of World War 2 the Post Office decided to adopt Kodak's scheme and the first airgraphs of the war were despatched from Cairo to Great Britain on 21 April 1941 arriving on 13 May. On arrival in England the films were sent to Kodak's Wealdstone factory where they were printed and handed, usually within 24 hours, to the Post Office who placed them in window envelopes, sorted and despatched them for normal delivery.

The first airgraphs from Great Britain to the Middle East were sent in August 1941. Special forms measuring 8 in by 11 in were available without charge at Post Office counters and when completed and a 3d stamp applied to the reverse side they could be handed in at any counter for transmission.

A collection of these should have examples ranging from the earliest airgraphs despatched in 1941 from the Middle East to Great Britain to the last ones sent in the summer of 1945. It should include some of the now rare unused original forms, especially those showing impressed or meter franking as this being on the back of the forms does not show on the final reproduction. The 'Targets' that separated the messages into groups going to the various destinations, similar routine and technical documents and Kodaks 'Recordograph' booklets should also be included. Other items to look out for are the special airgraphs sent by *The Aero Field* magazine on 16 November 1942 with Christmas greetings for that year, which gave details of the first transmission of photographic post by carrier pigeons during the 1870 Siege of Paris and was intended to be a souvenir of both events, and the final airgraph sent by *The Aero Field* to commemorate the last airgraph despatch of July 1945 which showed a page from the famous 'H. Crabtree' collection.

The 16 mm film used for photographing airgraphs was stored until the messages, which sometimes had to be repeated, finally reached their destinations and it was then disposed of. Although more than 350 million messages were transmitted examples of the original negative 16 mm film is very scarce indeed. Although it all ostensibly went through the usual channels I know at least one reel escaped official destruction and clips of this, for which I have been asked £5 a frame, make a very interesting addition to a collection.

A more readily available example of this type of film clip is seen on the souvenir postcard issued at the International Airmail Exhibition held in Great Britain on 4-7 July 1973 which displays a chip of microfilm that was

Mafeking Seige stamps produced by the cyanotype blueprint process. **Top** *The 1d bicycle stamp.* **Bottom** *3d Baden-Powell stamp.*

carried by carrier pigeon released from Kodak House, Hemel Hempstead, Hertfordshire, on 18 June 1973 to Windsor, Berkshire, to mark the 50th Anniversary of the Aero Philatelic Club of London and these can still be found quite inexpensively.

The USA postal authorities operated a similar system of airgraph called the 'V Mail' for the American forces. The V Mail forms were dual purpose. Where possible they were photographed, the negatives despatched and the microfilm messages reproduced and delivered as usual, but when sent to or from places where the microfilm apparatus was not available the original form was sent in the mail in the ordinary way. To facilitate this there was an address panel on both the front and the back of the forms and like the air letter forms they were designed to be reduced to size of an ordinary letter by three folds. As with the airgraph, Service units and other organizations produced their own designs and greetings forms, and collections of special Christmas airgraphs including official Christmas greetings form made available in 1943 and 1944, and the American's 'Mother's Day' V Mail, display some wonderfully inventive designs.

The designs of the three stamps issued by Israel in 1979 to commemorate the 11th 'Hapoel' Games which were the highlight of Israel's 31st anniversary celebrations were based on frames of 35 mm film. The motif of the films was different on each value; the £1.50 showing weight lifting, the £6 tennis and the £11 gymnastics. All on life size perforated 35 mm film frames, and although they were printed in considerable numbers, 1,822,000 of the first two values and 1,821,000 of the £11, they were withdrawn on 4 January 1980 and photographic collectors should try to find examples while they are still fairly inexpensive.

As is usual with Israeli stamps the tabs add interest and value to the stamps and collectors should also look for the special first day cover. Its design shows a motion picture cameraman perched on top of a very high extended ladder with his camera whilst photographing the Games. There is a set of the three tabbed stamps tied to the cover with the special Jerusalem dated handstamp and as an added bonus there is a *Jour d'Emission* cachet on the top left hand corner of the cover. This cover will incidentally serve to illustrate the different meanings sometimes given to the same term in America and Great Britain. In America the term *cachet* usually refers to the printed design or illustration on the left hand side of the cover, in this case the cameraman on his perch, whilst in Great Britain *cachet* refers to the special hand or machine mark applied to a cover to denote a particular usage, in this case again, the special Jerusalem cancellation and the Jour d'Emission corner print.

Stamp designs based on photographs are another fine source of collectable items. Many stamp designs have been based on or derived from photographs although the photographer has often not received credit for his work and even when the photographer is acknowledged there is often a difference of opinion amongst the authorities as to its value, but stamps displayed with the original photographs on which they are based make a great talking point in any collection.

The United States Postal Services manual says that their 5 cent stamp of 1923 is a 'Portrait of Lincoln from a photograph' whilst the American Scott and Minkus catalogues state that it is 'after an engraving' without mentioning the photographic original that it is based on although the Scott gives the

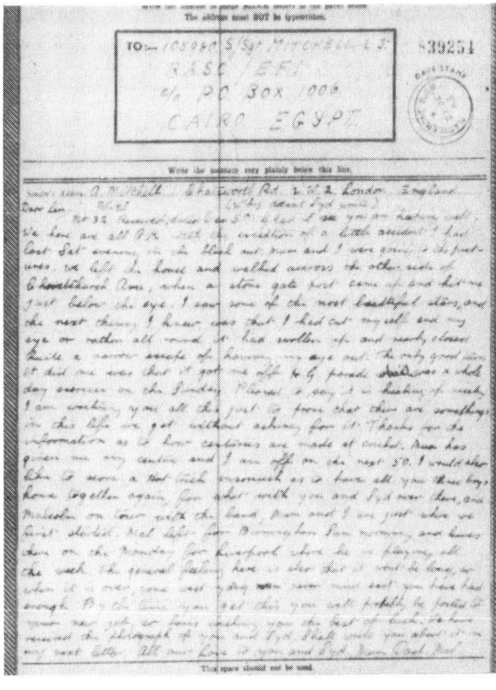

An airgraph sent to Staff Sergeant L.J. Mitchell by his mum, dad and brother whilst he was stationed in Egypt. Dated 21 December 1943. (Courtesy of L.J. Mitchell.)

date 1869 to the engraving and the Minkus names the artist as one G.F.C. Smillie.

The same postal manual credits two photographers for the portrait of Robert E. Lee on the USA 30 cent definitive stamp of 1955. The face on the stamp is reproduced from a photograph taken by Mathew M. Brady, the famed American Civil War photographer, which showed Lee in full uniform and the rest of the body in civilian clothes is from a photograph of Lee taken by L.C. Handy. To mix things up even further for us the catalogue credits the design of the 40 cent Marshall definitive as 'reproduced from a photograph taken by Harris and Ewing of a painting by Rembrandt Peale'.

Eight of Mathew Brady's photographic portraits have been used in the designing of American postage stamps but this record has now been surpassed by Jim Brandenburg the first photographer to be commissioned by the American postal to take photographs especially for stamp designs. Ten of his photographs of wild animals were used as a basis for the designs of the stamps in the USA wildlife booklet of 1981. One of these, the Bighorn Sheep design, was also used for all the stamps in the USA booklet of 20 cents stamps issued on 8 January 1982.

The many other famous photographers who have had American stamps based on their photographs range from Marcus Root, whose photographs

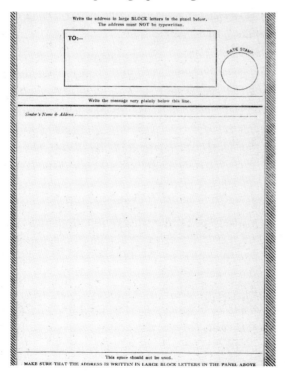

An unused airgraph form.

The Aero Field *magazine Christmas 1942 airgraph gave details of the similar system of microphotographs used during the Seige of Paris 1870-71.*

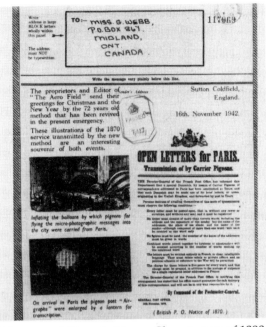

were used on the 10 cents Webster and 15 cents Henry Clay stamps of 1890, William Kurtz, whose photograph of Grant was used on the 5 cents stamp issued that same year, N.B. Sarony whose portrait of Sherman graced the 8 cents of 1893 and Orrin Dunlap whose photograph of Niagara Falls is used on the 5 cents of 1901 to Yousuf Karsh whose photograph of Winston Churchill was used for the 6 cents memorial stamp of 1965. Yousuf Karsh has told how he took this photograph of Churchill when Churchill sat for him in his Canadian studio. After talking for a little while Karsh suddenly leaned over and snatched the ever present cigar right out of Churchill's mouth whilst releasing the shutter at the same time to capture the 'Angry Lion's' glaring scowl.

Don Grossi's photograph of the victory march of American troops along the Champs Elysees in Paris with the Arc de Triomphe in the background was used as the basis of the 3 cents USA Army stamp of 1945 but some over enthusiastic stamp designer reduced the veracity of the photograph by adding six B-29 aeroplanes flying in formation over the scene although no B-29s had been flown in Europe at that time.

The most famous photograph used on an American stamp was the raising of the American Flag by six Marines on the top of Mount Suribachi, the high point of the Pacific island of Iwo Jima, taken by Associated Press photographer Joe Rosenthal. A small flag was originally raised and this was recorded by Marine photographer Staff Sergeant Louis Lowry who mentioned it to Rosenthal. Joe Rosenthal reached the peak of Mount

Suribachi as the Marines were taking down the original small flag and preparing to raise the larger 8 ft by 4 ft 8 in one into place. He took a number of photographs of the flag raising and the best of these, the famous Pulitzer prize winner was chosen for the design of the USA 1945 SG1071 3 cents Iwo Jima stamp.

Only two women photographers seem to have had their work used on American postage stamps. A portrait of Brien McMahon by Mrs Edith Glogau was used for the 3 cent stamp issued in 1962, and Martha Perske designed the coloured pencil drawing on the 1981 18 cents stamp commemorating the International Year of Disabled Persons from one of a series of photographers that she took of disabled people in a hosptial, only altering those parts of the photograph necessary to retain the anonymity of the person depicted.

It is estimated that more than 300 American stamp designs have been based on photographs. The first, and so far only, stamps of photographic interest issued in Great Britain have been a set of five stamps depicting photographs of four famous British film stars and of director Alfred Hitchcock, issued in 1985. I have hopefully suggested a series of stamp designs based on early photographs for an issue to commemorate the 150th anniversary of photography in 1989.

One can however go back to earlier than 1839 in a collection of postage

Left *An unused 'V Mail' form.*

Right *A first day cover depicting George Eastman, issued in the USA on 12 July 1954.*

stamps associated with the history of photography. This might commence with the stamps issued by Jordan, Pakistan and Quatar in honour of Alhazan the tenth century mathematician who used a camera obscura, a dark chamber with a small opening in one side to observe eclipses of the sun, and the stamps issued by Italy and other members of the EEC in honour of Leonardo da Vinci 1452-1519 who gave two clear descriptions of the camera obscura in his notebook. Your collection could continue with the stamp issued by Hungary in honour of Sir Isaac Newton 1642-1727 showing Sir Isaac and a diagram of image formation by a lens, even though it does not mention his title and gives his date of birth incorrectly as 1643, and the Austrian and German stamps honouring Johannes Kepler (1571-1630) for his description of the telescope lenses that were to become the telephoto lenses on our cameras.

The basic postage stamp for collectors of photographic philately is the stamp issued by France in 1939 to mark the 100th anniversary of the announcement of the daguerreotype process on 7 January 1839. It shows portraits of Niepce and Daguerre superimposed on the scene of Francoise Arago's announcement of the daguerreotype process at the meeting of the French Academy of Sciences.

Many other photographic notables are also commemorated on stamps. Ernst Abbe and Carl Zeiss honoured by the Deutche Demokratische Republik in 1956, L. Gevaert by Belgium in 1957, Samuel F.B. Morse, one of the earliest American daguerreotype artists, Oliver Wendell Holmes of stereoscope fame and James Clark Maxwell the English inventor who produced the world's first colour photographs by the USA, the Lumière Brothers by France and Mali, and George Eastman whose birth is commemorated on a USA 1954 3 cents stamp are some of the more important

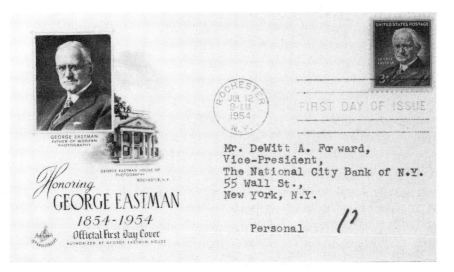

ones that collectors should look for and there are many more for the intrepid collector to discover.

A collection of photographic philately will inevitably have a large selection of motion picture items and the key stamp in this section must be the one issued by Belgium to commemorate the 1947 International Film Festival which honoured Joseph Plateau inventor of the Phenakistiscope, the first device to demonstrate the phenomena of persistence of vision upon which motion pictures are based. It can be followed by the USA stamp issued on 11 February 1947 and one from Hungary both honouring Thomas A. Edison who patented the kinetoscope and kinetograph, the first commercially successful motion picture devices. The USA stamp of 1954 commemorating the centenary of the birth of George Eastman whose innovative roll film developed for the Kodak camera made the Kinetoscope possible could also form part of this collection.

The 31 October 1944 USA stamp commemorating the 50th anniversary of motion pictures refers to the date of the opening of the first Kinetoscope parlour at 1,155 Broadway on 14 April 1894 but the first American public exhibition of projected motion pictures at Koster & Bial's Music Hall on 23 April 1896 was predated by the Lumière brothers in France who showed their first film *Lunch Hour at the Lumière Factory* at the Grand Cafe, Boulevard des Capucines, Paris, on 28 December 1895. Louis and Auguste Lumière are honoured on the French stamp issued on 12 June 1955 to commemorate the 60th anniversary of the birth of French motion pictures and the French film industry and on a more modern stamp issued by Mali in 1970.

Edison built the world's first film studio his 'Black Maria', a large rotating hut covered in black tar paper which could be turned to catch the light. He hired the first professional film actor, Fred Oth a speciality artiste who could produce sneezes to order, and the first American moving picture to tell a story *The Great Train Robbery* produced by Edwin S. Porter, one of Edison's cameramen, laid the foundations for the great Hollywood film industry. The centenary of Edison's birth was commemorated on a USA stamp but none of his motion picture innovations have so far been recorded on postage stamps although collectors will find that those early days are commemorated by the 50 cents stamp issued by France in 1961 in honour of Georges Méliès the great French pioneer film director.

George Méliès was the world's first great film maker. Transferring his allegiance from the theatre, where he was well established as a clever illusionist and magician, Méliès built a film studio and drawing upon his theatrical expertise made a series of films which established his position as one of the great geniuses of the early cinema. After making his first feature film *The Dreyfus Affair* based upon the injustice of the true life story, Méliès turned his talents to creating fantasy and science fiction for the silent screen. He made wonderfully inventive films based on stories such as Jules Verne's *20,000 Leagues Under The Sea, The Conquest of the Pole,* and *The Voyage to the Moon* a scene from which is shown on the screen in his commemorative stamp and following Méliès' lead many other film directors and producers have since then made films based upon the stories of Jules Verne including the award winning *Around the World in Eighty Days.*

D.W. Griffiths, the great early American director of motion pictures, is honoured on a USA stamp issued in 1975 and the USSR has also honoured one of their great classic film directors, Alexander Dovshenko, on a stamp. Walt Disney was pictured on a USA stamp in 1968 but the cartoon characters that he created have been depicted on stamps by many countries some of whom, although having little if anything to do with the cinema or cartoon films, have created a large selection of colourful stamps which have little value and are designed for collectors rather than for postal use. Anguilla, Antigua, Barbados, Dominica, Fujeira, Grenada, Grenadines of Grenada, Maldives Isl., Redonda, Saint Lucia, San Marino, Sharja, Togo and Turks and Caicos, are a few of the countries which have been guilty of creating this mountain of 'wallpaper' and collectors soon discover the difference between the issues of this kind and those of authentic postal interest.

A collection of Disney stamps can be extended to include stamps such as the one issued by Italy in 1954 in honour of Carlo Collodi the Italian author who created the little puppet Pinocchio featured in Disney's film of that name with Pinocchio pictured on that stamp. The stamps of China, Belize and Paraguay have depicted fairy story characters such as Cinderella, Little Red Riding Hood and Snow White who have all been shown in Disney cartoons. The 80 heller stamp in the series issued by Czechoslovakia for Expo '67 was designed by Jiri Tranka, a film maker who has created some of the world's best puppet films, and he based the design upon Hans Anderson's fairy tale *The Shepherdess and the Chimney Sweep.*

Jean Cocteau, the famous French film maker who has his signature on the 20 cents Marianne stamp that he designed, and Otto Preminger, who is featured on a 1971 stamp from Ajman, are amongst the few film directors and producers who can be collected on stamps but there are doubtless others in the philatelic roll of honour. Film stars have been honoured on many postage stamps. A delightful caricature of Charlie Chaplin dancing on a globe is shown on a Czechoslovakian UNESCO stamp. Will Rogers, one of the few artists to survive the transition from the silent screen to talking pictures, is shown on a 1948 USA stamp and on a few stamps of South American countries and the much loved French film stars Gerard Philipe and Raimu are each shown on a 50 cent stamp but in a series commemorating the theatre and not films issued by France in 1961.

Monaco has naturally issued several stamps featuring Princess Grace in her role as Princess of the Principality of Monaco which culminated in the black and white miniature sheet issued after her tragic death. Photographic collectors should also look for the 'culture' stamp issued by Monaco in 1971 which featured book, film and television.

Humphrey Bogart in *The Big Sleep* and *Maltese Falcon,* Raymond Burr as Perry Mason and Basil Rathbone as Sherlock Holmes can all be seen on a series issued by Nicaragua in 1972. Fujeira issued a set of movie star stamps and a souvenir sheet showing the famous comic team of Laurel and Hardy that same year and the USA Performing Arts series has featured many of the Hollywood stars including such great performers as Will Rogers in 1979, W.C. Fields in 1980, John, Ethel and Lionel Barrymore in 1982 and Douglas Fairbanks Senior in 1984.

International film festivals present yet another opportunity to create a small specialized collection of thematic motion picture philately. This might commence with a cinderella item, the brown label issued locally by Editions Lenoir for the first post war film festival at Cannes in 1946. The label showed a view of the port and had no face value although when it was subsequently overprinted and reissued in 1947 for the Grenoble Salon de Art it carried a 10 franc surcharge.

The following short list will give collectors some idea of what is available and what to look for when starting a film festival section in their collections and there are of course many more than this to be found.

1947   Belgium International Film Festival.
1951-64   Czechoslovakia, Karlova Vary International Film Festival
           (three stamps).
1962   South Korea, Federation of Motion Picture Producers, issued
           for the 9th Asian Film Festival at Seoul.

A postcard for the 1947 Film Festival and International Air Rally with a green cinderella label in the bottom right hand corner.

First day cover issued for the International Children's Film Festival in India, 1979.

1962	Italy, 30th Anniversary Venice International Film Festival.
1963	USSR, 3rd Moscow International Film Festival (after 1963 the Moscow and Karlova Vary Film Festivals were held on alternate years).
1964	Czechoslovakia, Karlova Vary International Film Festival.
1965	USSR, 4th Moscow International Film Festival.
1965	Bulgaria, Balkan Film Festival.
1966	Iran, 1st Children's Film Festival.
1967	USSR, 5th Moscow International Film Festival.
1969	USSR, 6th Moscow International Film Festival.
1970	Germany, 20th Berlin International Film Festival.
1972	Iran, Tehran International Film Festival.
1975	USSR, 9th Moscow International Film Festival.
1976	Czechoslovakia, Karlova Vary International Film Festival.
1977	India, New Delhi Film Festival.
1977	USSR, 10th Moscow International Film Festival.
1979	German Federal Republic, Oberhausen Short Film Festival.
1980	Tunisia, Carthage Film Festival.

Famous films have been featured on many postage stamps. In 1964 the USSR issued a stamp showing a scene from the famous Russian classic *Chapayev* and in 1965 three further stamps honouring the films *The Battleship Potemkin, The Young Guard,* and *Ballad of A Soldier* were issued and then two months later another two films *The Living and the Dead* and the Kosinetzer film of *Hamlet* were honoured on stamps.

Umm al Quain issued twelve stamps showing stills from award winning films to commemorate the introduction of the cinema into the Arabian Gulf and in 1969 Cuba issued four cinema stamps to celebrate the 10th anniversary of the Cuban motion picture industry which were artistically designed to represent different aspects of the industry: 1 cent the Cuban cinema, 3 cents newsreels, 13 cents movie pictures and the 30 cents *Lucia* representing feature films.

Collectors will also find the history of motion pictures recorded on the stamps of many countries and this short list will help to whet the appetite of photographic collectors.

Congo, 1971	History of motion pictures, four stamps.
Cuba, 1969	10 years of Cuban cinema, four stamps.
Dominica, 1981	Disney, 50th anniversary of Pluto, one stamp plus a souvenir sheet.
Egypt, 1977	50 years of Egyptian cinema.
Grenada, 1981	Disney 50th anniversary of Pluto, one stamp plus a souvenir sheet.
Grenadines of Grenada, 1981	Disney 50th anniversary of Pluto, one stamp plus a souvenir sheet.
Guatamala, 1981	50th anniversary of talking pictures.
Sweden, 1981	Souvenir sheet of history of Swedish cinema.
Togo, 1981	Disney 50th anniversary of Pluto, one stamp (this was issued with perforations of both 11 and 13.5) plus a souvenir sheet.
Turks & Caicos, 1981	Disney 50th anniversary of Pluto, 2 stamps plus a souvenir sheet.

A block of four Charlie Chaplain stamps from India.

| USA, 1977 | 50 years of talking pictures. |
| USSR, 1950 | 30th anniversary of the Soviet cinema. |

A thematic or topical collection should be a collection of world-wide stamps and postal history of one subject only and a collection of photographic postal history is no exception. Photography, however, includes many different sub-sections and subjects such as space stamps and covers in which collectors will find numerous items of photographic interest. The wonderful photograph of the earth seen from the moon depicted on the USA Apollo 8 commemorative 6 cents stamp of 1969, which was made from a photograph taken by one of the space crew astronauts Anders, Borman or Lovell, is an outstanding example of this. Collectors should also look for the 1969 souvenir sheet issued by the Republic of Rwanda in honour of the first men on the moon which shows a space suit clad astronaut using a camera whilst walking around the lunar module, the camera being placed for our convenience in a prominent position just above the centre of the stamp.

Countries from Afghanistan and Ajman to Umm al Quirain, Upper Volta and Uruguay who have little obvious connections with the advanced technology associated with space flight and lunar landings all jumped on the band wagon and issued postage stamps to commemorate this great event and many of the other notable happenings that have taken place during these early days in mankind's quest for the stars although often they do not seem to have been issued or used for any legitimate postal purposes. Bhutan, Central African Republic, Congo Republic, Grenada, Hungary, Liberia, Maldives, Rwanda, Togo, the USA, the USSR, and many other countries have all issued space stamps with many of them showing the moon vehicle roving around the surface of the moon and cameras can be seen in a number of these either attached to the moon vehicle itself or resting on the astronauts laps. In some cases the cameras are so small that they can only be seen properly with a magnifying glass but the USSR 1965 stamp showing cosmonaut A. Leonov with a camera is one of the better examples of this genre.

Those space stamps showing cameras are often found on cancelled to order covers especially prepared for collectors which often also have American type cachets which are sometimes real photographs of the astronauts with their cameras or photographs taken by them during space flights and whilst these make colourful additions to collections of photographic philately they are of very little value even if they are the more unusual examples that have actually been used postally. Because of this many collectors of photographic philatelic items prefer to keep to photographic postal history and try to specialize in collecting the letters of the early photographers and the manufacturers and suppliers of cameras and photographic equipment, covers that were used to send photographs through the post and advertising, cartoon and illustrated envelopes of photographic interest. The rarity of items such as this should not be off-putting to collectors but should rather add to their desirability and inspire the collector to further effort in the search for such lovely and scarce covers.

Collectors interested in stereoscopic photography will find that there are many other interesting items that can be added to their collections. These include three dimensional Victorian valentines and the envelopes that they were posted in, early stereoscopic postcards from the turn of the century, Thomas Brown and E. Osman Brown's 'Magic Post Cards' c 1908 which were printed in red and green ink as anaglyphic pictures which give a three dimensional effect when viewed through the appropriate red and green filters used in the viewer provided at the bottom of the card and the set of two anaglyphic commemorative postage stamps issued by Italy on 29 December 1956 to mark the first anniversary of that country's entry into the United Nations which were each printed with two superimposed pictures of a globe of the world printed in red and blue/green, so that when viewed with the appropriate viewer they combine into one stereoscopic picture of a globe, the symbol of UNO.

Collectors who wish to bring the stereoscopic section of their collections right up to date might also include examples of the several sets of commercial lenticular 3D postcards published in the 1960s and 1970s in Gibraltar, Japan, Spain and elsewhere which utilized a ribbed plastic surface to achieve the three dimensional effect. Similarly styled lenticular advertisement postcards produced in Great Britain in the 1960s, the fifteen different sets of lenticular 3D postage stamps issued by the Royal Government of Bhatan from the first set of Space stamps, issued 30 December 1967 to the last issued to date the set of eleven 3D mask stamps issued 23 April 1976 and the newest stereoscopic item, the lenticular postcard sized prints produced

A USA Apollo 11 first day cover 'cancelled to order' for collectors on 16 July 1969.

by the new four lens Nimslo 3D cameras can all be included in a stereoscopic collection.

Original artist's drawings, photographic essays and the various kinds of proof impressions are all rare and valuable collector's items and those few of them that are of photographic interest are very scarce indeed. Artist's proofs and de luxe proofs printed by the French Atelier de Fabrications des Timbres-Poste, the Government printing office in Paris, include several of great photographic interest depicting Daguerre, Niepce and other photographic pioneers and imperforate stamps of this kind, some in issued colours and others in single colours or various different colour combinations have also been produced for our edification.

Artist's proofs are printed on thin card and not in the issued colour of the stamp. Usually measuring about 5 in by 6½ in they are printed from the original unhardened die and only about twenty can be printed without damaging the die. Until 1958 only between twelve and 24 of each were issued, but since 1959 when the French Government controlled their printing between twenty and 28 of each have been made and since 1964 a new circular embossed seal *Control Printing Works of Postage Stamp* with a picture of an old hand printing press in the centre has been applied to further authenticate them.

Up to 600 de luxe sheets, which are similar to artist's proofs but in the issued colours of the stamp, and between 500 to 1,000 plate proofs, which are imperforated stamps not in the issued colour, are also printed and before 1939 colour essay proofs usually measuring about 4½ in by 5½ in were also made to assist in picking the most suitable colour for the new stamps. Numerous countries have produced these highly collectable items and photographic collectors will find many of photographic interest amongst them but do be careful to shop around and compare prices as they can vary enormously. Two American dealers who have recently quoted $125 and $225 respectively for a copy of the same Wallice & Future 1983 Niepce die proof give a good example of this and their prices for the de luxe sheets, imperforate pairs and trial colour pairs of the same stamps show equally great variations.

Many of the more specialized aspects of philately are of little importance to collectors of photographic antiques. Colour variations of stamps for instance, unless they are distinct colour shifts or greatly increase the value of the stamps, are mostly irrelevant to us and slight differences of perforations or watermarks have little bearing on our collecting theme, although stamps such as some of those of the Cannes Film Festivals which have been issued both perforated and imperforated can make nice little groupings in a collection.

Collectors should beware however of those countries that issue stamps to sell to collectors rather than for postal use. Such new issues are almost invariably offered in mint condition and the often limited postal services in the countries concerned are in stark contrast to the vividly coloured multi-offerings made to collectors. Some of the countries involved are artificial inventions designed to extract money from collectors and amongst countless others their almost endless lists of stamps showing Disney cartoon characters reflect their worthlessness to serious collectors.

Some of these stamp issuing countries have indeed been entirely fictitious some being small far off sections of the real world that were previously unheard of and which have no right to individual stamp issues whilst others such as Gerald M. King's *Wonderland* based on Lewis Carroll's *Alice's Adventures in Wonderland* have no real physical existence at all. Triggered off by the centenary of the book's first publication in 1965 Gerald M. King's first set of six cinderalla stamps based on Tenniel's original illustrations just 'grow'd' finally finishing up as a complete collection of 240 stamps including some blocks and pairs and over twenty covers complete with likely addresses and postmarks etc. Not all of these could be kept in a collection of photographic interest but examples of the Lewis Carroll 150th anniversary labels and cards together with one or two of his photographs make a delightful display for any collector of photographic philately.

Cinderellas, that is poster stamps, seals, or labels that look like stamps are now becoming a recognized collecting field and one that gives great scope to collectors of photographica. The original definition of cinderella material 'items that appear to be stamps but are not listed in the catalogues' is really no longer valid as many are now listed in catalogues and many collectors of cinderella material include other small items of similar ephemera in their collections so that 'cinderellas' afford many new fields of ancillary material for thematic collectors. Collectors of photographic antiques should not overlook this area of collectabilia, the number and variety of such items of photographic interest is surprisingly large.

It includes everything from labels awarded or used for advertising photographic exhibitions in the nineteenth and the early part of the twentieth century which were also stuck onto the backs of photographs to show that they had been exhibited and were sometimes also used postally like modern

From left to right: Niepce, Daguerre and Fox Talbot, three cinderella stamps by Bill Rodgers.

A rare wet plate or ferrotype camera for twelve 'gem' size photographs. There is no maker's name but it has been dated c 1875. Sold at Sotheby's Belgravia on 21 March 1975 for £850.

poster stamps and advertising stickers.

Collectors of photographic antiques will know that small gem size photographs were popular in the 1860s. Early carte de visite photographs are often seen with this small size image on them and special small albums were made to hold gem size photographic portraits. In the United States particularly gem size tintype photographs enjoyed considerable popularity and they were mounted in carte de visite or envelope type paper mounts, in small jewellery items such as broaches, cuff links, lockets and tie pins etc, or in small gilt frames much like the miniature ambrotype or daguerreotype portraits of earlier years.

Special multi-lens cameras such as the Wing or the Gem Box camera sold by the American Optical company which was fitted with sixteen lenses to take sixteen gem size photographs simultaneously on a 3¼ in by 4¼ in quarter plate led the way to the next items of great interest to collectors of photographic philately.

These were the postage stamp cameras which made a number of postage stamp sized copies of a carte de visite or cabinet size photograph on a single quarter plate. Typical examples were the nine-lensed Holborn Stamp Camera made by George Houghton & Sons in 1901 and sold for 12s 6d which made nine copies of a portrait placed behind a mask designed to give it the border and perforations necessary for the postage stamp effect in the grooves of a holder extending in front of the camera. The fifteen lens Royal Mail Stamp Camera sold by W. Butcher and Sons in 1908 for £1.05 which produced fifteen plain bordered copies of a photograph on a quarter plate negative which was overprinted with a special mask that supplied each postage stamp size portrait or view with the necessary ornamental border and perforations. These personal portrait stamps were produced by at least one photographer in 1866 and were available commercially from the end of the 1880s when they became very popular. They were used on envelopes and letters, on birthday invitation, Christmas and complimentary cards, on books, music and programmes and for many other purposes. In fact so many appear to have been made and sold that it is surprising to see how scarce and hard to find they have become today.

A number of postal authorities have also published advertisements on or in conjunction with their stamps. Photographic collectors will find many fascinating photographic advertisements published in this way and stamp booklets provide a number of fine examples. Although a prototype stamp booklet was made up by De La Rue in Great Britain in 1878 this was intended for revenue stamps. The first stamp booklets containing adhesive postage stamps were issued by Luxembourg in 1895 and the first British ones in 1904. Booklets have carried a vast variety of advertisements including a number of special interest to collectors of photographica. A term which collectors in this field may come across is se-tenant. This is a French term for which there is no precise English translation, meaning holding together or not separated. It is used to describe two different stamps or two varieties or two different values or a stamp and a label in an unseparated pair.

Photographic advertisements have appeared as se-tenant labels advertising *Satrap* photographic printing papers in German booklets of 5 pfennig and 10 pfennig Germania stamps and as similar labels advertising *Cinescope* with the Belgium 75 cent Albert I issue of 1932, on the tabs of New Zealand booklet panes in which three different types of stamps have carried Kodak advertisements and on the booklet interleaves of German East Africa fortunately on booklet III of 1913 which sells for about £100 today and not on the other booklets of that date which cost nearer £1,500 each, in the Series III edition 7 orange cover British booklet published August 1921, in the blue cover edition 13 of the same booklet issued November 1921, in a Series IV edition 120 booklet issued December 1929 and on the covers of a French booklet of twenty 10 cent stamps issued in 1922. There are many other examples waiting to be discovered by resourceful collectors. Collectors have sometimes been guilty of 'exploding' stamp booklets so as to spread out the covers, stamp pages and the inter-leaving pages onto an album page. Although this makes for a better display it greatly reduced the value of the booklets as, as in so many other cases, the whole is greater than the sum of its parts.

Photographic advertisements have also appeared on the advertising stationery that has been popular on the continent but collectors should be discriminating about these items as on a number of them the advertisements are very small and the prices very high.

Autographed covers, first day covers, maximum cards, miniature and special sheets, official announcements and posters, and postmarks, slogans and machine cancellations of photographic interest can all add colour and drama to your collection. Although some of them seem to be produced solely for the purpose of extracting money from collectors to the benefit of the revenue raising authority they can provide interesting, if low valued, items for collectors of photographic antiques.

Photographic and postal history both extend right up until today but many collectors will feel that modern stamps issued more for collectors than for postal use, spectacular although many of them are, have no great interest or value. Like many modern collectors items advertised as 'limited edition—send now to avoid disappointment' or 'this unique item will grace your collection and be cherished for generations' or in other glowing terms such items often prove to be unsaleable after the first flash of enthusiasm has been satisfied and the large numbers of remainders left over can often be purchased for coppers should you wish to pad out your collection but as

A personal portrait cinderella stamp stuck on to the page of an autograph album in 1886.

with all collecting, remember that one outstanding item in a collection is worth more than many inconsiderable ones regardless of their relative financial value. Even if the classic examples of photographic postal history seem expensive remember that restricting yourself to choice items only is the best way of affording and eventually building up a first class collection.

A collection of photographic philately should show how the history of the postal service and the history of photography were interwoven from the earliest days. The success of such a collection, like all collections, depends on the amount of effort put into it and although this effort is always equal to the amount of time and money spent, giving an equation $E = T + M$ it is up to the individual to determine whether to spend more time and less money on the collection or less time and more money as it is the total amount of effort and not the relative size of its parts that will determine the size and quality of the resultant collection.

The provenance of any expensive philatelic item, should be carefully checked. Collectors should also beware of the practice of some postal authorities who are known to have cancelled or postmarked whole sheets of stamps by machine in order to sell them to the trade at cheap prices or to clear their old stocks of mint stamps. Covers may also have been supplied 'cancelled to order' in this way.

The hardest thing for any dedicated collector to do is to reject any items

A first day cover celebrating the Fox Talbot centenary.

MR. CYRIL PERMUTT,
49, CRANBOURNE GARDENS,
LONDON N.W. 11

1877 = 1977

William Henry Fox Talbot
Scientist . Photographer . Classical Scholar
Centenary Year honouring the inventor of
the negative/positive photographic process
which is the basis of modern photographic systems
and also a pioneer of photoengraving (photogravure)
a method by which most stamps, including the
one on this envelope, are printed.

that are not in fine condition. Material which is in perfect condition usually costs more but will be easier to exchange or even sell should the need or occasion arise but items of only average or poor condition are often impossible to sell or swap. A stamp that has been repaired or doctored in any way is a bad buy because no matter how skilfully the repair has been done the item has been spoiled and will never have any real value to a serious collector.

Cleaning a stamp or cover with white breadcrumb or a soft artist's eraser is quite permissible, pressing between two sheets of clean blotting paper will often work wonders and the judicious trimming or splicing of a tatty cover to improve its appearance in your collection is often a good idea but collectors should only do this with the greatest of care and discretion. The removal of fiscal cancellations or overheavy postmarkings, the adding of margins or perforations, the filling of thin spots or pinholes or the adding of postmarks is something that should never be done as such restoration or betterment is akin to fraud in creating something that was not originally there.

The arrangement of items in a collection of this kind is always a matter of personal taste and there are no hard and fast rules. The first few stamps and covers might well be arranged in alphabetical order of countries but subthemes will soon take over. Collectors will probably need sections for Victorian Great Britain and then for later items, several for other countries with the United States and Canada probably predominating, separate ones for cinema, cinderella, microphotography, 3D items and picture postcards of photographic interest. The collection will keep growing and needing rearranging, which as all collectors know is half the fun of collecting.

If you intend to collect only single stamps of photographic interest then a bound album will suffice but if you wish to make your collection more exciting and interesting by adding multiples, covers, post cards, items of photographic postal history and other philatelic items you will need individual pages held in a loose leaf binder. Loose leaf pages, transparent protective covers and hard covers for them are available from many dealers and modern mounting strips have replaced stamp hinges for most discerning collectors, many of whom only collect stamps that are unmounted mint and with the original gum.

A collection should be stored in a cool dry room with the albums in their slip covers standing on end like books and not piled up flat upon each other. Stamps and covers are very fragile, they should be aired regularly and should be constantly checked and rearranged. This will help to prevent mould or rust forming or spreading and will also help to prevent mint stamps from sticking to each other or to other items in the collection.

Dealers will often tell you that buying stamps and items of postal history is an investment—but beware of the Greeks bearing gifts! The catalogue price or the price which dealers ask for their precious gifts often bears little relation to what they are prepared to pay when asked to buy them back. It is every collector's painful experience that everything offered for sale is rare, scarce and valuable but when returned to the sellers one finds that there are many of the same items in stock, that the one which has just been sold to you as 'perfect' has some slight invisible defect or flaw and that the dealers are only interested in having it back if you are prepared to accept a very cheap price.

With this in mind this chapter on collecting photographic philately is ending with two sound pieces of advice; firstly as when collecting any photographic antiques be a careful buyer, picking out only choice items for your collection and secondly only collect those things which you fall in love with and wish to keep for ever.

Chapter 11

More collectable photographic antiques

Collectors will understand that there are many other aspects of collecting photographic antiques that we have not discussed here, many of which would fill a book of their own.

A comprehensive collection of exposure meters for instance might well fill a small museum. The first actinometers and photometers had been made by the early part of the eighteenth century long before photography was invented but the early photographers seemed unaware of this.

In his first manual Daguerre said that the time necessary for the production of the image may be in Paris between three and at the most thirty minutes. He called attention to the time of the year and the hour of the day, the state of the weather and the colouring of the subject as factors that the photographer should take note of in determining the correct exposure. These ideas are followed up in the exposure table published by Daguerre's assistant, Hubert, in December 1839 which is one of the earliest items of photographic collectabilia in this field.

Jean-Baptiste Francois Soleil of Paris published details of an actinometer that was the first photographic exposure meter on 25 May 1840. A wet paste of silver chloride smeared 1 mm thick onto a white card was exposed in a short tube at the side of the subject of the photograph and the time taken for the silver chloride paste to darken to a slate grey was the correct exposure time for the daguerreotype plate in the camera which also made this the first photographic incident light meter.

In his *Essai d'Optique,* Paris, 1729, Pierre Bouguer was the first to show that the eye could be used to establish the equality of brightness of two adjacent surfaces. Early photographers developed several methods of using the size of the pupil opening in the eye as a measure of the light in the 1840s and many examples of exposure tables, calculators and meters had been described and brought into use by the time that Scott Archer announced his wet collodion process in 1852, but in 1854 London wet plate photographers were still being advised to memorise couplets such as

'when the wind is in the East
double the exposure least'

to help them to gauge the correct exposure for their plates.

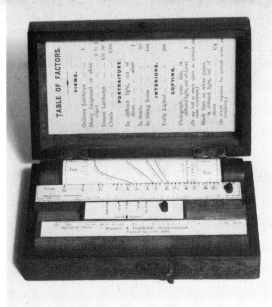

A Hurter & Driffields Actino-graph. The mahogany case is 4½ in long and the piece was made in England in 1888. Sold at Sotheby's Belgravia on 26 June 1981 for £90.

Professor J. W. Draper suggested the first optical extinction-meter in 1857. This was a triangular glass vessel with black painted sides filled with a blue liquid. In 1860 Boison proposed a photometer in which the sensitive paper was exposed through a slot until it matched an adjacent tint. Measuring the effect of light upon the electric conductivity of a thermo-electric pile with a galvanometer was suggested by Harrison in 1868 and the similar effect of light on the electric conductivity of selenium noted by Willoughby Smith in 1873 led to E.T. Roll developing the first battery-type selenium photoelectric light meter using a wet cell and a sensitive galvanometer to measure this effect in 1875.

As these devices were only practical in a laboratory few were made and they are hard to find but every collector will be able to locate an example of the Radiometer or Sun Engine invented by Crooke in 1873 which was put forward for possible use as an exposure meter providing that someone could devise a way to count the revolving vanes which become a complete blur in direct sunlight.

Very early examples of exposure meters and tables dating from the first decades of photography are extremely rare today but following the intro-duction of dry plate and flexible roll film photography in the 1880s a great variety of exposure assisting devices were made to supply the greatly increased demand and many of these can still be found by collectors today. These highly collectable items of photographic history include actino-meters, exposure calculators and tables, extinction type meters, optical exposure meters and the more modern photometers and photo-electric cell type meters.

The simplest of these are exposure tables and calculators and whilst fairly modern ones abound collectors should look for Victorian examples such as the original Hurter and Driffield box form Actinograph of 1888 or the vulcanite Ilford exposure meter of 1893 a disc type calculator based on Scott's tables of 1880 which were used by photographers in conjunction with homemade actinometers for many years and were themselves derived from data published by Bunsen and Roscoe in 1862.

Extinction type meters which measure the light reflected by the subject by comparing it through an adjustable shaded wedge or a series of holes of diminishing sizes with a standard provided, such as the German Ica Diaphot of 1924 and the Austrian Cinephot of 1928 and Dremscop of 1932 are still to be found fairly easily. The more interesting French Decoudon optical exposure meter of 1887 is much more rare. Decoudon's photometer was a commercial version of a method of through the lens metering on the ground glass screen of the camera, using a step-wedge which had been introduced some years earlier by Storey and Roper. Although the circular metal Decoudon meter was well made few seem to have survived the passing years.

Actinometer exposure meters measure the available light by noting the time taken for a special printing out paper to darken to a standard shade and the highly collectable British Watkins exposure meters are excellent examples of these. They range from the first Watkins standard exposure meter of 1890 through the well known Watkins Junior exposure meter 1893, the Watkins Watch Form actinometer 1899, the Watkins Dial 1900, the Watkins Bee 1902, the Watkins Fall roll film meter 1924 and the many varieties of each of these that were made through the years. The Bee was the most famous of all the Watkins meters and the one that collectors will see most often. It was made with ordinary glass and with blue glass, in two silver plated versions, the Queen Bee which was slightly larger than the standard model and another which was slightly smaller and deeper than the standard Bee.

Small leather wallets containing a selection of interchangeable dial faces were also sold for the standard Bee so that the Focal Plane Bee can be found with a fresh face as the Autochrome meter and again as the colourplate meter leaving a wonderfully complex trail for the collector to follow.

A Kinematograph Bee meter for professional motion picture cameramen which had a ball and chain timing device in the middle was followed in 1927 by a Junior model for use with smaller amateur cine cameras, one referring specifically to the Filmo cine camera and there were many other versions of both the Bee and the other watch form meters that Watkins produced. In all Watkins produced some 27 actinometers most of them from 1890 onwards in the 52 years of the Watkins Meter Company's existence and putting together a complete collection of them would be a wonderful project for the collector of photographic antiques.

The more modern optical meters which compare the brightness of a part of the subject with the light of the filament of a miniature electric bulb and the photo-electric cell light meters are also an important part of the development of light meters. Collectors should look for examples of the first commercial photo-electric light meter that were marketed in the United States in 1932, the Weston a general purpose model, the Rhamstine Electrophot and the twin cell Weston 617 which were the first to be especially designed for photographic work and also the early Weston models 627 of 1933 and 650 of 1934.

Early camera lenses are also well worth collecting in their own right and their development from the first plano-convex crown glass lens which Niepce used with its convex surface facing the plate and with a stop in contact with it to the complex types that were developed by lens manufacturers such as Goerz, Taylor-Hobson and Zeiss by the end of the nineteenth century is a fascinating story. Even less technically minded collectors fall in love with the gleaming brass and glass of early camera lenses and we often purchase them using the excuse that one day we will find the lensless camera that they belong to. This of course seldom happens but it gives us a happy excuse to look for more of these lovely photographic antiques.

A collection of shutters will also make an interesting item in a collection of photographic antiques. Until the 1850s simple lens caps were used to make the exposure in almost every camera, although I do have one early experimental photographic camera obscura c 1839 that has a simple hand held sliding drop shutter built in front of the lens. Exposure times for the early photographic processes were very long and even when improvements made it possible for J. Werge to take an instantaneous daguerreotype of New York Harbour in 1854 he still used a lens cap to make the about one

An advertisement for 'The New Weston Universal Exposure Meter' Model 617, first produced in 1932, which appeared in the British Journal of Photography Almanac *for 1933.*

A rare Beck-Steinheil tele-photo lens, Unofocal Series II, 6 in f4.5 No 12552. Made in England in 1895. Sold at Sotheby's Belgravia on 22 February 1980 for £60.

third of a second exposure and it was not until the end of the 1850s that shutters came into regular use.

Wooden drop-shutters, introduced by L. Price in 1858, were the first to become popular. A collection should commence with examples of these and of the simple hinged flap shutters introduced in the early 1860s that were especially used on stereoscopic cameras where one long flap could expose both lenses simultaneously.

The 1860s and 1870s saw the introduction of many different types of shutters, some fitted in front of and some behind the lens, but the real burst of invention and innovation came again with the introduction of dry plates and roll film in the 1880s, but although Lancaster introduced the first model of their rotary shutter in 1882, drop shutters and flap shutters were still being made well into the early part of the twentieth century. Earlier examples had been described and a few were made but the first real practical form of roller blind shutter in which a variable slot passes across the film usually in the focal plane was suggested by B.J. Edwards in 1882 and was first marketed by Thornton-Pickard in 1892.

With the continual improvement in emulsions smaller detective and hand cameras became very popular with amateurs and the most famous of all was of course George Eastman's No 1 Kodak Camera of 1888 which was fitted with a cylindrical shutter for instantaneous exposures and a lens plug to use instead of the time honoured lens cap for time exposures. The second model of the No 1 Kodak made in 1889 had a reciprocating shutter and it has been estimated that up until World War 2 the Eastman Kodak Company had used more than fifty different shutters on its cameras and that does not include the many different types that have been used for specialist cameras and for cameras made overseas, which all helps to show what a wonderful field Kodak shutters and the many Kodak cameras make for modern collectors.

Collectors of Kodak cameras can refer to publications such as *The Kodak Collector* by Alan R. Feinberg and *The Snapshot Photograph* by Brian Coe and

Paul Gates. Leica collectors have *The Leica Collectors Guide* compiled by D.R. Grossmark and the various other publications of Hove Photo Books one of England's leading Leica specialists whilst collectors of Zeiss Ikon cameras have *Zeiss Ikon Cameras 1926-1939* which is also a Hove Photo Book, but there are several other exciting fields of collecting cameras which are not covered by such excellent publications.

There are for instance the Vest Pocket Kodak '16 on 127' roll film cameras that proliferated in the 1930s. The Leica had shown that with the post-war improvements in emulsions and lenses small negatives could produce good photographs but the Leica was expensive and difficult to load and the 35 mm film was not as readily available as the ubiquitous roll film.

The first camera to take sixteen 4 cm by 3 cm negatives on 127 film was the Zeiss Ikon Kolibri of 1930. Two versions were marketed, a better one fitted with an f 3.5 Tessar lens in a Compur shutter and a cheaper one with an f 4.5 Novar lens in a Telma shutter, and collectors should try to find an example of each. Like the Leica the Kolibri had a rigid body and the lens pulled out on a tube but the Kolibri had a streamlined shape with a collapsible view finder at one end. The f 3.5 Tessar lens compared favourably with the Leica's f 3.5 Elmar and its Compur shutter had the slower speeds that were missing on all the early Leicas except those collector's joys the Compur Leicas.

The Kolibri was followed by the Nagel Pupille fitted like the Leica with an f 3.5 Elmar lens, the Baby Ikonta, the Foth Derby, Korelle, Rodenstock Ysella, Zeca Goldi and many other collectable '16 on 127' cameras. These included oddities like Zeiss Ikon's Baby Box Tengor of 1930 which was made in two models with either an f 11 Prontar lens in a cheap T and I shutter or an f 6.3 lens in a Derval shutter, and the British Ensign Multex which only lasted from 1936 to 1938 as although it was nicely made and was available with a range of standard lenses its prices brought it into the Leica league and it could not compete with the Leica's prestige and immense range of accessories and lenses.

The vast majority of cameras have had black bodies. This has led to many collectors specialising in the lovely gleaming wood and brass Victorian cameras and the wooden tropical and the brown and tan leather covered presentation models of the dry plate and roll film cameras that were being made until the late 1930s but it is the few cameras that were made in exciting ranges of colours that have become a must for collectors.

Henry Ford is reported to have said about his cars: 'You can have any colour you want, as long as it is black' and most camera manufacturers seem to have emulated him but several have tried to increase their sales by producing a few of their cameras with more colourful coats. The earliest coloured camera that I know of is a blue Expo Watch camera the American version of the British Ticka which were both made well before World War 1, and the same manufacturer was also responsible for the Expo Easy Load box camera of 1928 which was made in black, green, red, tan, and silver, and which like the Expo Watch camera was cartridge loading.

A Marion & Co Ltd brass bound tropical single lens reflex camera with maroon leather hood and bellows. Sold at Phillips on 29 October 1980 for £880.

The 1920s brought out a rash of highly collectable coloured cameras as all the major and many of the minor camera manufacturers struggled for a share of the diminishing market. Ansco introduced special red covered sports models of their No 2 and 2A Anscos and their No 0 Buster Brown cameras in 1924, the Ansco Vanity camera in blue, green, orange, and red in 1928, the golden brown leather covered Ansco Royal Cameras in 1929 and their Vogue Model Antar box cameras were made in blue, green, red, and tan.

Kodak were once again one of the most prolific producers of coloured cameras. Their range included the Vanity Kodaks of 1928 which were their Vest Pocket Kodak series III cameras made in blue, brown, grey, green, and red with matching silk lined cases and described by their advertising department as 'these gloriously colourful Kodaks, the loveliest gift creations, available in Bluebird, Jenny Wren, Sea Gull, Cockatoo, and Redbreast'; the Vanity Kodak Ensemble which contained a Vanity Kodak Model B, lipstick, compact, mirror, and change pocket; the Kodak Petite 1929, a vest pocket Kodak Model B made in blue, grey, green, lavender, and old rose; the Kodak Coquette a Kodak Petite with matching lipstick holder and compact, and the green Boy Scout Kodak 1930, the Girl Scout Kodak 1929, and the Camp Fire Girls' Kodak 1931.

A collection of the coloured Kodak cameras should also include the No 2 Portrait Brownie of 1929 which was advertised for 17s 6d in black or 19s 6d in any of the six colour finishes although I only know of it in blue, brown, grey, green, and red; the Rainbow Hawk-Eye cameras of 1929 in blue, green, rose, tan, and also in black; the Beau Brownie of 1929 in blue, green, rose, tan, and black, all with the delightful Art Deco enamelled front, one of the more than half a million anniversary Hawkeye cameras that George Eastman gave away to any children whose twelfth birthday fell in 1930 and the several different versions of the No 1 and No 1A Pocket Kodaks that were made in colours as well as the standard black in 1929 and 1930.

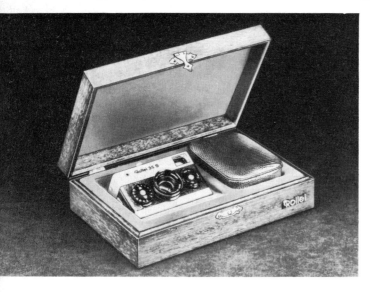

The Golden Rollei 35 S of 1979 was produced to celebrate the fiftieth anniversary of the introduction of the first model Rolleiflex camera. It was heavily plated in 24 carat gold and the normal leather covering was replaced by African lizard skin with pouch case and strap to match. It was priced at £395 and is worth much more today. (Courtesy of Rollei (UK) Ltd.)

Houghton-Butcher produced a range of coloured cameras in England at about that time commencing with the tropical model of their Watch Pocket Carbine which did not have the customary teak body of tropical models but were made of brass with a beautiful oxidised copper finish and matching Russian leather bellows, and carrying on with their black or brown leatherette covered Box Ensign 1926, the black, blue, or red Duo-Ensign which could take normal or close-up photographs, and including the All Distance Ensign box camera in black, blue, brown, and red, and the All Distance Pocket Ensign which was a folding companion to the box camera.

The Coronet Camera Co of Birmingham made their Coronet Midget, the moulded bakelite subminiature that is so sought after by collectors today, in five colours black, green, red, and tan in 1935 and in blue in 1936 so making it possible for us to collect a complete set.

The coloured cameras par excellence for collectors are without a doubt the special gold cameras that have been made in limited numbers so that both their price and their rarity add to their collectable value. At the turn of the century Adams and Co, the London camera manufacturers would use 18 carat gold for the dark slides, metal parts and screws of their special order cameras if requested. Fifteen years ago I was offered two of these cameras for £750 each and although that was much too much for them then as they were not in the best of condition they would doubtless bring much more than that today and few collectors can hope to find one now.

The Luxus Leicas of 1930 with their gold plated metal parts would probably fetch that sort of price today. Even one of the 1,200 gold plated Tessar lensed Rollei 35 Gold Cameras made in 1969 to celebrate the production of a million and a half Rollei 35s or one of the 1,500 alligator or snakeskin covered gold plated Rollei 35 Gold Cameras with its Sonnar lens that were produced in Singapore to celebrate the two millionth Rollei 35 will fetch £500 or £600. A collection of these and some of the other gold plated cameras that have been issued more recently such as the Leica M4-2 Gold of 1979 listed at just under £6,000 fitted with a gold 50 mm f 1.4 Summilux lens, the Contax RTS Gold of 1980 which is valued at about £3,000, the Gold Tessina subminiature listed at £325 the Alpa IIsi Gold of 1981 listed at just under £4,000, the Pentax LX Gold of 1981 listed at £4,500, the Mamiya M645 Gold and its big brother the RB67 Gold made in limited numbers in Japan both with gold plated metal parts and lizard skin covers which sold for approximately £1,200 and £1,500 respectively would attract the attention of many people not otherwise interested in photographic antiques.

Even the small gauge cine cameras designed for the amateur market kept up with the craze for coloured cameras. In 1928 the 16 mm Bell and Howell Filmo 75 with its attractive filagree embossed casing was available in silver birch and walnut brown, the Cine-Kodak Model B was produced in grey

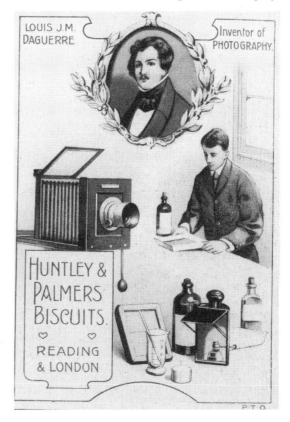

An example from a set of eight Huntley & Palmers trade cards issued free between 1885 and 1910. This set was sold at Sotheby's Belgravia on 1 June 1979 for £80.

and brown and the QRs Combination Movie Camera/Projector was sold in brown or green, all of course in addition to the standard black models. Collectors will be able to add even more colours to a selection of these cine cameras with the black, blue, brown, and grey versions of the Model BB Cine-Kodak of 1929 and the Cine-Kodak Model K of 1930 and the coloured versions of the Campro camera-projector of 1927 and the Midas of 1933.

Devotees of photographic collectabilia have even found items of interest amongst the humble cigarette and trade cards that so many school children have collected. They were introduced in the United States in the 1870s to stiffen the soft paper cigarette packets and prevent the cigarettes from being crushed and were first used in 1876 in packets of Capadura cigars made by R.C. Brown and in packets of Marquis of Lorne cigarettes in 1878. The first British cards were a pair of oval cards held together by a stud which were printed with a calendar for 1884 and the parcel post charges of that time and issued with Richmond Gem cigarettes.

By 1890 W.D. & H.O. Wills and John Player and Son were issuing advertising cards with their cigarettes and photography entered the picture in 1894 when Ogdens put their new Guinea Gold cigarettes on the market with an ongoing series of small black and white photographs in the packets. Instead of being a set of a defined number of cards this series of photographs carried on for over fourteen years and eventually contained more than 8,000 different photographic illustrations.

Many cards produced by the colour lithographic process were based on real photographs but the most interesting ones for us were those in series devoted to famous inventors and inventions which featured the pioneers of photography such as Niepce, Daguerre and Fox Talbot. Niepce and

Left *A trade card depicting Niepce issued by Chocolat Guerin-Boutron in the late nineteenth century.* (Courtesy of Bill Rodgers.)

LE GALANT PHOTOGRAPHE
Pourquoi dérober sous le satin qui la frôle
L'harmonieux contour de votre blanche épaule

Right *A French postcard of 1908.*

Daguerre are also featured in a series of 84 trade cards issued in France in packets of Chocolat Guerin-Boutron and a series of 'Les Trucs du Cinema', Tricks of the Cinema, was issued with jars of Veritable Extrait de Viande Lieberg in France at the beginning of the twentieth century.

Collectors will know that both lithographic and photographic picture postcards of photographic interest can be found ranging from the comic 'wish you were here' seaside postcards to photographers advertising postcards and fine collections of these have been made and although the days when good examples could be picked up for a few pence each have long gone excellent opportunities for collectors still remain.

The photographic picture postcard became extremely popular at the beginning of the twentieth century and there seem to have been professional postcard photographers in every seaside resort, village and high street throughout the Western World and it is mostly the work of these pro-

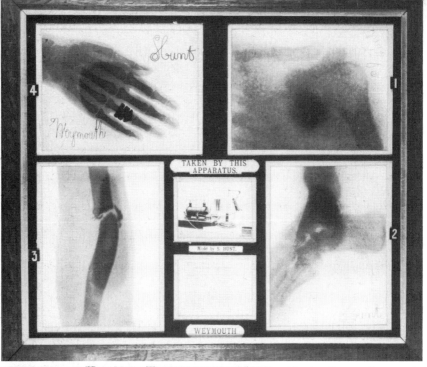

Above X-ray photographs taken by S. Hunt soon after the publication of the first English translation of Professor W.C. Roentgen's paper in Nature on 23 January 1896. (Courtesy of Sotheby's Belgravia.)

Left The golfer Dennis Shute swinging his club. A bromide print, 9¼ in by 7½ in, from a multiple exposure negative made with the aid of a strobe light. It was taken by Harold E. Edgerton in collaboration with Kenneth J. Gemeshausen and Herbert Grier in 1935. Sold at Sotheby's Belgravia on 28 June 1978 for £300.

fessional photographers that we find today. In 1902 the Eastman Kodak Company joined in the picture postcard boom by issuing a postcard size photographic paper and in 1903 they marketed their Folding Pocket Kodak No 3a which took 3 ¼ in by 5 ½ in postcard size negatives, which made it easy for amateur photographs to make their own picture postcards.

Some collectors have been fascinated both by the early classic photographs taken by the pioneers of X-ray photography and the apparatus that they used to make them with and have built up most interesting collections around them.

Following on Sir William Crookes' classical experimental investigations on the discharge of electricity through high vacua, William Conrad Roentgen discovered a silent invisible beam which he called a new kind of ray and later named X-rays. In his first paper published on 28 December 1895 he reported on an experimental X-ray photograph that he had taken of a human hand.

Like all new photographic inventions this opened the way to a new field of photographic collectabilia but although early X-ray photographs and X-ray tubes such as the Crookes tube of 1895 and the Jackson tube designed by Sir Herbert Jackson in 1896 which had a much smaller X-ray source and so made a far better defined image are extremely scarce today their value has as yet not been fully realised and although they are rarely seen these days when they are found they can still be purchased for a relatively reasonable price.

Electric flash photography has produced remarkable photographs that are also sought for by collectors today. William Henry Fox Talbot took the first electric flash photographs. He demonstrated these at the Royal Institution in London in June 1851 by using the spark produced by electrical discharge to photograph a piece of paper attached to a rapidly spinning wheel.

Many other scientists and innovative photographers experimented with flash photography and all their photographs are worth looking for and preserving. Names to look for in this field include Nadar, Professor A.M. Worthington, who published *A Study of Splashes* illustrated with his flash photographs in 1908, and Ernst Mach and Charles V. Boys who took high speed photographs of bullets in motion. It was Professor Harold Edgerton who revolutionized flash photography when he showed the first results taken with his new very short duration flash equipment in 1937. Made with exposures as short as a hundred thousandth of a second given by electronic flash instead of a shutter, and a special camera synchronized to stroboscopic flash, Edgerton's single flash and stroboscopic high speed multiple exposure photographs were published in *Flash: Seeing the Unseen with Ultra-High-Speed Photography* in 1938 and even now nearly fifty years later they are still exciting images. Although they are now rare examples of Edgerton's book and his photographs still occasionally come to light at sales of photographica and would be delightful additions to any collection.

Photoceramics provide collectors with another interesting source of photographic antiques. Several ways of reproducing photographs in carbon were publicized in the 1850s and using these the carbon photograph could be fired into the surface glaze of ceramic plaques, glasses, plates, and vases of all kinds and the process was used for both family protraits and pictures of famous people.

Collectors will also find Victorian photographs printed on to milky white opal glass that had been coated with a special emulsion. Opal photographs were mostly portraits and later cheaper examples were made on artificial ivory and celluloid instead of the opal glass. Ground glass was also used to make transparent photographs like giant lantern slides which were framed and hung in front of windows. Usually scenic views or posed artistic pictures they were often hand tinted to add to their decorative effect. Bristol blue glass was used for ambrotypes by a very few photographers but are extremely rare.

The small cases used for early photographs are another kind of photographic antique that most collectors are unable to resist. The early professional portrait photographers adapted the cases used by artists for miniature portraits to hold the new daguerreotypes, the occasional talbotypes, and then in turn ambrotypes and albumen prints. Originally made of wood covered with morocco leather and lined with silk they gradually evolved into cheap cases made of paper or card with a wooden frame and a lining of plain or embossed velvet, and soon other kinds of miniature cases made of celluloid, metal, papier mache or wood, and covered or decorated with card, cloth, leather, mother of pearl or tortoiseshell, and often hand painted were being made for the flood of photographs that the popularity of the new art brought about.

Collections have been made of all these different kinds of miniature cases both with and without their original photographic contents although those containing the photographs are naturally more precious to us. The most

Left *'Drop of Milk'. A set of three studies, each 6¼ in by 4½ in, taken by Harold E. Edgerton in collaboration with Kenneth J. Germeshausen and Herbert Grier in 1935.* (Courtesy of Sotheby's Belgravia.)

Right *A sixth plate black leather case, gilt-embossed with a protrait of Daguerre and the credit 'As taken by Meade & Brother Albany NY'. It contains a portrait of a young boy taken in 1850 and was sold at Christie's South Kensington on 30 June 1977 for £220.*

important ones are the plastic cases made in the United States of America from 1853 until the end of the 1860s when the albumen paper prints and tintypes which had become overwhelmingly successful no longer needed the protection that they afforded.

Called Union Cases, these plastic cases were the first examples of the commercial use of thermo-plastics and although they were mass produced their elaborate and often beautiful designs makes them very collectable items today. They were made in most sizes from one-sixteenth plate to whole-plate but the examples that are found by collectors these days are usually the standard one-sixth and quarter-plate that were the most popular. Very small and very large Union Cases were produced in much smaller numbers and are very rare, as are the wall frames made of the same thermoplastic material which held one or sometimes two or four or more of the magic images.

Samuel Peck, a daguerrian artist of New Haven, Connecticut, is credited with the introduction of the Union Case. In 1851, together with the Scoville Manufacturing Company, he registered a new business, Samuel Peck and Company for the purpose of manufacturing daguerreotype cases. They commenced with wood and leather and then papier-mache cases, but by May 1852 Peck was experimenting with various compounds and he marketed his first Union Cases early in 1853, although his patents were not granted until 3 October 1854.

Peck used gum shellac mixed with sawdust or similar material and

Left *A leather daguerreotype case from Antoine Claudet's original studio in the Adelaide Gallery on the Strand.* (Courtesy of Sotheby's Belgravia.)

Right *'The landing of Columbus'—a whole plate Union Case made of brown thermoplastic in 1858. Sold at Sotheby's Belgravia on 28 June 1978 for £130.*

colouring for his compound which held a much better impression than the leather covering of earlier types of cases. His great competitor Alfred P. Critchlow, an Englishman who had emigrated to Massachusetts in 1843, began to manufacture plastic daguerreotype cases in 1853 together with two partners, Samuel Hill and Isaac Parsons. He used his own formula, a mixture of lampblack, shellac and wood resin which he called Florence Compound.

The hinges of the early Union Cases were their weak point and both Peck and Critchlow patented improved hinges in 1856. The patent dates on the labels in Union Cases will help collectors to date them and as the more popular designs were made for many years the wear and tear of the dies meant that later examples were less distinct and showed less detail in their impression. A new type of hinge patented by Edward G. Kinsley and Samuel Parker Junior on 1 January 1858 was used for Union Cases manufactured by Wadhams Manufacturing Company. A new stronger and more water resistant compound, made of a mixture of equal parts by weight of cannel coal, a hard bituminous coal, ivory black and shellac was patented by Mark Tomlinson 24 August 1858.

The exotic oriental appearance of the images in early Japanese photographs makes them as popular to collectors today as they were to the Victorian collectors who bought and treasured them a hundred years ago, but because of the difficulty of translating and spelling the sometimes poorly reported Japanese names and dates there is still some uncertainty about the early history of photography in Japan.

In the May 1976 issue of the American magazine *Modern Photography* Koyasu Masabao claimed that the earliest surviving daguerreotype portrait made in Japan which was found in 1975 was taken in 1841 but other sources

have suggested that this portrait was taken in 1857, one even giving the date as 2 November of that year. What is certain is that Eliphalet Brown Jr, who accompanied the famous Commodore Matthew Perry 1853-54 USA expedition to Japan which led to the opening up of the then feudal Japan to foreigners and foreign ideas, took the first photographs of Japan that can now be positively dated. All other Japanese photography follows from this. Eliphalet Brown began making daguerreotypes in Okinawa as soon as the expedition arrived there in May 1853 and he took further series of daguerreotypes wherever he was permitted ashore.

The first native Japanese photographer Renjo Shimooka is believed to have learned the art of photography in 1856 from a 'Dutchman' Henry Hensken who was serving in the American diplomatic corps in Japan at the time and Japanese interest in photography seems to have stemmed from about that time. For many years a Japanese called Ushida had a virtual monopoly of the art. He charged $75 USA for carte de visite size ambrotypes and was the only supplier of photographic goods in the country. Ushida too reputedly gained his knowledge of photography from a 'Dutchman' but it must be remembered that before Commodore Perry's expedition the Dutch explorers and traders were the only Westerners that the Japanese had seen and everyone of European stock was called a 'Dutchman' or less complimentarily in their own language 'the Barbarians from the south', the Dutch have first reached Japan via the South Pacific.

Ushida sold many of his photographs to foreigners and world famous photographers visited Japan to record its people and sights. Their photographs sold well in the west and gave further encouragement to the growing band of Japanese photographers who often learned the art from the Westerners.

Being treasured by their contemporary collectors, many early Japanese photographs have survived and they often come up for sale today. A group of eighteen Japanese albumen prints each approximately 8¾ in by 11 in taken by Felice Beato in the early 1860s sold for £605 at Sotheby's on 24 June 1983. A group of 32 photographs by Felice Beato and twelve by W. Saunders, all albumen prints mostly hand tinted and measuring 8¼ in by 10¼ in sold for £2,090 in the same rooms on 12 March 1982. Fifteen Japanese portraits, albumen prints approximately 3½ in by 5.5/16 in each, taken by the Japanese photographer Sohutamarko in the early 1870s were sold at Sotheby's for £165 on 29 October 1982. These are all typical examples of the early Japanese photographs that are still available to modern collectors.

It is perhaps significant that the earliest Japanese illustrations showing cameras in use, in the catalogue of the Pentax Gallery Tokio's prestigious photographic museum, are both dated 1863. The earliest photographic illustration shown is of a man using a Kodak camera in 1888. The earliest cameras on display are a Stirn's waistcoat detective camera dated 1886 and a half plate Lancaster's Instantograph dated 1898.

Konishiroku Photo Ind Co Ltd of Tokyo, Japan, who were originally named Konishi, claim to be the oldest photographic firm in Japan, having been founded in 1873. They say that their Cherry Portable of 1903 was the first camera manufactured in Japan and they carry on with an impressive list of Japanese 'firsts': Japan's first single lens reflex camera, the Sakura Plano Reflex of 1907; the first Japanese camera with a telephoto lens, the Ideal Telephoto of 1909; the first Japanese camera with parallax correction, the Lily of 1916; the first camera made there using modern manufacturing techniques, the Pearlette Vest Pocket of 1925; and the Record camera, the first Japanese 35 mm camera were all produced by what is now the Konica Corporation.

For most collectors the early part of this century provides the most interesting collectable Japanese cameras and as they were almost entirely made for their home market their rarity in the West contrasts vividly with their more ready availability in their home country. The Japanese copy Leica and copy Contax cameras make lovely additions to the collections of those who specialize in these types of cameras. Cameras made during the post-

'The Coiffeur'—one of a group of sixteen Japanese hand coloured albumen prints, mostly 9¼ in by 7¼ in, taken in 1870. Sold at Sotheby's Belgravia on 21 March 1980 for £480.

An example from an album of Japanese albumen prints, mostly 10¼ in by 8¼ in, taken in 1880. Sold at Sotheby's Belgravia on 29 October 1982 for £330.

A replica of the Cherry Portable Camera of 1903. The Cherry was the first Japanese mass produced amateur camera, it took 2¼ in by 3¼ in plates in its simple drop plate mechanism. (Courtesy of the Pentax Gallery and Museum, Tokyo.)

A Doryu 2 16 mm Pistol Camera of 1954. The handgrip held 'bullets' resembling revolver cartridges containing flashpowder and an igniting chemical. When loaded a striker fired the flash powder but it was considered 'advisable to keep the camera at arms length to avoid severe facial burns'. (Courtesy of the Pentax Gallery and Museum, Tokyo.)

An Echo 8 cigarette lighter camera of 1951. It produced 6 mm by 6 mm negatives on one half of a section of 16 mm film and became well known when one was used by Audrey Hepburn in the film Roman Holiday. *(Courtesy of the Pentax Gallery and Museum, Tokyo.)*

World War 2 period which were stamped 'Made in Occupied Japan' and many subminiature and toy cameras made in Japan are also fruitful fields for collectors and although they are found more readily in the United States than in Europe their very scarcity only adds to the fascination that these exotic eastern cameras hold for collectors.

Collectors of photographic antiques will not need to be reminded of the value of keeping a photographic record of the more valuable items in a collection but they should be careful not to keep the photographs in the same place as the collection itself.

Collecting photographic antiques is an enjoyable and progressive occupation. We continuously learn more about the history of photography, early photographers, and the various photographic processes and as we discover new facts and become more knowledgeable about the subject we derive more and more pleasure and profit from our activities.

Collectors will find that joining a collector's society or group such as the Historical Group of the Royal Photographic Society or any of the kindred organizations that have come into being all over the world is a wonderful way to learn more about collecting photographic antiques and where and how to find photographic collectabilia. As we meet other collectors, join societies and make new friends for many of us collecting photographic antiques will become a lifetime occupation with constantly widening horizons and constant new discoveries. Some collectors are indeed lone wolves who look upon all other collectors as predatory enemies to be avoided at all costs less they follow us and beat us to a treasure. But many of us have become good friends over the years, helping instead of competing with each other, and I am indebted to many fellow collectors for pointing out or passing on to me many fine photographic antiques that were surplus to their own requirements.

We may not locate a daguerreotype or wet plate camera, an early book or a priceless photograph every day, but as every collector knows the thrill of the hunt can often be as exciting as the successful ending. So good luck, happy hunting, and above all keep on collecting.

LANCASHIRE LIBRARY

Index